THE STATE OF THE WORLD'S CHILDREN 2005

Thank you

This report has been prepared with the help of many people and organizations, including the following UNICEF field offices: Angola, Argentina, Bangladesh, Benin, Bolivia, Botswana, Brazil, Burundi, Cambodia, Cameroon, China, Colombia, Côte d'Ivoire, Democratic Republic of the Congo, El Salvador, Ethiopia, Georgia, Ghana, Guatemala, Guyana, India, Indonesia, Iraq, Jamaica, Jordan, Lesotho, Madagascar, Malawi, Malaysia, Mexico, Mongolia, Mozambique, Myanmar, Nepal, Nigeria, Occupied Palestinian Territory, Pakistan, Panama, Papua New Guinea, Paraguay, Peru, Philippines, Romania, Republic of Moldova, Senegal, Serbia and Montenegro, Sierra Leone, Somalia, South Africa, Sri Lanka, Sudan, Suriname, Timor-Leste, United Republic of Tanzania, Uruguay, Venezuela and Zimbabwe. Input was also received from UNICEF regional offices, the UNICEF Innocenti Research Centre and UNICEF Supply Division.

Sincere thanks to H.M. Queen Sylvia of Sweden, Dr. Bina Agarwal and Professor Joseph Stiglitz for their special contributions.

ISBN 92-806-3817-3

The Library of Congress has catalogued this serial publication as follows:
The State of the World's Children 2005

UNICEF, UNICEF House, 3 UN Plaza,
New York, NY 10017, USA

E-mail: pubdoc@unicef.org
Website: www.unicef.org

Cover photo: © UNICEF/HQ91-0914/Roger LeMoyne

THE STATE OF THE WORLD'S CHILDREN 2005

Childhood Under Threat

Carol Bellamy
Executive Director
United Nations Children's Fund

THE STATE OF THE WORLD'S CHILDREN 2005

CONTENTS

With a foreword by Kofi A. Annan, Secretary-General of the United Nations vii

1 CHILDHOOD UNDER THREAT

2 CHILDREN LIVING IN POVERTY

CHILDHOOD

3 CHILDREN CAUGHT UP IN CONFLICT

4 CHILDREN ORPHANED OR MADE VULNERABLE BY HIV/AIDS

5 A CHILDHOOD FOR EVERY CHILD

UNDER THREAT

"Only as we move closer to realizing the rights of all children will countries move closer to their goals of development and peace."

Kofi A. Annan

FOREWORD

© UN/DPI/Sergey Bormeniev

The Millennium Declaration, adopted in 2000 by all countries as a blueprint for building a better world in the 21st century, was a landmark document. It captured the aspirations of the international community for a world united by common values, striving to achieve peace and a decent standard of living for every man, woman and child. In such a world, the years of childhood hold a special place as an ideal we all hope to realize – a place in which all children are healthy, protected from harm and surrounded by loving and nurturing adults who help them grow and develop to their full potential.

But as *The State of the World's Children 2005* makes clear, for nearly half of the two billion children in the real world, childhood is starkly and brutally different from the ideal we all aspire to. Poverty denies children their dignity, endangers their lives and limits their potential. Conflict and violence rob them of a secure family life, betray their trust and their hope. HIV/AIDS kills their parents, their teachers, their doctors and nurses. It also kills them.

With the childhood of so many under threat, our collective future is compromised. Only as we move closer to realizing the rights of all children will countries move closer to their goals of development and peace. When nations gather in 2005 for the five-year review of the implementation of the Millennium Declaration, I hope they will bear that in mind, and be ready to take far-reaching decisions that can translate our aspirations into reality.

Kofi A. Annan
Secretary-General of the United Nations

1

Childhood Under Threat

Millions are losing out on their childhood

Pictures of childhood: boys and girls scavenging in the rubbish piles of Manila, coerced into carrying an AK-47 in the jungles of Democratic Republic of the Congo, forced into prostitution on the streets of Moscow, begging for food in Rio de Janeiro, orphaned by AIDS in Botswana. Pictures that are replicated again and again – different lives, different countries, but hauntingly similar images – as millions of children grow up in poverty, are caught up in armed conflict or are orphaned and made vulnerable by HIV/AIDS in these beginning years of the 21st century.

Contrast the experiences of these children with the ideal of childhood as a time when children are allowed to grow and develop to their full potential: healthy children in school and at play, growing strong and confident with the love and encouragement of their family and an extended community of caring adults, gradually taking on the responsibilities of adulthood, free from fear, safe from violence, protected from abuse and exploitation.

Childhood is the foundation of hopes for a better future

In the first instances, childhood is an empty word and a broken promise. In the second, childhood is the foundation of the world's hope for a better future. The gap between the reality and the ideal of childhood is the focus of this year's report on *The State of the World's Children*: what childhood means for children, what childhood means for countries, and what must be done if the rights of all children are to

Summary

ISSUE: Childhood means more than just the time between birth and the attainment of adulthood. It refers to the state and condition of a child's life: to the **quality** of those years. As the most widely endorsed human rights treaty in history, the Convention on the Rights of the Child, adopted by the UN General Assembly in 1989 and ratified by all but two countries, in effect represents a global consensus on the **terms** of childhood. Although there is not absolute agreement on the interpretation of each and every provision of the Convention, there is substantial common ground on what the standards of childhood should be.

There have been significant advances since the Convention was adopted in the fulfilment of children's rights to survival, health and education through the provision of essential goods and services, and a growing recognition of the need to create a protective environment to shield children from exploitation, abuse and violence. Worryingly, however, in several regions and countries some of these gains appear in danger of reversal from three key threats: **poverty**, **armed conflict** and **HIV/AIDS**. The rights of over 1 billion children are violated because they are severely underserved of at least one or more of the basic goods and services required to survive, grow and develop. Millions of children are growing up in families and communities torn apart by armed conflict. In sub-Saharan Africa, HIV/AIDS has led to rising child mortality rates, sharp reductions in life expectancy and millions of orphans. Although the problem is most acute in Africa, HIV prevalence rates are also rising in other parts of the world.

These are not the only factors that undermine childhood, but they are certainly among the most significant, with profoundly damaging effects on a child's chances of survival and development after the early years of life. The harm they cause lingers well beyond the years of childhood, increasing the likelihood that the next generation will be affected by the same threats. Moreover, as damaging as the major threats are by themselves, when two or even three coincide, the impact on children's lives is devastating.

ACTION: There are those who dismiss as utopian the conviction that the majority – let alone all – of the world's children could actually experience such a childhood as the ideal that infuses the Convention: one of love, care and protection, in a family environment, with ample scope to survive, grow, develop and participate. UNICEF is not among them. But swift and decisive action is required to reduce the poverty that children experience, protect them from armed conflict and support those orphaned or made vulnerable by HIV/AIDS. Every one of us has a role to play in ensuring that **every** child enjoys a childhood.

The world comes to recognize the importance of childhood

1919 The international legal recognition of children's rights owes much to an Englishwoman, Eglantyne Jebb. She launches the Save the Children Fund in response to the post-war misery of thousands of children around Europe. However, her sights are set even higher than immediate relief, and in 1920 she moves to Geneva to form the Save the Children International Union (later to become the International Union for Child Welfare).

1924 The League of Nations adopts the Geneva Declaration of the Rights of the Child, drafted by the International Union for Child Welfare. The Declaration establishes children's rights to the means for material, moral and spiritual development; special help when hungry, sick, disabled or orphaned; first call on relief when in distress; freedom from economic exploitation; and an upbringing that instils a sense of social responsibility.

1948 The UN General Assembly passes the Universal Declaration of Human Rights, which refers in article 25 to childhood as "entitled to special care and assistance."

1959 The UN General Assembly adopts the Declaration of the Rights of the Child, which recognizes rights such as freedom from discrimination and the right to a name and a nationality. It also specifically enshrines children's rights to education, health care and special protection.

1979 The UN declares 1979 the International Year of the Child. The greatest achievement of the year is to set in motion a process of much longer-term significance: The UN General Assembly agrees that a working group comprising members of the UN Commission on Human Rights, independent experts and observer delegations of non-member governments, non-governmental organizations and UN agencies should be set up to draft a legally binding Convention.

1989 The UN General Assembly unanimously approves the Convention on the Rights of the Child, which enters into force the following year.

1990 The World Summit for Children is held in New York. It includes 71 Heads of State and Government. The leaders sign the World Declaration on the Survival, Protection and Development of Children as well as a Plan of Action for implementing the Declaration, setting goals to be achieved by the year 2000.

1994 The International Year of the Family reaffirms that programmes should support families as they nurture and protect children, rather than provide substitutes for such functions.

1999 The Convention concerning the Prohibition and Immediate Action for the Elimination of the Worst Forms of Child Labour (ILO Convention 182) is adopted.

2000 The UN Millennium Development Goals incorporate specific targets related to children, including reducing the global under-five mortality rate by two thirds and achieving universal primary education over the period 1990 to 2015. The UN General Assembly adopts two Optional Protocols to the Convention on the Rights of the Child: one on the involvement of children in armed conflict, the other on the sale of children, child prostitution and child pornography.

2002 The UN General Assembly holds a Special Session on Children, meeting for the first time to specifically discuss children's issues. Hundreds of children participate as members of official delegations. World leaders commit themselves to building 'A World Fit for Children'. They reaffirm that the family holds the primary responsibility for the protection, upbringing and development of children and is entitled to receive comprehensive protection and support.

be protected, if the Millennium Development Goals are to be met, and if we are to be successful in building a world fit for children and for all of us.

Childhood defined

Childhood is more than just the time before a person is considered an adult

Meaning much more than just the space between birth and the attainment of adulthood, childhood refers to the state and condition of a child's life: to the **quality** of those years. A child who has been kidnapped by a paramilitary group and compelled to bear arms or forced into sexual slavery cannot have a childhood, nor can a child put to hard labour in a garment workshop in the capital city, far from family and home village. Children living in abject poverty without adequate food, access to education, safe water, sanitation facilities and shelter are also denied their childhood.

What then do we mean by childhood? The quality of children's lives can vary radically within the same dwelling, between two houses on the same street, between regions and between industrialized and developing countries. The closer children come to being full-grown, the more cultures, countries, and even people within the same country differ in their views of what is expected of children and on the level of adult or legal protection they require. Yet, despite intellectual debates about the definition of childhood and cultural differences about what to expect for and from children, there has always been a substantial degree of shared understanding that childhood implies a separate and safe space, demarcated from adulthood, in which children can grow, play and develop.

A new beginning for childhood

A new definition of childhood based on human rights is reflected in the Convention on the Rights of the Child, adopted by the United Nations General Assembly in 1989. The Convention is the first international human rights treaty to bring together the universal set of standards concerning children in a unique instrument, and the first to understand child rights as a legally binding imperative.[1]

The Convention represents the culmination of a process of recognizing the rights of children and the special status of childhood that gained significant momentum as the 20th century progressed. Work on the Convention began in earnest in 1979 and spanned a decade. It involved exhaustive negotiation and research into differing cultural interpretations of childhood. The process of negotiating, drafting and approving the Convention brought governments, international agencies and non-governmental organizations to agreement around the moral necessity of protecting children's rights.

The Convention on the Rights of the Child

The impact of the Convention on the Rights of the Child on the status of children has been as profound as its consolidation of the rights of children.

The Convention defines childhood as a separate space from adulthood. Historically, the needs and obligations of children were not well differentiated from those of adults. Like adults, able-bodied children traditionally engaged in arduous labour and were often combatants in battle.[2] But the Convention, citing the "special care and assistance" that children require, recognizes that what is appropriate for an adult may not be suitable for a child. This is why, for instance, it sets a minimum age for recruitment into the armed forces and participation in armed conflict. Its recognition of childhood as a 'separate space' means that even when children face the same challenges as adults, they may require different solutions.

The terms of childhood: Children's rights

According to the Convention on the Rights of the Child, every child has the right to:

	Articles[a]
Non-discrimination	2, 30
Actions taken in their best interests	3, 18
Survival and development	6
Identity	7, 8
Family relations and parental guidance	5, 7, 8, 9, 10, 18, 21, 25
Protection from illicit transfer and illegal adoption	11, 21
Freedom of expression, thought, conscience and religion	12, 13, 14
Freedom of association and peaceful assembly	15
State protection of privacy, home, family and correspondence	16
Access to appropriate information	17
Protection from abuse and neglect	19
Special protection and assistance if deprived of the family environment	20, 22
Protection from armed conflict	22, 38-39
Special care if disabled	23
Health and access to health-care services	24
Benefit from social security	26
A decent standard of living	27
Education	28-29
Rest and leisure, play and recreation, culture and the arts	31
Protection from child labour, trafficking, sexual and other forms of exploitation, and drug abuse	32-36, 39
Protection from torture and deprivation of liberty	37-39
Dignity and worth, even if the child has infringed the law	40

[a] Articles refer to articles 1-40 of the Convention of the Rights of the Child. Those cited refer explicitly to children's rights or the obligations of States parties to children.

© UNICEF/HQ02-0474/Donna DeCesare

The Convention asserts the role of the family in children's lives. The family is the fundamental unit of society and the natural environment for the growth and well-being of its members, particularly children. Under the Convention, countries are obliged to respect parents' primary responsibility for providing care and guidance for their children and to support parents in this regard by providing material assistance and support. States are also obliged to prevent children from being separated from their families unless the separation is judged necessary in order to ensure the child's best interests.

The Convention declares that all children have rights regardless of their circumstances. Children have often been considered the property of their parents; any inherent value was thought to derive from their potential economic productivity. Even when laws were passed that benefited children, they were often motivated by a desire to safeguard family property rights rather than children themselves.[3] The Convention recognizes that children are the holders of their own rights. And because these rights are invested in the child's own person, the child is no longer a passive recipient of charity but an empowered actor in her or his own development. Children have the right to influence decisions that affect their lives – in accordance with their age and maturity.[4]

The Convention views the child as both an individual and a member of a larger community. The Convention commits nations to guarantee individual rights: no child is more important than another, and children are entitled to freedoms "without discrimination of any kind." Yet while children are uniquely vulnerable and deserve particular protection, they are also to be "prepared to live an individual life in society." The Convention emphasizes the need to respect children's "evolving capacities." Adults are expected to create spaces and promote processes designed to enable and empower children to express their views, to be consulted and to influence decisions

The protective environment

The protective environment is made up of interconnected elements that individually and collectively work to protect children from exploitation, violence and abuse. While many of the responsibilities for the creation of a protective environment lie with the government, other members of society also have duties. The key elements of the protective environment include:

- **Capacity of families and communities:** All those who interact with children – parents, teachers and religious leaders alike – should observe protective child-rearing practices and have the knowledge, skills, motivation and support to recognize and respond to exploitation and abuse.

- **Government commitment and capacity:** Governments should provide budgetary support for child protection, adopt appropriate social welfare policies to protect children's rights, and ratify with few or no reservations international conventions concerning children's rights and protection. Ratification of the two Optional Protocols to the Convention on the Rights of the Child would be an important demonstration of the commitment to protect children from armed conflict and exploitation.

- **Legislation and enforcement:** Governments should implement laws to protect children from abuse, exploitation and violence, vigorously and consistently prosecute perpetrators of crimes against children, and avoid criminalizing child victims.

- **Attitudes and customs:** Governments should challenge attitudes, prejudices and beliefs that facilitate or lead to abuses. They should commit to preserving the dignity of children and engage the public to accept their responsibility to protect them.

- **Open discussion including civil society and media:** Societies should openly confront exploitation, abuse and violence through the media and civil society groups.

- **Children's life skills, knowledge and participation:** Societies should ensure that children know their rights – and are encouraged and empowered to express them – as well as given the vital information and skills they need to protect themselves from abuse and exploitation.

- **Essential services:** Services for victims of abuse should be available to meet their needs in confidence and with dignity, and basic social services should be available to all children without discrimination.

- **Monitoring, reporting and oversight:** There should be monitoring, transparent reporting and oversight of abuses and exploitation.

Key to building the protective environment is responsibility: All members of society can contribute to protecting children from violence, abuse and exploitation.

See References, page 99.

in all matters affecting them in accordance with their age and development.

The Convention lays down the terms of childhood. As the most widely endorsed human rights treaty in history, the Convention effectively represents a global consensus on the **terms** of childhood. Although there is not absolute agreement on the interpretation of each and every provision of the Convention – some of the States parties have issued declarations and reservations clarifying their national positions on one or more aspects of the rights – there is substantial common ground on what the standards of childhood should be.

The Convention identifies obligations to the child. A child's experience of life – childhood – especially in their earliest years, is largely determined by the care and protection they receive, or fail to receive, from adults: from the family and also from the wider community, including States parties. It is the responsibility of all duty bearers for children – governments, international organizations, civil society, families and individuals – to ensure that children's rights are fulfilled and protected. When children are left unprotected and vulnerable to exploitation and abuse, their childhood is undermined. A protective environment is pivotal to governments' and societies' commitment to ensuring that no child is deprived of the material, spiritual and emotional resources needed to achieve their potential or participate as full and equal members of society.

Creating a protective environment

Children have the right to grow up in an environment that protects them. Successful protection increases children's chances of growing up physically and mentally healthy, confident and self-respecting, and less likely to abuse or exploit others, including their own children. Child protection is also closely linked to other aspects of a child's rights. The right to health is not enjoyed by an immunized child who is constantly beaten; a schoolchild taunted or abused for her or his ethnicity does not fully benefit from the right to an education; an adolescent sold into prostitution has the right to freedom criminally violated.

Despite the near universal ratification of the Convention on the Rights of the Child, and the addition of two Optional Protocols, both of which address protection rights, child protection is weak in much of the world. While governments appear to agree with the principle that children should not be abused, trafficked, exploited or exposed to hazardous labour, their commitment to creating and sustaining a protective environment for children is less clear.

Creating a protective environment, based on the ideal childhood of the Convention, is not just about changes in laws and policies; it is also about altering attitudes, traditions, customs and behaviours that continue to undermine children's rights (*see Panel: The protective environment, page 6*).

Surviving childhood

Improvements since the Convention was adopted

In the years since the Convention was adopted, the world has seen concrete results. For example, there have been substantial increases in the provision of essential goods and services, such as immunization, insecticide-treated mosquito nets and oral rehydration salts, that children require if they are to survive and remain healthy. Between the early 1990s and 2000, the global under-five mortality rate declined by 11 per cent; in the decade to 2000, underweight prevalence among children under five fell from 32 to 28 per cent in developing countries, and global access to safe drinking water rose from 77 to 82 per cent. Child deaths from diarrhoea, the foremost killer of children at the beginning of the 1990s, declined by half during the decade, saving an estimated 1 million lives.[5] The Global Polio Eradication Initiative, launched in 1988, helped reduce the number of polio cases from 350,000 that year to fewer than 700 at the end of 2003.[6]

There is still much to be done to create a world fit for children

The 190 governments that convened at the UN General Assembly Special Session on Children in May 2002 pledged to accelerate progress on child development. World leaders unanimously embraced a set of time-bound goals: promoting the best start and healthy lives for children; providing quality education; protecting children against abuse, exploitation and violence; and combating HIV/AIDS. These commitments were reflected in a new international compact – 'A World Fit for Children'.

The vision of 'A World Fit for Children' complements the Millennium Development Goals (MDGs), adopted just 20 months earlier at the UN Millennium Summit. The MDGs, which encompass eight primary goals to be achieved by 2015, have become central objectives for all countries, UN agencies, including UNICEF, and bilateral donors and international financial institutions. The goals have a strong focus on children and the realization of their rights.

Reaching the Millennium Goals will require a stronger focus on children and the realization of their rights.

The Millennium Development Goals and childhood

Failure to achieve the MDGs will have tragic consequences for children

Progress is behind schedule for almost all of the MDGs. UN agencies, the World Bank, the Organisation for Economic Co-operation and Development and others have repeatedly voiced their concern that nearly all of the MDGs – and therefore most of the goals in 'A World Fit for Children' – will not be met unless there is a concerted effort by donors and governments.

Failure to achieve the MDGs will have tragic consequences for children, particularly those in developing countries. Millions will see their childhood violated through ill health or death from preventable diseases. Millions more will see their futures compromised because of governments' failures to provide them with an education, and the

Failure to achieve the Millennium Development Goals: Implications for childhood

FACTOR	GOAL	TARGETS, 2015	PROGRESS, 1990-2003/04
Poverty	*Eradicate extreme poverty and hunger*	Reduce by half the proportion of people living on less than a dollar a day. Reduce by half the proportion of people who suffer from hunger.	**Mixed.** On current trends and projections, this goal and its related targets will be achieved in aggregate terms, mostly owing to strong economic growth in China and India. However, most sub-Saharan African countries will in all likelihood miss these targets.
Primary education	*Achieve universal primary education*	Ensure that all boys and girls complete a full course of primary schooling.	**Mixed.** Several regions are on target to meet this goal, including Central and Eastern Europe and the Commonwealth of Independent States (CEE/CIS) and Latin America and the Caribbean. East Asia and the Pacific have almost met the target a full decade ahead of schedule. Shortfalls appear likely across sub-Saharan Africa.
Gender equality	*Promote gender equality and empower women*	Eliminate gender disparity in primary and secondary education preferably by 2005, and at all levels by 2015.	**Insufficient.** Despite significant progress towards gender parity in primary schools, shortfalls are still likely in about one third of developing countries at the primary level and over 40 per cent of countries at the secondary level.
Child survival	*Reduce child mortality*	Reduce by two thirds the mortality rate among children under five.	**Seriously off track.** The fourth MDG is commonly regarded as the furthest from being achieved. Only one region – Latin America and the Caribbean – is on track, although substantial progress has been made in several East Asian countries.
Families and women	*Improve maternal health*	Reduce by three quarters the maternal mortality ratio.	**Seriously off track.** Only 17 per cent of countries, accounting for 32 per cent of the developing world's population, are on track.
Health	*Combat HIV/AIDS, malaria and other diseases*	Halt and begin to reverse the spread of HIV/AIDS. Halt and begin to reverse the incidence of malaria and other major diseases.	**Seriously off track.** HIV prevalence is rising in many countries. While prevalence rates are highest in southern Africa, the rate of increase is sharpest in Europe and Central Asia, and absolute numbers are large in China and India. Malaria is proving difficult to contain, while the global incidence of tuberculosis is rising.
Water and sanitation	*Ensure environmental sustainability*	Reduce by half the proportion of people without sustainable access to safe drinking water and basic sanitation.	**Mixed.** The world is on track to meet the target for drinking water, as global access to improved drinking water sources increased from 77 per cent in 1990 to 83 per cent in 2002. However, progress in sub-Saharan Africa has fallen short. Sanitation remains an even greater challenge: on current trends, the target will be missed by a margin of more than half a billion people.

number of children orphaned or made vulnerable by HIV/AIDS will continue to rise.

Threats to childhood

The advent of the Convention on the Rights of the Child was a landmark in human history, and its subsequent ratification by all but two of the world's countries is a remarkable testament to the universally shared vision of what childhood should mean. The concept of childhood, then, has never been stronger, clearer or more detailed.

The childhood of millions does not match the Convention's vision

Yet childhood remains under threat. The powerful vision of children's rights set forth in the Convention and reinforced in 'A World Fit for Children' contrasts starkly with the actual childhood of most of the world's children. Around 29,000 under-

IMPLICATIONS FOR CHILDHOOD

As children experience poverty as an environment that is not conducive to their development, rather than merely a lack of income, achieving the income target will make only a moderate contribution to ensuring that every child enjoys a childhood. China and India are on track to meet the income target, but are falling behind on MDGs directly related to children, especially reducing child mortality. Halving hunger will have a pronounced impact, as malnutrition is a contributing factor in over half of under-five deaths in developing countries.

Around 121 million children, the majority of them girls, do not attend school and are denied their right to an education, a right to which their governments committed themselves under the Convention on the Rights of the Child. The price of failure to meet the second MDG will be that 75 million children – 70 per cent of them in sub-Saharan Africa – will be denied their right to a primary education in 2015.

Gender parity in primary and secondary education will be the first of the MDG targets to be missed, in part because of much slower progress on secondary enrolment. UNESCO estimates that 76 countries are unlikely to reach gender parity at primary and secondary school levels by 2005. Based on current trends, parity will not be met in 54 countries by 2015.

Every day, 29,000 under-fives die from largely preventable diseases, resulting in 10.6 million deaths each year. The best current estimate is that the MDG for reducing under-five mortality will remain unmet in sub-Saharan Africa and CEE/CIS well into the 22nd century.

Over half a million women die from the complications of pregnancy and childbirth each year, and 15 million women suffer injuries, infections and disabilities in pregnancy or childbirth. Infants have a lower probability of survival without the care of their mothers. Without a concerted effort to save mothers' lives, millions of children will be denied maternal love and care during childhood.

Over 2 million children under 15 are infected with HIV. Based on current trends, the number of children orphaned by AIDS in sub-Saharan Africa will exceed 18 million by 2010. With infection rates rising and the long latency period complicating efforts to estimate prevalence rates, this crisis for children will persist for decades. Malaria will continue to be a major cause of child deaths, as the availability and use of nets and medicines are limited by behavioural and financial constraints. Poor nutrition will leave children vulnerable to tuberculosis in many countries.

Access to safe water and sanitation is critical to child survival. The lack of access to decent sanitation facilities is particularly pronounced in rural areas of developing countries. Unless progress accelerates markedly, over half a billion children – one in every three children in the developing world – will continue to be denied access to any sanitation facilities whatsoever.

See References, page 99.

Figure 1.1 **Poverty, armed conflict and HIV/AIDS threaten child survival**

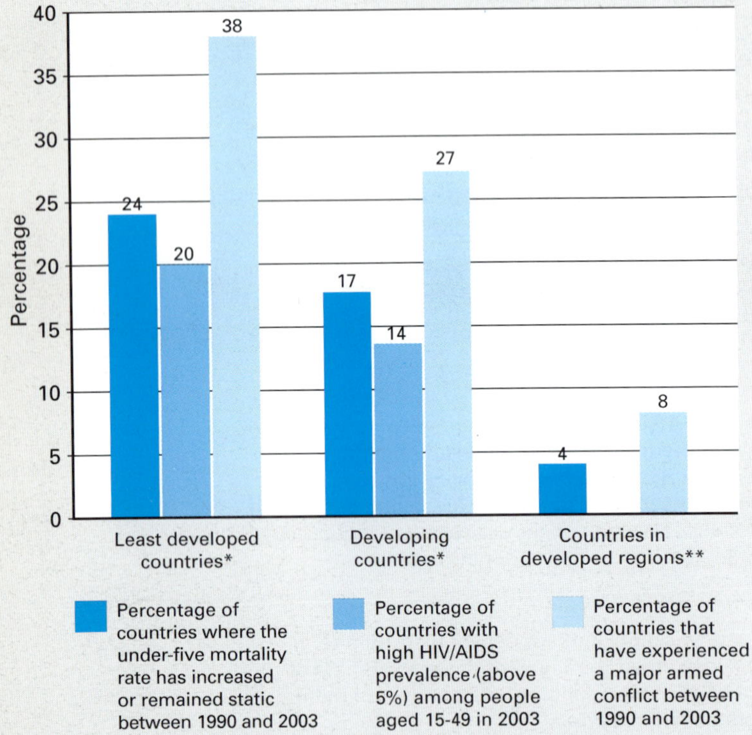

* See Statistical Tables, page 140, for a listing of countries in each category.

** There is no established convention for the designation of 'developed' and 'developing' countries or areas. In common practice, Australia, Canada, Europe, Japan, New Zealand and the United States are considered 'developed'.

Source: UNICEF; SIPRI/Uppsala Conflict Data Project; UN Statistics Division.

fives die every day from causes that are easily prevented, such as diarrhoeal dehydration, acute respiratory infections, measles and malaria.[7] The lives of over 1 billion children are blighted by poverty, despite the wealth of nations.

Poverty, armed conflict and HIV/AIDS are grave threats to childhood

Worryingly, in several regions and countries some of the advances in fulfilling children's rights of recent decades – e.g. reductions in child mortality rates, increasing net primary school enrolment, and important strides in creating a protective environment for children – appear at risk of reversal from three key threats: **poverty**, **armed conflict** and **HIV/AIDS** (*see Figure 1.1, left*). Other threats to children's survival and development persist largely because of poverty, armed conflict and HIV/AIDS.

- **Poverty** is the root cause of high rates of child morbidity and mortality. The rights of over 1 billion children – more than half the children in developing countries – are violated because they are severely underserved of at least one of the basic goods or services that would allow them to survive, develop and thrive. In the developing world more than one in three children does not have adequate shelter, one in five children does not have access to safe water, and one in seven has no access whatsoever to essential health services. Over 16 per cent of children under five lack adequate nutrition and 13 per cent of all children have never been to school.

- **Armed conflict**. As civil strife proliferates – and civilians become its main causalities – millions of children are growing up in families and communities torn apart by armed conflict. Many have been forced onto the front lines. Since 1990, conflicts have directly killed as many as 3.6 million people; tragically, more than 45 per cent of these are likely to have been children.[8] Hundreds of thousands of children are caught up in armed conflict as soldiers, are forced to become refugees or are internally displaced, suffer sexual violence, abuse and exploitation, or are victims of explosive remnants of war.

- **HIV/AIDS**. AIDS is already the leading cause of death worldwide for people aged 15 to 49; in 2003 alone, 2.9 million people died of AIDS and 4.8 million people were newly infected with HIV.[9] Over 90 per cent of people currently living with HIV/AIDS are in developing countries. In sub-Saharan Africa, HIV/AIDS has led to rising child mortality rates, sharp reductions in life expectancy and millions of orphans. Although the problem is most acute in this region, prevalence rates are also rising in other parts of the world.

When 1+1 is more than 2

Poverty, armed conflict and HIV/AIDS are not the only factors that undermine childhood but they are certainly among the most significant, with profoundly damaging effects on a child's chances of survival. The harm caused by each of these threats lingers well beyond the years of childhood and increases the likelihood that the next generation of children will be affected by the same threat. And as damaging as these three major threats are by themselves, when two or even all three coincide the impact on children's lives is devastating.

The vision of childhood that unites countries and peoples is at odds with the one that most children in the world actually experience. Into this gap between the ideal and the reality, between the Convention and convention, more young lives plunge with every passing day. And with each child that falls into this chasm, a little more of the world's shared future is compromised. Not one of the Millennium Development Goals – those idealistic objectives of the international community – will be attained if childhood continues under the current level of attack. Not one.

© UNICEF/HQ-00-0050/Jim Holmes

The quality of childhood is largely determined by the care and protection children receive – or fail to receive – from adults.

Advancing childhood, advancing humanity

Faced with such assaults on children, it is worth refocusing on what the key terms of childhood should be as agreed to by the 192 States parties to the Convention on the Rights of the Child. Children have the right to survival, food and nutrition, health and shelter. Children also have the right to be encouraged and educated, both informally and formally, from birth. Children have the right to a loving, understanding family environment where the primary concern is their best interests, that provides guidance appropriate to their evolving capacities and prepares them to live an individual life in society in a spirit of peace, dignity, tolerance, freedom, equality and solidarity. Children have the right, and must be afforded the opportunity, to recreation and play, and to engage in sport and cultural activities rather than be subjected to violence and exploitation. Where they experience work, it should be as a positive contribution to the family and community that increases their own self-respect and sense of empowerment, and contributes to their learning rather than detracts from it.

There are those who dismiss as impossibly utopian the conviction that the majority – let alone all – of the world's children could actually experience such a childhood. UNICEF is not among them.

Threats to Childhood

Countries reducing their under-five mortality rate by an average annual rate of less than 1%	Poverty GNI per capita (US$) 2003	Major armed conflict at some time during 1990–2003	HIV/AIDS Adult (15–49 years) prevalence rate 2003
1 Afghanistan	250†	●	no data
2 Angola	740	●	3.9
3 Azerbaijan	810	●	<0.1
4 Belarus	1590		no data
5 Botswana	3430		37.3
6 Bulgaria	2130		<0.1
7 Burkina Faso	300		4.2
8 Burundi	100	●	6.0
9 Cambodia	310	●	2.6
10 Cameroon	640		6.9
11 Central African Rep.	260		13.5
12 Chad	250	●	4.8
13 Congo	640	●	4.9
14 Congo, Dem. Rep.	100	●	4.2
15 Côte d'Ivoire	660		7.0
16 Gabon	3580*		8.1
17 Georgia	830*	●	0.1
18 Iraq	2170†	●	<0.1
19 Jamaica	2760*		1.2
20 Kazakhstan	1780		0.2
21 Kenya	390		6.7
22 Korea, Dem. People's Rep. of	765		no data
23 Latvia	4070		0.6
24 Liberia	130	●	5.9
25 Mauritania	430		0.6
26 Nigeria	320		5.4
27 Papua New Guinea	510		0.6
28 Russian Federation	2610*		1.1
29 Rwanda	220	●	5.1
30 Saint Vincent and the Grenadines	3300		no data
31 Sao Tome and Principe	320		no data
32 Senegal	550		0.8
33 Sierra Leone	150	●	no data
34 Somalia	130†	●	no data
35 South Africa	2780		21.5
36 Swaziland	1350		38.8
37 Tajikistan	190	●	<0.1
38 Tanzania, United Rep. of	290		8.8
39 Togo	310		4.1
40 Turkmenistan	1120*		<0.1
41 Tuvalu	no data		no data
42 Ukraine	970*		1.4
43 Uzbekistan	420		0.1
44 Zambia	380		16.5
45 Zimbabwe	480†		24.6

Data shown in blue meet the definitions of 'Threats to childhood'.

† Indicates data that refer to years or periods other than those specified in the column heading, differ from the standard definition or refer to only part of a country.

* Included in poverty column because of stagnant or negative GDP per capita average annual growth rate, 1990–2003. Gabon: –0.2; Georgia: –2.7; Jamaica: 0.0; Russian Federation: –1.5; Turkmenistan: –1.3; Ukraine: –4.7.

Source: For conflict data: Adapted from SIPRI/Uppsala Conflict Data Project.

Millennium Development Goal 4 (MDG 4) calls on countries to reduce by two thirds, between 1990 and 2015, the under-five mortality rate.

Of the 98 countries that are 'off track' to meet the goal, 45 are 'seriously off track': reducing their under-five mortality rate by an average annual rate of less than 1%. The vast majority of these suffer from one or more of the three major threats to childhood: high rates of poverty, conflict or HIV/AIDS.

MDG 4: The goal implies a 4.4% target average annual rate of reduction.

Threats to childhood for the purposes of this map:

Poverty – $765 or less GNI per capita in 2003, or stagnant or negative GDP per capita average annual growth rate, 1990–2003.

Conflict – Major armed conflict at some time during 1990–2003. Note: Data from SIPRI/Uppsala Conflict Data Project except for the Russian Federation. The United Nations has stated that the situation in the Republic of Chechnya is not an armed conflict within the meaning of the Geneva Conventions and the Additional Protocols thereto (ref: United Nations General Assembly/Security Council Corrigendum A/58/546/Corr.2-S/2003/1053/Corr.2).

HIV/AIDS – Adult (15–49 years) prevalence rate over 5%, 2003.

When 1 + 1 Is More Than 2

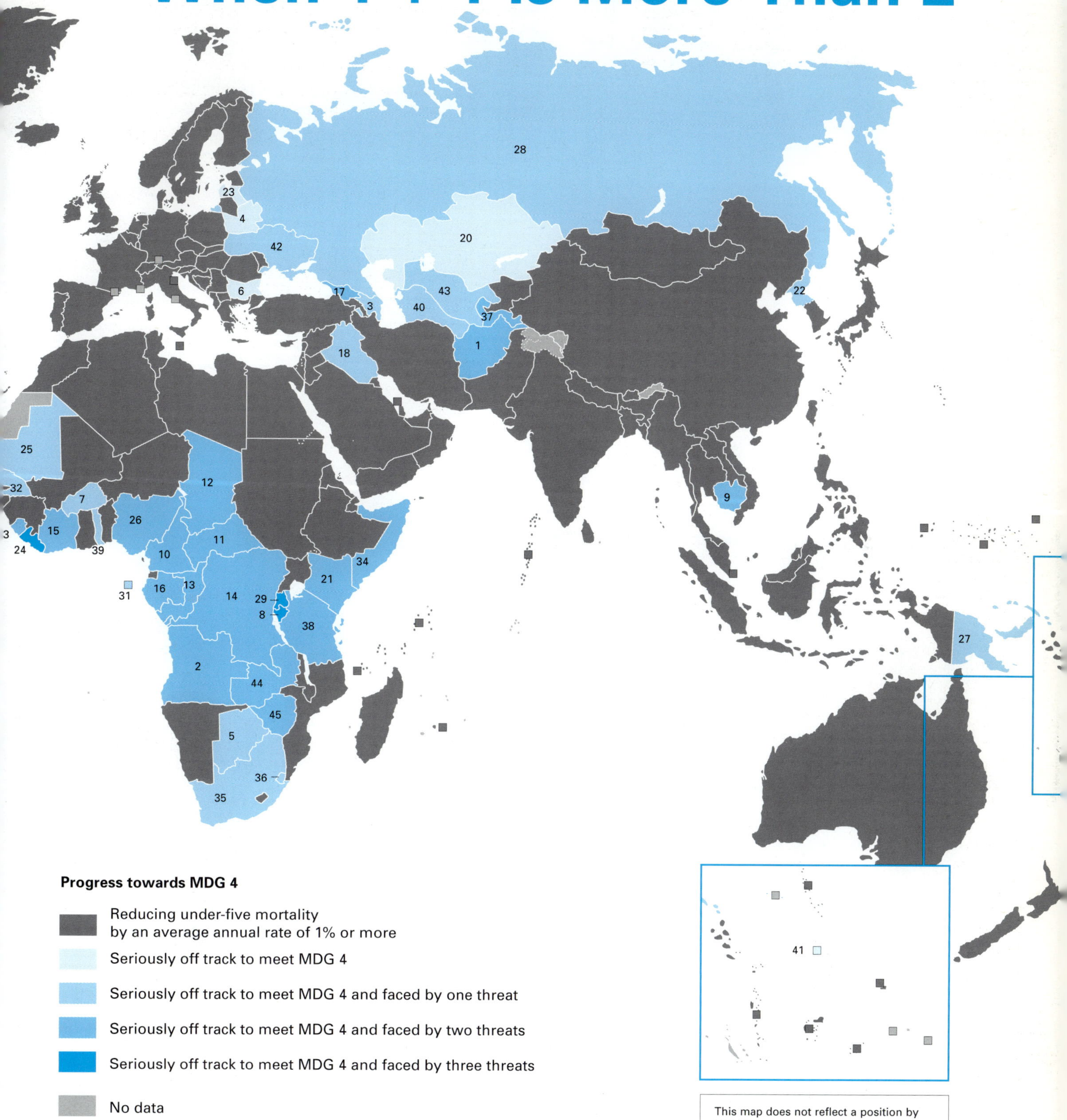

This map does not reflect a position by UNICEF on the legal status of any country or territory or the delimitation of any frontiers.

Dotted line represents approximately the Line of Control in Jammu and Kashmir agreed upon by India and Pakistan. The final status of Jammu and Kashmir has not yet been agreed upon by the parties.

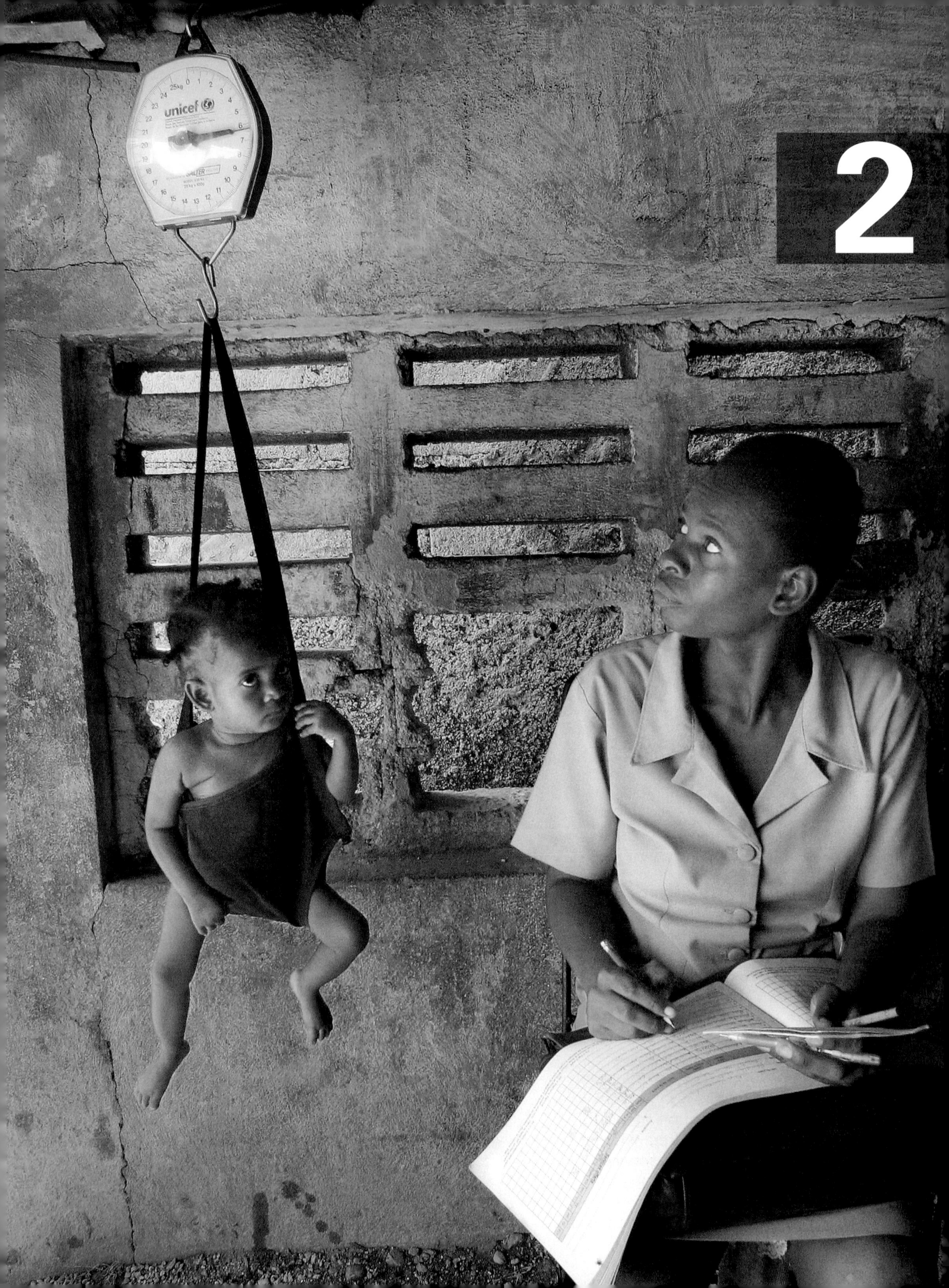

2

Children Living in Poverty

Poverty wears a multitude of faces and has numerous dimensions. It threatens all aspects of childhood by depriving children of the capabilities needed to survive, develop and thrive. It entrenches or widens social, economic and gender disparities that prevent children from enjoying equal opportunities and undermines protective family and community environments, leaving children vulnerable to exploitation, abuse, violence, discrimination and stigmatization. Poverty inhibits the capacity of families and communities to care for children. It also poses a threat by exacerbating the effects of HIV/AIDS and armed conflict.

Poverty in childhood is a root cause of poverty in adulthood. Impoverished children often grow up to be impoverished parents who in turn bring up their own children in poverty. In order to break the generational cycle, poverty reduction **must** begin with children.

Poverty denies children both essential goods and services and opportunities

Reducing child poverty means fulfilling children's rights to the goods and services necessary for their survival, normal growth and development. It also means improving the opportunities for disadvantaged children to participate in society. These two concerns support each other; together, they offer a platform for tackling child poverty as a human rights issue. Without first meeting the survival, health and education rights of children, without providing essential goods and services such as access to safe water or adequate nutrition, it is impossible to talk about equal opportunities. Yet, even when these

Summary

ISSUE: Children living in poverty face deprivations of many of their rights: survival, health and nutrition, education, participation, and protection from harm, exploitation and discrimination. Over 1 billion children are severely deprived of at least one of the essential goods and services they require to survive, grow and develop. Millions of children are severely deprived of nutrition, water, sanitation facilities, access to basic health-care services, adequate shelter, education and information. Gender discrimination is both a visible outcome and an underlying factor of severe deprivation. Even in countries where absolute deprivation is low, relative deprivation in terms of family income and wealth implies unequal opportunities for children.

Children whose rights to safety and dignity are denied are also impoverished. Each year, tens of millions of children are the victims of exploitation, violence and abuse, which rob them of their childhood, preventing them from fulfilling anything close to their full potential.

ACTION: The many dimensions of poverty mean that an integrated, multifaceted approach is required to reduce it, including the following actions:

- **Define and measure child poverty.** Accept that child poverty cannot be understood only in terms of family income. Responses to it should be based on how children experience poverty.
- **Ensure that poverty-reduction strategies prioritize actions to protect childhood.** Poverty-reduction strategies should have a strong focus on fulfilling children's rights and addressing key issues of deprivation and protection for children and their families.
- **Expand basic social and education services and ensure universal access.** Countries successful in improving access to basic health care and education for children are ready to spend more on social services, even in times of economic or financial crisis.
- **Set targets and mobilize stakeholders.** All stakeholders must be engaged to meet development targets – the world is falling behind on the Millennium Development Goals and 'A World Fit for Children' – which address many of the dimensions of poverty that children experience.
- **Promote the family.** Families form the first line of defence for children: the further away children are from their families, the more vulnerable they are to risks.
- **Eliminate gender discrimination.** Pursuing labour market and fiscal policies that address economic insecurity among women also help to diminish child poverty.
- **Encourage local solutions and community participation.** Developing countries successful in reducing poverty are increasingly promoting community participation. Children should be encouraged to contribute to the debate on ways to reduce poverty.

rights are met, children will still be relatively deprived if they are not able to take advantage of equal opportunities, and they will be at risk of exploitation if a protective environment is not in place.

Lessons from countries that have made headway in reducing poverty suggest that a comprehensive approach is required, consisting of the following five key steps:

- Confront the issue of poverty conceptually
- Quantify poverty according to the conceptual definition
- Demonstrate the need and scope for action
- Mobilize stakeholders around clear goals
- Maintain awareness and build partnerships to sustain the attack on poverty and its underlying factors.[1]

Understanding poverty from a child's perspective

Understanding how children experience poverty is essential to the design of effective poverty-reduction strategies. Inspired by international conventions and pioneering research, this chapter follows the five-point framework outlined above. It begins by introducing a globally applicable concept of what should be considered poverty from a child's perspective. With this in mind, it then examines new, internationally comparable data that measure the poverty children experience. While significant gaps remain in knowledge – which the international community should urgently address – it is clear that current evidence offers many lessons and, overall, highlights a huge scope for action. Reviewing the positive experiences of countries that have managed to reduce the poverty that deprives children of their childhood, the chapter concludes that the international community possesses the knowledge necessary to eliminate the most disturbing aspects of child poverty. The Millennium Development Goals and 'A World Fit for Children' provide clear targets around which stakeholders – donors, governments, communities, international agencies – can structure national development plans or Poverty Reduction Strategy Papers (PRSPs), reflected in government budgets and external support. What is needed is higher political priority: better awareness of how children experience poverty and corresponding action from all stakeholders.

Defining child poverty

Poverty is more than material deprivation

The United Nations views poverty as "a human condition, characterized by the sustained or chronic deprivation of the resources, capabilities, choices, security and power necessary for the enjoyment of an adequate standard of living and other civil, cultural, economic, political and social rights."[2] While poverty encompasses deprivation of basic goods and services, it also includes deficiencies in other vital elements of human rights – such as rest and recreation and protection from violence and conflict – that expand people's choices and enable them to fulfil their potential. Because children experience poverty as an environment that is damaging to their mental, physical, emotional and spiritual development, expanding the definition of child poverty beyond traditional conceptualizations, such as low household income or low levels of consumption, is particularly important.

Children's experience of poverty has different dimensions from that of adults

Child poverty is rarely differentiated from poverty in general and its special dimensions are seldom recognized. UNICEF has long argued that children are often hardest hit by poverty. Since the best start in life – especially in the first few years – is critical to the physical, intellectual and emotional development of every individual,

Poverty deprives children of their rights

Children living in poverty are deprived of many of their rights: survival, health and nutrition, education, participation, and protection from harm, exploitation and discrimination.

Survival: Poverty threatens childhood in the most tangible way of all: by jeopardizing a child's right to survival. Always a core concern of the international development community, the battle to save infant lives, to safeguard the health of mother and child, remains a key priority for UNICEF. One child out of every six born in the least developed countries dies before the age of five, compared with one child out of every 167 born in rich countries.[a] On average, a child from the poorest 20 per cent of the population in a developing country is at least twice as likely to die before the age of five as a child from the richest 20 per cent.[b] The most impoverished – usually rural – areas have few or no health-care facilities and few means of transporting people for medical assistance.

Health and nutrition: Poverty threatens childhood by exposing millions of children to diseases that could be easily prevented or cured through inexpensive medicines and vaccines. Two million children under the age of five still die every year because they were not immunized with commonplace vaccines.[c] Around 7 out of every 10 deaths among children under the age of five in developing countries can be attributed to a few main causes: acute respiratory infections, diarrhoea, measles or malaria. Malnutrition contributes to about half of these deaths.[d] Micronutrient deficiencies also play a role: A child deficient in vitamin A, for example, faces a 25 per cent greater risk of dying.[e] Even when it does not threaten life itself, malnutrition in early childhood can cause stunting or disability and hinder brain development and children's capacity to learn, hampering their ability to accrue skills that are critical to their life chances. Lack of access to clean water and proper sanitation spreads disease, aggravates malnutrition and weakens health.

Education: Over 121 million primary-school-age children are out of school. They are deprived of their right to education by poverty, either because their families cannot afford school fees, because scant national resources stand in the way of adequate school facilities, or because they have to work to put food on the table. Girls, who are often the first to be withdrawn from school in times of financial distress, constitute the majority of this group. Even when girls do successfully enrol in school, their subsequent achievements may be lower because of persistent gender stereotypes or because household responsibilities frequently interrupt their attendance.[f]

Protection: In addition to threatening children's lives, poverty increases their vulnerability to other dangers, providing fuel for violent and exploitative conditions that include hazardous child labour and child trafficking. The predators who sell children into slavery or sexual exploitation do not seek their prey in comfortable suburbs; they look in the poorest shanty towns or the most underprivileged rural areas, where grinding poverty can heighten children's vulnerability to protection abuses.

Participation: Children who lack access to health care, education and security will also lack the capacity to contribute to family and community decisions. National and international development projects often portray children as recipients of charity, rather than as active participants in determining their own futures, and too often fail to integrate children's voices into the strategies that are designed to benefit them. Yet just as poverty silences children, poverty reduction can empower them. For example, in countries like Honduras and Viet Nam, consultations sponsored by Save the Children have enabled children and young people to make valuable contributions to policies, including Poverty Reduction Strategy Papers, formulated by adults.[g]

poverty in early childhood can prove to be a lifelong handicap. Children are disproportionately represented among the poor. Developing countries tend to be rich in children, and income-poor families generally have more children than wealthier families. Yet research dealing with child poverty has not progressed far enough, and many matters of definition and measurement have yet to be resolved.

A working definition of children in poverty

As a step towards enhancing poverty-reduction strategies, *The State of the World's Children 2005* proposes the following working definition of children in poverty:

Children living in poverty experience deprivation of the material, spiritual and emotional resources needed to survive, develop and thrive, leaving them unable to enjoy their rights, achieve their full potential or participate as full and equal members of society.

This definition suggests that the poverty children experience with their hands, minds and hearts is interrelated. Material poverty – for example, starting the day without a nutritious meal or being forced to engage in hazardous labour – hinders cognitive capacity as well as physical growth. Living in an environment that provides little stimulation or emotional support to children, on the other hand, can remove much of the positive effect of growing up in a materially rich household. By discriminating against their participation in society and inhibiting their potential, poverty not only causes children suffering – it also disempowers them.

Poverty deprives children of their rights

Highlighting the ways poverty prevents children from realizing their full potential and participating as equal members of the community is a key step towards reducing it. Children living in poverty face deprivations of many of their rights: survival, health and nutrition, education, participation, and protection from harm, exploitation and discrimination *(see Panel: Poverty deprives children of their rights, page 17).* These deprivations cause suffering in the short term and hinder development in the long term. They tend to be associated with three underlying factors: low household income; poor physical infrastructure, often due to low levels of public investment; and weak institutions.

Measuring child poverty

The many dimensions of poverty – including mortality, morbidity, hunger, illiteracy, homelessness and powerlessness – are difficult to compress into a single measure. One of the most widely used measures of poverty is the $1 a day per person benchmark expressed in purchasing power parities, introduced in 1990 by the World Bank.[3] Together with a measure on hunger, this is one of two targets employed in the Millennium Development Goals for measuring progress on poverty reduction.[4]

The UN Development Programme's human development index and its derivative poverty measure, the human poverty index, are powerful competitors to income measures of human well-being. They focus, respectively, on human capabilities and human deprivations.[5] Attainment of the survival, health, education and gender-related targets of the Millennium Development Goals would significantly reduce poverty as measured by the human poverty index. Comparisons between the human development index and income measures of poverty such as per capita gross domestic product (GDP per head) have shown that countries with the same level of per capita income can have very different levels of human development.[6] This suggests that low-income countries have some scope for addressing illiteracy or poor health even if they fail to generate rapid economic growth.

While important for measuring poverty in broad terms, neither the income measure

Operational definitions of deprivation for children

As a compromise between theoretical considerations and available data, the concrete ways of defining severe deprivation for children in the study conducted by the University of Bristol and the London School of Economics were:

Nutrition: Children whose height and weight for their age were more than three standard deviations below the median of the international reference population.

Water: Children who only had access to surface water for drinking or who lived in households where the nearest source of water was more than 15 minutes away.

Sanitation: Children who had no access to a toilet of any kind in the vicinity of their dwelling.

Health: Children who had not been immunized against any diseases, or young children who had recently suffered from diarrhoea but had not received any medical advice or treatment.

Shelter: Children in dwellings with more than five people per room or with no flooring material.

Education: Children aged between 7 and 18 years old who had never been to school.

Information: Children aged between 3 and 18 years old with no access to radio, television, telephone or newspapers at home.

Of these, only deprivation of education and information can be answered in simple binary terms; the others are matters of degree. As practically all children have access to some food or water, for example, the researchers had to draw an arbitrary line in the continuum of deprivation, setting a point at which the degree of deprivation could be considered 'absolute' and few would question that these conditions are unacceptable. Indeed, it is reasonable to conclude that even less severe deprivations than those referred to above could undermine children's survival and harm their human rights.

See References, page 100.

Figure 2.1 **Severe deprivation among children in the developing world, by different deprivations**

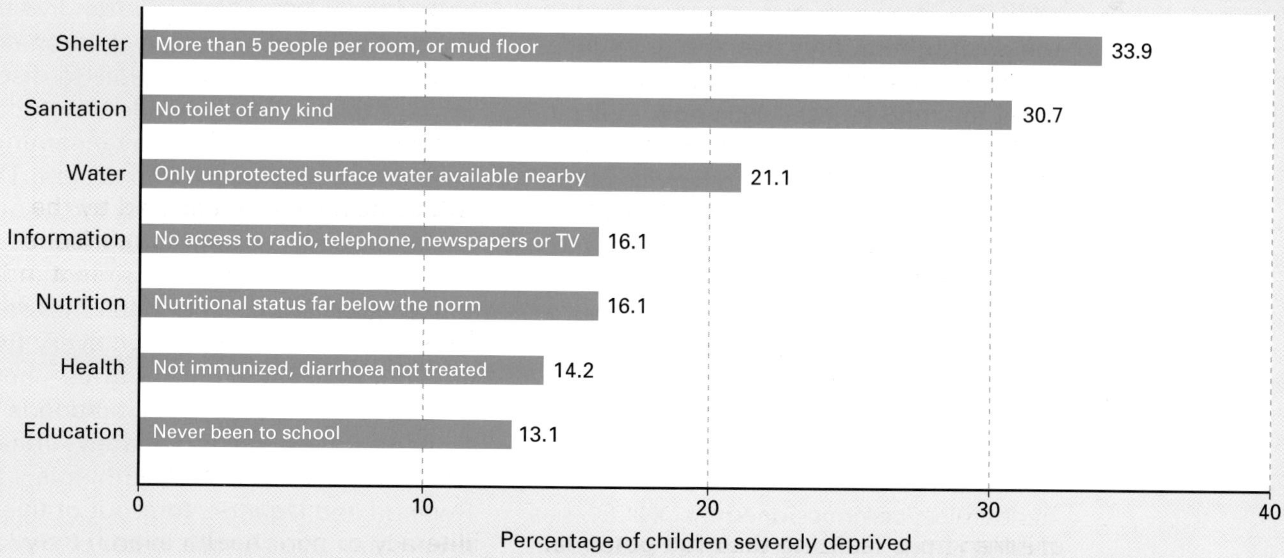

Age ranges: Education: 7-18 years old; Information: over 3 years old; Nutrition: under 5 years old.

Sources: Gordon, David, et al., *Child poverty in the developing world,* The Policy Press, Bristol, UK, October 2003. **Note:** The data used in the original study have been updated using Demographic and Health Surveys (DHS) and Multiple Indicator Cluster Surveys (MICS).

© UNICEF/HQ02-0298/Giacomo Pirozzi

employed by the World Bank nor the UN Development Programme's composite indices have been specifically designed to assess child poverty. And, for all their merits, neither quantifies how many children live in poverty nor focuses directly on the deprivations of their rights.

Child poverty as severe deprivation

The notion of **deprivation** focuses attention on the circumstances that surround children, casting poverty as an attribute of the environment they live and grow in. Household statistical surveys carried out since the mid- to late-1990s now make it possible to compare the levels of deprivation of essential goods and services that children experience across countries.[7] The impetus for this investigation derived from the commitment of the 117 States attending the 1995 World Summit for Social Development to tackle poverty as a human rights issue.

A recent empirical study by the University of Bristol and the London School of Economics, commissioned by UNICEF, has looked at how children in developing countries are affected by severe deprivations in seven areas: adequate nutrition, safe drinking water, decent sanitation facilities, health, shelter, education and information.[8] The study used a stricter interpretation of 'severe deprivation' than is normally employed in such investigations *(see Panel: Operational definitions of deprivation for children, page 19).* For example, a child severely deprived of an education means here a child who has never attended school, rather than the more widely used concept of 'non-completion of primary education'. The researchers relied on these highly restrictive definitions to ensure that they measured deprivation at a level that undeniably undermines children's rights.

One billion children are suffering from one or more forms of extreme deprivation

The study concluded that over 1 billion children – more than half the children in developing countries – suffer from at least one form of severe deprivation. The fact that every second child is deprived of even the minimum opportunities in life is alarming. Moreover, using these criteria, the study found that about 700 million children suffer two or more forms of severe deprivation.

Nutrition deprivation: Over 16 per cent of children under five in the developing world are severely malnourished. Nearly half of these 90 million children live in South Asia. Many of these children are anaemic, weak and vulnerable to disease; most of them already had low weight at birth; some of them will have learning problems if they ever go to school. They will probably remain among the poorest of the poor throughout their lives.

Water deprivation: About 400 million children – on average one in every five children in developing countries – have no access to safe water. The situation is particularly severe in sub-Saharan Africa: here, in countries such as Ethiopia, Rwanda and Uganda, four out of five children either use surface water or have to walk more than 15 minutes to find a protected water source. Rates of severe water deprivation are considerably higher in rural areas (27 per cent) than in urban

Figure 2.2 Severe deprivation* among children in the developing world, by region

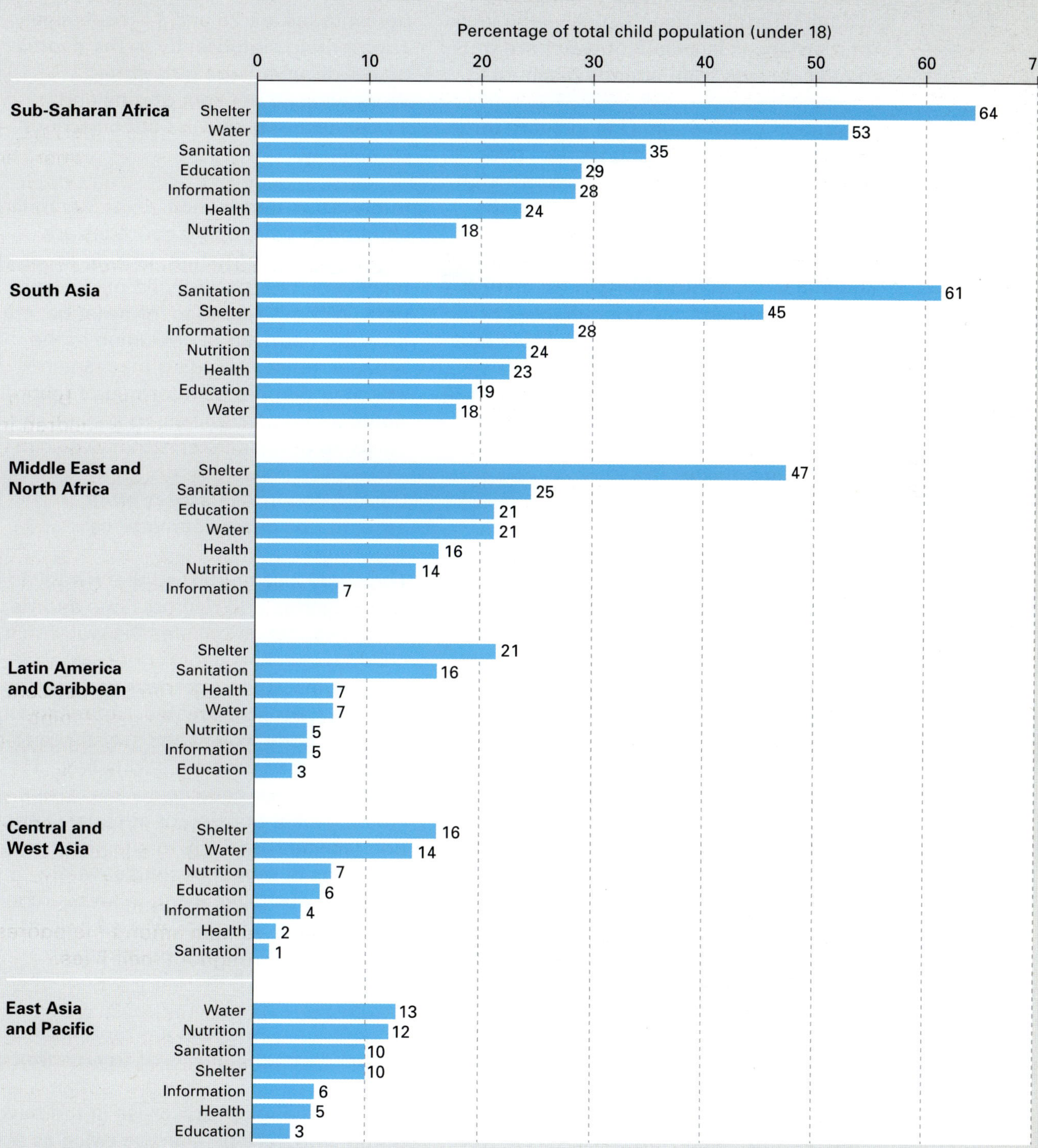

* See Figure 2.1, page 19, for definitions of the deprivations.

Age ranges: Education: 7-18 years old; Information: over 3 years old; Nutrition: under 5 years old.

Sources: Gordon, David, et al., *Child poverty in the developing world,* The Policy Press, Bristol, UK, October 2003. **Note:** The data used in the original study have been updated using Demographic and Health Surveys (DHS) and Multiple Indicator Cluster Surveys (MICS).

ones (7 per cent). A lack of safe water is a major cause of disease, but also affects children's productivity and attendance in school. Children – mainly girls – who walk long distances in search of water are often in effect barred from attending school.

Sanitation deprivation: One in every three children in the developing world – over 500 million children – has no access whatsoever to sanitation facilities; again, the problem is particularly pronounced in rural areas. Without access to sanitation, children's risk of disease rises dramatically, further jeopardizing their chances of survival and often reducing the likelihood that they will be able to take full advantage of schooling. For example, millions of school-aged children are infected by intestinal worms, which have been shown to sap learning ability.

Health deprivation: Around 270 million children, or just over 14 per cent of all children in developing countries, have no access to health-care services. In South Asia and sub-Saharan Africa, one in four children either does not receive any of the six principal immunizations or has no access to treatment if they suffer from diarrhoea.

Shelter deprivation: Over 640 million children in developing countries experience severe shelter deprivation, with those in sub-Saharan Africa clearly the most deprived. However, the lack of access to proper shelter is also widespread in both South Asia and the Middle East and North Africa; in the latter region, rural children are more than four times more likely than their urban counterparts to be shelter deprived.

Education deprivation: Over 140 million children in developing countries – 13 per cent of those aged 7-18 years – have never attended school. This rate is 32 per cent among girls in sub-Saharan Africa, where 27 per cent of boys also miss out on schooling, and 33 per cent among rural children in the Middle East and North Africa. The gender gap is greatest in the latter region: 34 per cent of girls and 12 per cent of boys there have never attended school. In South Asia these percentages are 25 and 14 respectively, contributing significantly to the overall global disadvantage girls suffer. Worldwide,16 per cent of girls and 10 per cent of boys miss out on school completely.

Information deprivation: Over 300 million children in developing countries are deprived of information, lacking access to television, radio, telephone or newspapers. Without access to information, children are deprived of education in the broader sense, including mechanisms enabling them to be informed of their rights and opportunities, as well as the ability to participate effectively in society.

Deprivation in one aspect often accentuates other deprivations

The study also confirmed that disadvantages overlap and reinforce one another. A lack of sanitation pollutes the water that children use, and poor nutrition makes them vulnerable to sickness and diarrhoea – which then go untreated, further reducing their body weight and resistance to disease. Children who are poorly fed, frequently ill or have no access to safe water, decent housing or adequate sanitation facilities are likely to encounter more problems in school. A child severely deprived of shelter, living in an overcrowded home and an impoverished neighbourhood, may not be able to absorb an education even if there is a school nearby.

Children in rural areas are more exposed to these extreme forms of deprivation

Children living in rural areas in the developing world are on average twice as likely to be severely deprived of essential goods and services as their urban peers. They are also almost twice as likely to suffer severe nutritional deprivation and three times as likely to never attend school. Of course, not all urban children enjoy the

Figure 2.3 **Severe deprivation among children in the developing world, by country income group***

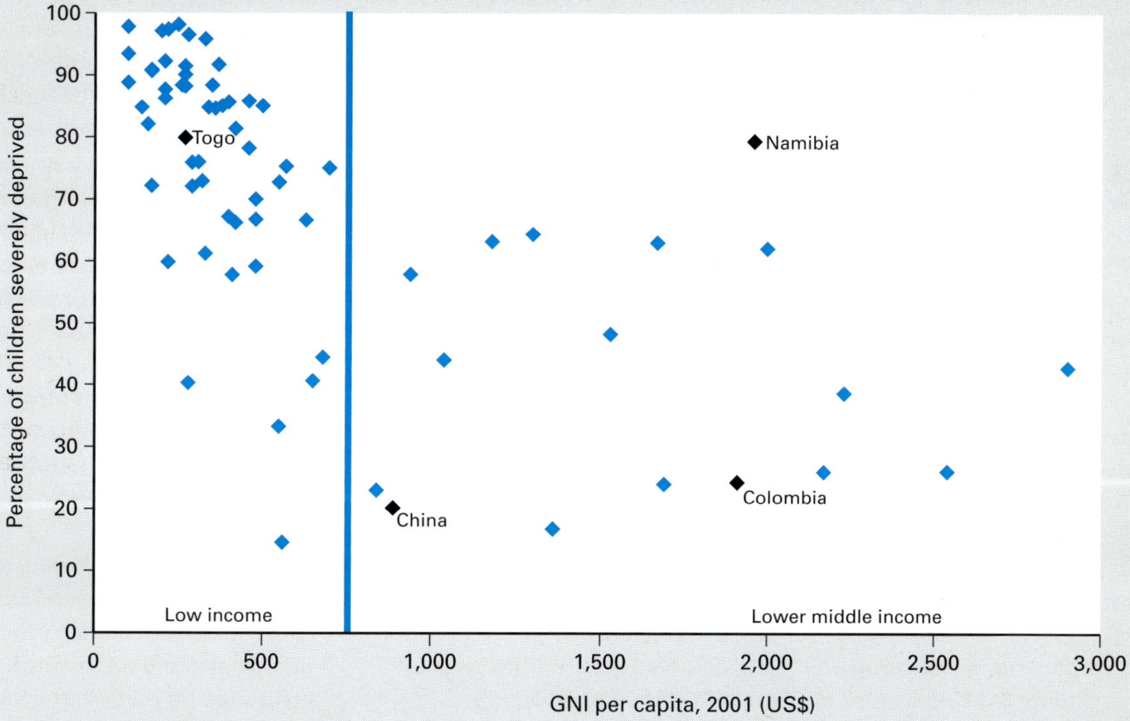

Low income: $745 or less (GNI per capita, 2001)
Lower middle-income: $746-$2,975 (GNI per capita, 2001)

*Selected countries

Source: Gordon, David, et al., *Child poverty in the developing world,* The Policy Press, Bristol, UK, October 2003. **Note:** The data used in the original study have been updated using Demographic and Health Surveys (DHS) and Multiple Indicator Cluster Surveys (MICS).

same living conditions. For instance, children who live in squatter settlements may fare even worse than their rural counterparts.[9]

Severe deprivation among children is not just an issue for low-income countries

The study by the University of Bristol and the London School of Economics focused on the deprivations of essential goods and services experienced by children in developing countries. A disturbing finding is that many of the children in extreme poverty live in countries with fairly high levels of national income. Figure 2.3 above shows aggregate levels of severe deprivation among both low- and middle-income countries. National income is clearly a factor: On average, low-income countries tend to have higher rates of deprivation than middle-income countries. Yet a significant number of children in middle-income countries are still exposed to severe deprivations. For example, while China and Colombia's levels of deprivation are roughly the same, per capita GNI is far higher in the latter. Conversely, although Colombia and Namibia have similar levels of per capita income, their levels of deprivation differ markedly. Namibia's level of deprivation is similar to Togo's, a far poorer country.

Gender discrimination is an underlying factor of severe deprivation

Poor access to education, food or health-care services has particular implications

Children's welfare and mother's property *by Bina Agarwal*

The development of human capabilities in childhood rests greatly on the ability of the family and of the State to ensure that children are free from deprivation. Children born into families that have little access to property, especially physical property such as land or housing, begin life with a considerable disadvantage. In the rural areas of many developing countries, the ownership of even a small plot of land can substantially reduce the risk of a family falling into extreme poverty. In an urban context, impoverished neighbourhoods tend to be associated with poor quality housing and overcrowding.

Recent research suggests that while family assets have a positive effect on children's well-being, it is the assets that belong to the mother that make the greatest difference. Evidence from many parts of the world shows that women, especially in poor households, spend most of the earnings they control on essential goods and services that serve the household's needs – particularly those of children. In contrast, men tend to spend a significant share of their earnings on personal goods, such as alcohol and tobacco. Even more striking are findings that a mother's ownership of assets makes a significantly greater contribution to a child's well-being than the ownership of these assets by the father. In urban Brazil, for instance, a study found that child survival probabilities improved markedly when asset income accrued to the mother than when it accrued to the father. The positive impact on the health of daughters was especially high. Children in rural India were found more likely to attend school and receive medical attention if their mother owned more assets. Among marginal farmer households in Kerala in south India, the mother's cultivation of a home garden – the harvest of which she controlled – was found to have a consistently high positive impact on child nutrition.

Apart from differences in spending patterns, mothers who own assets such as land also have greater bargaining power in the home. This can lead to a more equitable distribution of benefits along gender lines, even from the income the father controls. Recent research also shows a substantially lower incidence of marital violence against women who own land or property. This has positive implications for children, since children witnessing domestic violence tend to suffer from greater emotional and behavioural problems than other children.

Women's lack of property or property rights can also affect children's welfare when HIV/AIDS threatens. In many countries, especially in sub-Saharan Africa, the children of widows whose husbands have died of HIV/AIDS have been left destitute, because customary inheritance laws disinherit the mothers, leaving them landless and homeless.

Women's and children's welfare is affected not only by the ownership of private assets, but equally by their access to community assets such as forests and clean water. Children (especially girls) are their mother's main helpers in the collection of firewood, fodder and water. Scarcity increases this burden, and can even cause some to drop out of school or never attend school in order to help their mothers. The scarcity of community assets can also pose health risks for children. Lack of safe drinking water is a major cause of disease that affects children's productivity and school attendance. Firewood scarcity arising from deforestation forces women to substitute with inferior fuels such as weeds and crop waste. Firewood itself is associated with smoke-related diseases: inferior fuels compound this risk for children working or playing in smoky kitchens.

In many regions, decentralized community forestry management has further aggravated rather than reduced this problem, especially among poor families. In South Asia, for instance, many recently constituted community forest management committees, although meant to be inclusive and democratic, are, in practice, largely controlled by men who typically pay little attention to women's and children's needs for forest resources. Many of these committees have banned entry into local forests. While this has helped to regenerate the forests, it has also increased the time and energy expended by women and children, especially girls, on gathering firewood and fodder, or forced a shift to inferior fuels, with negative effects on the work burdens, schooling and health of children.

In summary, women's access to both privatized assets, especially land and housing, and to community assets, such as forests, is often a key factor determining the survival, health, education and physical security of children, and especially of girls. Enabling women to access these assets must thus become a primary objective of development strategies in general and poverty-reduction strategies in particular.

Access can be strengthened in several ways: by increasing the rights of women to parental and marital property; by ensuring that all government transfers of property and land go equally to both men and women, either through joint or individual titles; and by promoting schemes that enable groups of women to jointly access land and housing. This list is not exhaustive and there are many other innovative ways in which governments and communities can increase women's access to land and other property. Similarly, improving women's and children's access to community resources such as forests and water will require enhancing women's participation in the management of these resources. Basically, increasing the mother's access to land, housing and community resources will directly benefit children's welfare and help create a more child-supportive environment, both at home and in the community.

Dr. Agarwal is Professor of Economics at the Institute of Economic Growth, University of Delhi, and author of the award-winning and widely influential book *A Field of One's Own: Gender and Land Rights in South Asia* (Cambridge University Press, 1994). She has also written many papers on poverty, gender inequality, property rights and environmental management, among other subjects. She is currently President of the International Association for Feminist Economics and Vice-President of the International Economic Association.

for women and their children. The large disparities in most regions between the numbers of girls and boys who have never attended school are telling evidence of the discrimination that girls and women face. Gender discrimination is widely recognized as a major contributor to children living in poverty. How resources are earned, valued and distributed depend on power relationships between men and women within the household as well as within society[10] *(see Panel: Children's welfare and mother's property, page 24).*

Enabling women to access private and community assets must become a primary objective of poverty-reduction strategies.

Child poverty and the breakdown of protection for children

Poverty denies children safety, dignity and protection

Children living in poverty do not only experience material deprivation. Emotional and spiritual impoverishment are also abrogations of their rights. However, these dimensions of child poverty and their interaction with material deprivation and lack of family and community resources are poorly researched and documented, and internationally comparable data related to child protection is still sparse.

The Convention on the Rights of the Child makes it clear that it is the duty of governments and parents to provide the **protective environment** required to ensure that all children experience childhood in safety and dignity. It is equally clear that millions of children worldwide are being denied this protection. These children are just as impoverished as those whose rights to survival, health and education are threatened by a lack of essential goods and services.

Each year, tens of millions of children are the victims of exploitation, violence and abuse. They are abducted from their homes and schools and recruited into armed conflicts. They are trafficked and forced to work in prostitution and sweatshops. They are needlessly deprived of parental care and forced into early marriage. They are subjected to violence and abuse in the home, school and community. The effects of these abuses are far-reaching and enduring; they rob children of their childhood, preventing them from achieving anything close to their full potential.

Material deprivation exposes children to exploitation and abuse

Many child protection abuses are linked to deeply entrenched material deprivations. One of the most obvious ways in which material poverty facilitates exploitation and abuse is through child labour. It creates economic need that can force vulnerable children – such as those caught up in armed conflict, or orphaned or made vulnerable by HIV/AIDS – into hazardous labour, often at the expense of their education and recreation. Currently, 180 million children are thought to be engaged in the worst forms of child labour.[11]

Child protection abuses reinforce the generational cycle of poverty

Material deprivation makes children more vulnerable to trafficking and commercial sexual exploitation. An estimated 1.2 million children are trafficked every year;[12] 2 million children, the majority of them girls, are sexually exploited in the multibillion-dollar commercial sex industry.[13]

While poverty exacerbates child protection abuses, it is equally true that abuse often forces children into material deprivation or exacerbates their existing poverty. Violence and abuse at home can force children onto the streets, where their poverty is likely to become entrenched. Discrimination can be an obstacle to learning at school and can cause children to drop out. Exploitation generates poverty by keeping children out of school, in poor health and subject to further psychological and physical abuse.

Children in the criminal justice system face special risks

Poverty often leads children into contact with the law, and criminal justice systems that are not receptive to the rights of children accused of crimes can perpetuate poverty. When children are accused of crimes such as theft of food or detained for begging, poverty is frequently the underlying cause. And when the response to children accused of crimes is detention, they are separated at an early age from their families and the wider community, and are unlikely to learn the life skills necessary to function effectively in society and to escape poverty in adulthood. Even after their release, they are often stigmatized and may have difficulty reintegrating into the community – conditions that contribute to their further marginalization and poverty later on. In all these cases, the legacy of poverty does not stop with one generation but may affect several generations to come.

Families provide the best protection

Families form the first line of defence for children; the further away children are from their families, the more vulnerable they are. Children separated from their families, both those living or working on the streets and those in institutions, are more likely to be marginalized, abused and live in poverty in adulthood. Those living on the streets are left unprotected against violence and exploitation. They are also at greater risk of contracting HIV. Children in institutional care, while ostensibly protected from the most obvious protection abuses, are segregated from one another according to age and sex and from other people in their communities. This inhibits the development of vital social skills as well as community support and interaction.

The fight against poverty stands a good chance only when children are freed from exploitation, violence and abuse. Unfortunately, there is no quick-fix solution: A child cannot be immunized against abuse. But there is something that can be done. We can begin by ensuring that all children live in a strong protective environment.

Child poverty as relative deprivation

Children can experience poverty even if they are not severely deprived or abused

Growing up in families whose material conditions are close to the 'norms' in the community is important for children. Research on how children themselves experience and feel about poverty suggests that relative deprivation – when children do not have access to the same opportunities as other children – hurts young people in poor and rich countries alike. Deprivation of goods and services that adults might not always regard as 'essential' can be viewed differently by children, who may feel they are denied the lifestyles and opportunities available to other children.[14]

Relative deprivation means unequal opportunities for children to survive, grow and thrive

Relative deprivation in terms of family income and wealth is a factor in absolute deprivations of essential goods and services that children require to survive, grow and develop, and can therefore have grave implications for them. A recent study of 43 developing countries has shown that, on average, children of families in the bottom wealth quintile of the population are more than twice as likely to die before reaching the age of five than children living in families in the top quintile.[15] In Brazil, children whose per capita family income is less than half the minimum wage are three times more likely to die before their fifth birthday, 21 times more likely to be illiterate and 30 times more likely to live in a home without an adequate water supply.[16] While low family income often interacts with other aspects of poverty – such as limited parental education, and rural or slum environments – to undermine children's rights to survival and access to health care and educational services, studies have shown that it can be a determinant of child health and education achievement independently of these other factors.[17]

In this context, it is particularly disturbing that income inequalities across countries and among households within the same country have risen in the past decade despite periods of rapid economic growth in many developing countries.[18] Large segments of the population in China and India have received only modest benefits from the rapid economic growth of recent years.[19] Similarly, research on child poverty in the Organisation for Economic Co-operation and Development (OECD) countries has shown that the proportion of children living in relative poverty – defined as households where income was less than half of the national median – has risen since the late 1980s *(see Figure 2.4: Child poverty in OECD countries, page 28)*.

Child poverty has risen in relative terms over the last decade in some affluent countries

In 11 of the 15 OECD countries for which comparable data are available, there have been notable increases in child poverty rates over the course of roughly the last decade. At the beginning of the millennium only three countries – Finland, Norway and Sweden – enjoyed a rate of child poverty of less than 5 per cent. And in only four countries – Canada, Norway, the United Kingdom and the United States – has the share of children living in low-income households seen even a modest reduction over the past decade. With the exception of Norway, these countries still have relatively high levels of relative child poverty, owing to a higher base of comparison in the late 1980s.

Strategies for tackling child deprivation

The statistical evidence on children living in poverty presents a bleak picture.

Figure 2.4 Child poverty in OECD countries*

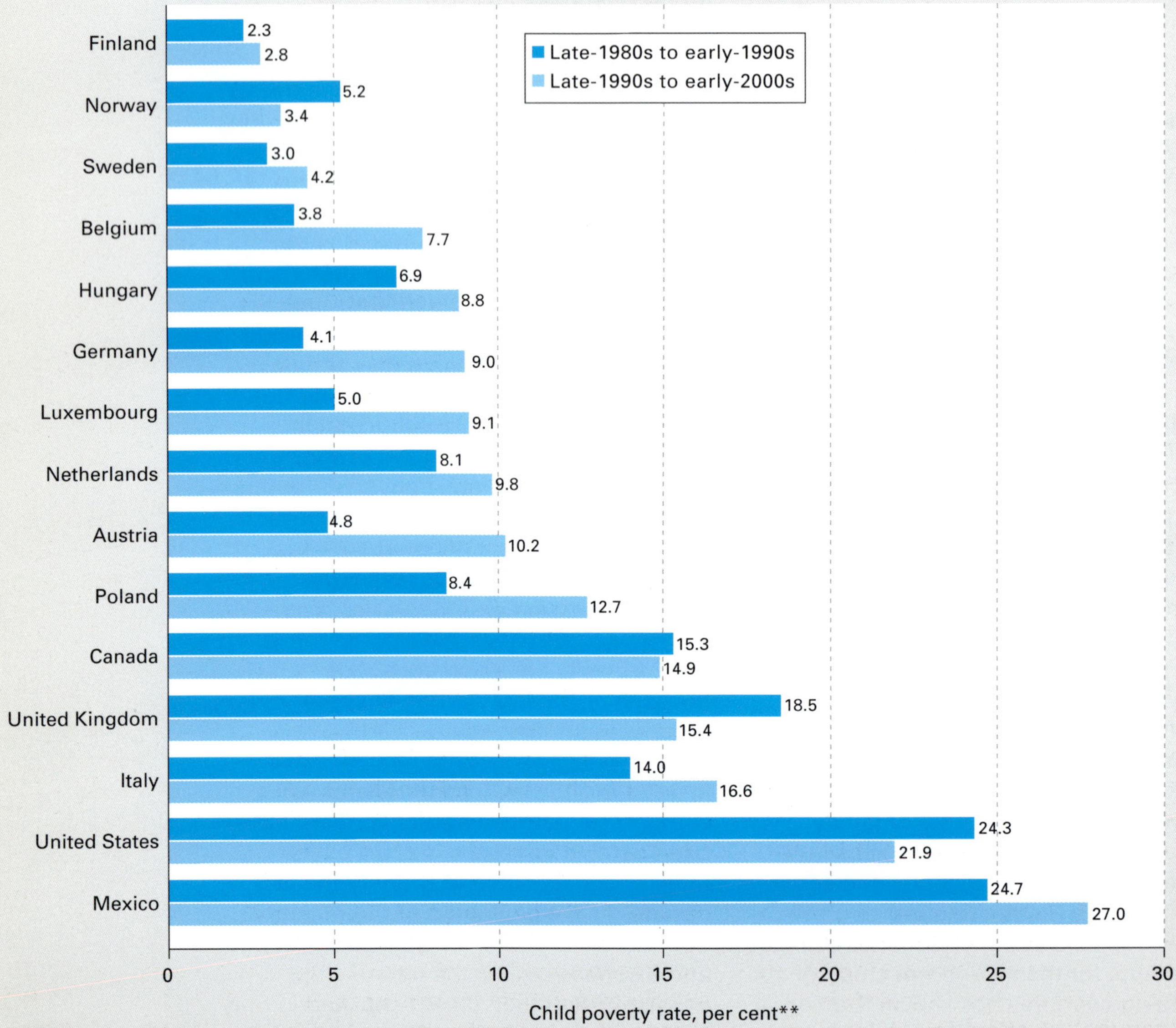

* Selected countries

**Child poverty rate refers to the percentage of children living in families whose income is less than 50 per cent of the median adjusted disposable income for all persons.

Source: Luxembourg Income Study, 2000.

It confronts us with staggering rates of severe child deprivation that will hinder further progress in reducing child mortality rates and in improving health and nutrition, education and protection. It shows rising rates of relative deprivation that translate to disadvantaged children who gain little or nothing from increased average household incomes and better public services. It demonstrates the extent to which the lack of a protective environment imperils children and places them at risk of exploitation, abuse and violence.

These numbers and trends call into question the commitment of national and local governments, the private sector and the international community to act on the

Millennium Development Goals and 'A World Fit for Children'. They also call into question the determination of all duty bearers, including parents and communities in addition to the aforementioned parties, to reduce child poverty. All this is even more disturbing as much of the experience and knowledge about how to act on child poverty is already on hand.

Harnessing globalization and economic growth for children

Economic growth needs channelling in order to reduce child deprivations

Countries that have significantly and sustainably reduced poverty have done so by simultaneously addressing economic and social issues rather than giving exclusive priority to macroeconomic stability or economic growth. There is evidence that even rapid economic growth can be slow to produce positive returns in terms of social development. A key example of this is the under-five mortality rate, whose average annual rate of reduction has slowed sharply in both China and India since 1990 despite robust economic growth in both countries over the same period.[20] Countries successful in improving access to basic social services for children are ready to spend more – as Costa Rica, Malaysia and Mauritius, for example, have consistently done over the past few decades.[21] While economic growth is clearly required to attain the Millennium Development Goals, a recent World Bank study has found that the two sub-Saharan African countries expected to have the best poverty-reduction performance by 2015 stand out because of their more equitable income distribution rather than their pace of economic growth.[22]

Investing in children will bring economic rewards as well as human development

Recent evidence suggests that in developing countries, investing in human capital – including education – attracts foreign capital from investors seeking gains from a dynamic and well-educated workforce.[23] Similarly, economic recovery and foreign direct investment have been associated with good education systems and a well-trained workforce in several economies that made the transition from planned systems to market economies during the 1990s.[24]

Countries that protect children's rights even in times of crisis will benefit from higher human development levels. A World Bank report showed that Cuba – a country with a high level of human development despite a moderate level of per capita income – cut defence spending sharply in the 1990s while broadly sustaining health and education expenditure.[25]

Debt relief and reduced defence spending could free up resources

Recent initiatives by international financial institutions to contain high indebtedness in the least developed countries – principally through the Heavily Indebted Poor Countries Initiative as well as efforts to prevent further high indebtedness – are welcome and necessary. Many developing countries are often already spending more on debt service than on education or health. Several countries spend more than 10 per cent of their gross domestic product on servicing debt, and currently 38 countries qualify for the initiative because they are both extremely poor and heavily indebted.

Meanwhile, the world is currently spending almost 1 trillion dollars on defence annually. This is much more than the estimated annual cost of US$40-70 billion required to meet the Millennium Development Goals by 2015. Many of the world's poorest countries continue to budget far more for military armaments and personnel than for health or education; diverting even a fraction of this expenditure to health or education would provide them with millions of dollars for social investment. It will be interesting to observe in the coming years the economic and social outcomes of countries such as Bolivia, Botswana, Ghana, Kenya and Malaysia, where education commands a far higher proportion of gross national income than military spending.

Promoting local solutions and participatory planning for development

With the Millennium Development Goals and the Monterrey Consensus driving the international agenda, the world community is now firmly committed to good governance in the broadest sense: promoting human development through transparent public budgets, wide-scale consultations and participatory planning processes. This means rejecting the idea that the world is divided into two blocks of poor and rich countries with asymmetric objectives or responsibilities. It means that those who will implement plans should actually own them, learn from the experiences of other countries and share their own experiences.

Poverty Reduction Strategy Papers are becoming the principal focus for poverty reduction in the least developed countries

Since 1999, national governments in low-income countries have been required to draw up Poverty Reduction Strategy Papers (PRSPs). These must satisfy a set of key criteria in order for countries to qualify for aid or loans from international financial institutions and have been a tool to gain access to debt concessions under the Heavily Indebted Poor Countries Initiative. PRSPs have enshrined poverty reduction as a pre-eminent goal of national and international policy and are increasingly used to promote the Millennium Development Goals.

Using Poverty Reduction Strategy Papers to better promote and protect childhood

The ongoing development of PRSPs – and the growing debate about how to make them more effective, equitable and participatory – represents a significant opportunity. PRSPs rarely make a full transition from a narrowly economic or sectoral perspective to a human rights approach, which would include an emphasis on personal freedom, democracy and social participation alongside fiscal agendas, budget transparency and accountability. Similarly, experience so far shows that the concerns of children, youth and women do not feature strongly and tend to be secondary to the macroeconomic objectives.[26] PRSPs with a strong focus on fulfilling children's rights would address key issues for children and their families, country-specific causes of child poverty and methods to expand opportunities for children.

UNICEF is working with governments and partners to ensure that priorities for children, such as immunization, free education and legislative initiatives to protect the rights of children, are built into PRSPs. However, problems relating to governance, including poor functioning and corruption in public institutions and weak civil society organizations can prevent an enabling environment where child rights, including the right to health and education, can be realized. Efforts to build the capacity of duty bearers in a developing country will therefore need to address constraints of insufficient public resources, governance and quality basic amenities.

Integrated and comprehensive national and community programmes

The threat to childhood from poverty is multipronged. The response has to be similarly all-embracing, starting with an integrated approach to early childhood that will greatly improve the chances that every child will both survive and thrive.

Aggregate public expenditure on support for families and young people correlates closely with the incidence of relative child poverty in OECD countries *(see Figure 2.5, Social expenditure and child poverty in OECD countries, page 35).* Well-developed government-funded institutions can prevent high rates of social exclusion and related risks for children and youth. The cost of having similarly complex welfare systems is sometimes seen as prohibitive in poorer countries. However, middle-income countries could clearly do more, and international assistance, federal initiatives and innovative local solutions can remove part of the costs for governments in developing countries.

The Oportunidades programme, launched in Mexico in 1997, grants cash transfers on the condition that members of a household are certified as attending school and health clinics. The results have been significant and consistent. Over the last five years the programme has doubled its outreach and it is currently on target to pass the mark of serving 5 million families. In rural areas covered by the scheme, there has been a 57 per cent rise in visits to health clinics and significant reductions in under-five morbidity. School attendance and completion have also been boosted *(see Panel: Oportunidades: A poverty-reduction programme that works, page 32)*.

In Madagascar, a comprehensive child survival programme is helping to reduce under-five mortality. One-third of the country's children under the age of five are moderately or severely underweight. But the root of the problem lies in causes other than a lack of food and includes poor feeding practices, malaria, diarrhoea and other recurrent illnesses. The programme includes activities to vaccinate every child, to ensure that every mother and newborn is protected by insecticide-treated mosquito nets and to provide free oral rehydration packs. Mothers are encouraged to breastfeed their babies: The benefits include fewer illnesses and better nutrition for their infants. They are also counselled on how to improve nutrition and supplement their children's diets with vitamin A, schools are provided with latrines and safe drinking water, and health workers are trained on how to manage the treatment and prevention of childhood illnesses.

Integrated approaches have also proven successful in middle- and high-income market economies – where poverty often manifests itself through educational disadvantage, frequent illness, obesity, teenage motherhood, high unemployment rates for young people, drug abuse and crime.

Gender perspectives could improve the efficiency of poverty-reduction schemes

Having a gender perspective in public interventions is important in rich and poor countries alike. The OECD countries that have the lowest rates of child poverty as measured by family income both secure generous support for families with children and have high labour market participation rates among women. Higher employment rates among women (including those who are single parents) have contributed to reducing child poverty in the 1990s in a number of OECD countries.[27]

The highly flexible labour market in the United States and the effective legal protection against gender discrimination in the Nordic countries may not be available to women in other countries. Nonetheless, pursuing labour market and fiscal policies that address economic insecurity among women and diminish persistently high levels of inequality can help reduce poverty. The Oportunidades programme highlighted above, for example, owes much of its success to the fact that in almost every case the cash transfer is paid to a woman. This strengthens her position within the family and increases the likelihood that the money is used to purchase food and other essentials.

Strengthening the protective environment for children

Developing legislation and local initiatives to fortify the protective environment for children will result in both economic development and the fulfilment of child rights. A recent study by the International Programme on the Elimination of Child

Oportunidades: A poverty-reduction programme that works

© UNICEF/HQ04-0567/Mauricio Ramos

Oportunidades works directly with women and families like this one to provide scholarships, basic health care, hygiene education and nutritional supplements.

Since 1997, a large-scale, innovative government programme called Oportunidades has been making a difference in the life of millions of Mexican children and their families.

Oportunidades reached 4.2 million families in 2003, which accounts for three out of four families living in capacity poverty (defined below), and the budget approved for 2004 will include 5 million households. In the short term, the programme strives to improve these families' health and education status. In the long run, it hopes to enable families to rise above the poverty level through education, which will improve their income and employment prospects. The merits of Oportunidades as a social policy and poverty-reduction strategy can be seen in recent external evaluations, which found improvements in school attendance and completion, maternal and child health, socio-economic conditions and household income in the areas of intervention (see *Key Achievements, next page*).

The programme focuses on families living in 'capacity' poverty (*pobreza de capacidades*), in which income is less than that needed to cover basic food, health and education needs, a situation that affects 5.6 million families (25.3 per cent of Mexican households). The programme addresses these specific needs by providing cash transfers directly to mothers to enable them to pay for school attendance for children, buy food and schools supplies and provide adequate nutrition and health-care visits for the entire family. Oportunidades requires that schools and health clinics certify that children are attending school and that family members are actually utilizing health services. Through constant monitoring, the programme continuously assesses its own effectiveness and results.

Low operating costs – less than 6 per cent of the programme's budget – coupled with thorough evaluation mechanisms have also made Oportunidades a highly reputable and efficient operation, and the first such scheme to survive intact through two administrations. Oportunidades was born under the name 'Progresa' during the administration of former President Ernesto Zedillo (1994-2000). Under the incumbent President, Vicente Fox, Oportunidades has remained the government's most important social programme. Not only did it continue despite the huge changes in the political landscape that have taken place in recent years, but the Mexican Congress has also annually enlarged its budget. The Fox administration has increased funds for high schools, incorporated families in urban and metropolitan areas into the scheme, and improved its operational and supervision systems.

Oportunidades is jointly implemented by the Ministries of Social Development, Education and Health, as articulated in the National Plans for Development, Education and Health for 2002-2006. The coordinated efforts of the ministries have proven effective in increasing the programme's efficiency, expanding its reach and avoiding duplication of efforts. In 2002, the Inter-American Development Bank signed a US$1 billion financing package with the Mexican Government for three years, to be renewed in 2005 for an additional three years and another US$1 billion. This funding will ensure the continuation of Oportunidades until 2008.

Some key features of the programme include:

- **Scale and sustainability:** In 1997, the programme (then called 'Progresa') reached 300,705 families in 13,000 localities in 12 states. In 1998, its first full year of operations, the programme was expanded to reach 1.6 million families. It has continued to grow every year. In 2004, it will reach 5 million families (25 million people), and has been already allocated a budget of more than US$2.5 billion.

- **Targeting:** Oportunidades in 2003 operated in 70,436 localities, 96 per cent of which are marginalized, isolated rural areas of under 2,500 inhabitants. In 2002, cities of up to 1 million inhabitants with a medium, high or very high level of marginalization were included in the programme. In rural areas, family eligibility is based on a household census (Encuesta de Características Socioeconómicas de los Hogares). In urban areas, poor families can apply by filling out a socio-economic survey at information centres set up for this purpose.

- **Gender focus:** One programme priority is to improve the condition of women by strengthening their position in the family and in society through increased access to information and knowledge and active participation in decision-making processes. Some 98 per cent of heads of household receiving cash benefits are women, which is intended to increase their autonomy and ensure that the money received is used for the family, i.e. to buy food and pay for school supplies. In education, the scholarships at secondary (grades 7 to 9) and upper-secondary (grades 10 to 12) levels are higher for girls than for boys, with the objective of reducing the gender gap in attendance at these levels.

- **Young people:** The cash amount of scholarships gets progressively higher as students move on to higher grades in order to compensate for higher levels of school dropouts as children get older and enter the work force. In the 2003/04 academic year, 1.4 million secondary and 535,000 upper-secondary school students received scholarships.

A separate component of the programme called Young People with Opportunities (Jóvenes con Oportunidades) provides a savings account for those completing the 12th grade and wishing to go on to higher education, start a business, obtain health insurance coverage or acquire a home.

- **Evaluation mechanisms:** A regular evaluation of programme management, results and impact is part of the Oportunidades strategy, including evaluations of educational, health and nutritional interventions and evaluations of poverty levels. Related indicators include women's condition; family spending and consumption patterns; family health and nutritional status; children's educational attainment; young people's entry into the labour market; demographic variables; and target efficiency (municipalities, localities and families).

Key Achievements

Education

- In the third year of primary school, a 14.8 per cent reduction in girls' dropout and a 22.4 per cent reduction in boys' dropout in rural areas.
- In the third year of primary school, 14.2 per cent fewer girls and 9.6 per cent fewer boys failed to graduate in urban areas.
- A 25 per cent increase in secondary school attendance in rural areas (32.2 per cent for girls and 17.1 per cent for boys).
- A 5 per cent increase in first-year secondary-school attendance in urban areas (7 per cent for girls and 3 per cent for boys).
- An 85 per cent increase in first year upper secondary-school attendance in rural areas (79 per cent for girls and 90 per cent for boys).
- A 10 per cent increase in first year upper secondary-school attendance in urban areas (11.2 per cent for girls and 9.1 per cent for boys).

Health and nutrition

- A 57 per cent increase in health clinic visits in rural areas.
- A 45 per cent increase in health clinic visits for nutritional monitoring of children under five, in rural areas.
- Maternal mortality in municipalities incorporated in Oportunidades was 11 per cent lower than in non-incorporated municipalities.
- A 12 per cent reduction in under-5 morbidity.
- Child mortality rates in municipalities incorporated in Oportunidades were 2 per cent lower than in non-incorporated municipalities.

See References, page 100.

Labour offers convincing evidence that, over a 20-year period, the economic benefits of eliminating child labour would far exceed the costs.[28] The model envisages urgent action to eliminate the worst forms of child labour, such as bonded labour and the criminal exploitation of children in prostitution. Income-transfer programmes that offer financial benefits to families living in poverty with school-age children would help to defray the costs of transferring their children from work to school.

In Brazil, the Bolsa Escola initiative provides a minimum monthly salary to poor families that agree to keep all their 7- to 14-year-olds enrolled in and recording 90 per cent attendance in school.[29] Brazil's 1990 Statute of the Child and Adolescent stands as one of the most advanced pieces of national legislation on child rights. Here, the protective environment approach to child protection has succeeded in dramatically reducing the incidence of child labour – the number of working children aged 5-15 fell by some 2.2 million between 1995 and 2002.[30]

Involving children

Children themselves help us understand what child poverty means. 'Young Lives' is an international research project conducted by the Institute of Development Studies in the United Kingdom that is recording changes in child poverty over 15 years. Through research in Ethiopia, India, Peru and Viet Nam, the project aims to reveal the links between international and national policies and children's day-to-day lives. The project includes a strong participatory element and has already showcased, for example, children's writings about their experiences of poverty, education and child labour.

In Serbia and Montenegro, impoverished by more than a decade of strife, inter-ethnic tension and economic crisis, UNICEF has been working with the government and local non-governmental organizations on a participatory study of child poverty that has made a point of consulting children as well as their parents. The research eschews the dry traditional techniques of polls and questionnaires and involves children in discussions that are set up like games.

While younger children focus on the lack of supplies such as books, toys and playgrounds, older children also mention problems with the way institutions operate. Parents emphasize income poverty more than children, believing it to be the source of all other problems. But the research has shown, above all, that poverty affects the fulfilment of a wide range of basic child rights, from education to health, from play to adequate living standards.[31] And, as one child from Serbia and Montenegro says: "Finally someone has remembered to ask how we feel about all this."

The way forward

Poverty is one of the three greatest threats to childhood in the world today. But the lines of response to child poverty are clear – provided the international community has the political and economic will to pursue them. From the evidence reviewed above, the following key lessons emerge:

- Reaching the Millennium Development Goals would go a long way to reducing the material poverty that children experience in developing countries. The Millennium Development Goals and policies specifically designed to benefit children are interrelated and mutually reinforcing strategies. Many of the deprivations children face can be addressed by a positive change in their family income and better access to basic social services. However, strong arguments can be made for prioritizing action on reducing the many dimensions of the poverty that children experience. This will require greater awareness, concepts that tackle child poverty as a multidimensional issue, better monitoring and sharing of lessons, and efforts to build a broad coalition of agents.

Figure 2.5 Social expenditure and child poverty in OECD countries*

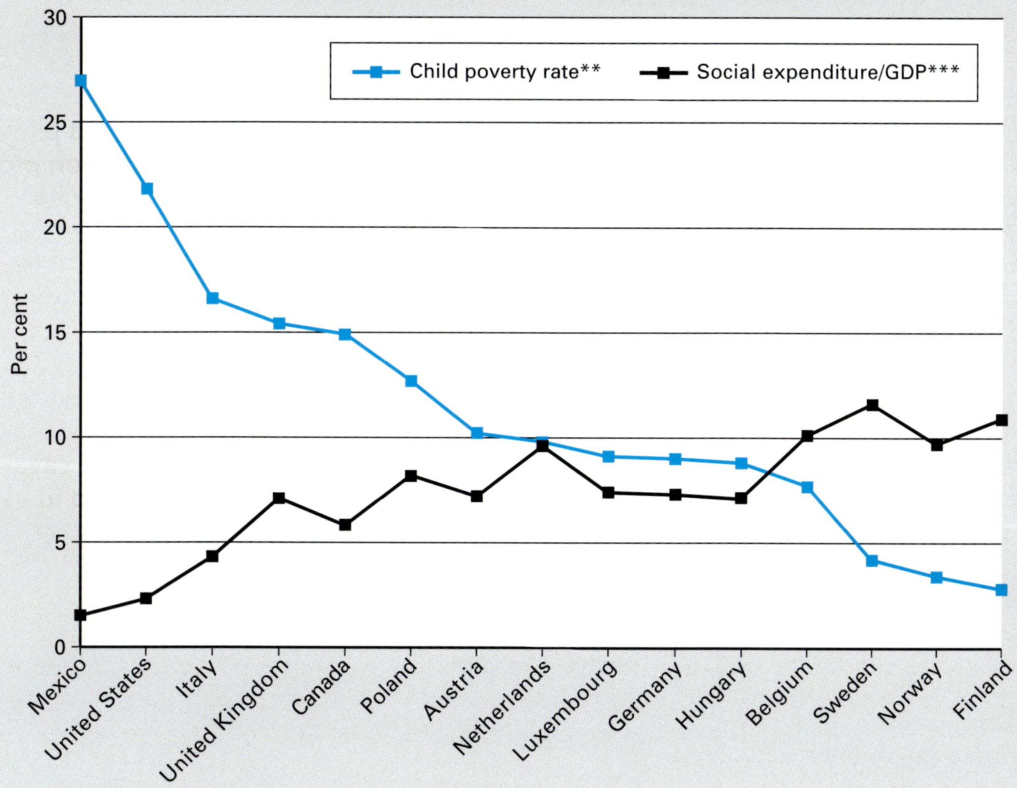

* Selected countries; late-1990s to early-2000s

** Child poverty rate refers to percentage of children living in families whose income is less than 50 per cent of the median adjusted disposable income for all persons.

*** Social expenditure figures are based on family and other related social benefits, including incapacity-related benefits, active labour market programmes, unemployment, housing and other social policy benefits to the working-age population as a percentage of GDP. Figures for Belgium and the United States do not include housing. Figures for Mexico do not include unemployment benefit.

Sources: Poverty rate from Luxemburg Income Study, 2000. Social expenditure as a percentage of GDP from OECD Social Expenditure database, 2004.

- Protecting childhood from poverty is a global as well as a national responsibility. Severe deprivations that deny children the right to survive, grow, develop and participate are concentrated heavily in lower-income countries, which have fewer resources to confront these challenges. In addition, poor countries generally have less capacity to protect themselves from external shocks such as commodity price fluctuations or adverse climatic conditions. National and local governments need to demonstrate commitment and capacity to act on child poverty; the best results can be achieved from multipronged action from national as well as international actors.

- Interventions that address child deprivations need to be designed and owned locally; families and children must be part of the solution. The evidence reviewed underlines the importance of building interventions on sound country-based, locally-situated, gender-sensitive analyses, rather than on the basis of 'one-size-fits-all' agendas. Without a good understanding of the country conditions or local family context, for example, health or education interventions focused on children may fail to deliver the desired results.

- Strengthening the protective environment for children at every level, from the family right through to the level of national and international initiatives must be a priority for poverty-reduction strategies.

- Resolve conflict and combat HIV/AIDS, which both contribute to the poverty children experience and combine with it to undermine their childhood.

The Multiple Dimensions of Child Poverty

Poverty threatens every right, depriving children of the capacities they require to survive, develop and thrive. Children living in the countries highlighted on this map face some of the worst deprivations of essential goods and services: More than one third of all children are malnourished, lack basic immunizations, or are not enrolled in or attending school. In 13 countries, less than half the population has access to improved drinking water and adequate sanitation facilities.

Income-poverty measures are a good indication of where the problem lies. Most countries with high levels of deprivation suffer from low levels of per capita income. But income-poverty measures cannot adequately convey how children actually experience poverty. India and Senegal have very similar levels of per capita income, for instance, but children in India are more at risk from malnutrition while children in Senegal are more likely to miss out on an education. Eighty-nine per cent of children in Peru receive the DPT3 vaccine, while only 65 per cent of children in the Dominican Republic do – but the per capita income in the former country is less than 4 per cent higher than in the latter.

Poverty embodies the multidimensional nature of the threats to childhood: Each deprivation exacerbates the effect of the others, and when two or more coincide, the effects on children can be catastrophic. Children who must walk long distances to fetch water have less time to attend school – a problem that particularly affects girls. Children who are not immunized or who are malnourished are much more susceptible to the diseases that are spread through poor sanitation. These and other deprivations, such as lack of adequate shelter and access to social services, inhibit children's ability to achieve their full potential. Until every child realizes their right to education, nutrition and health care, childhood will continue to be under threat.

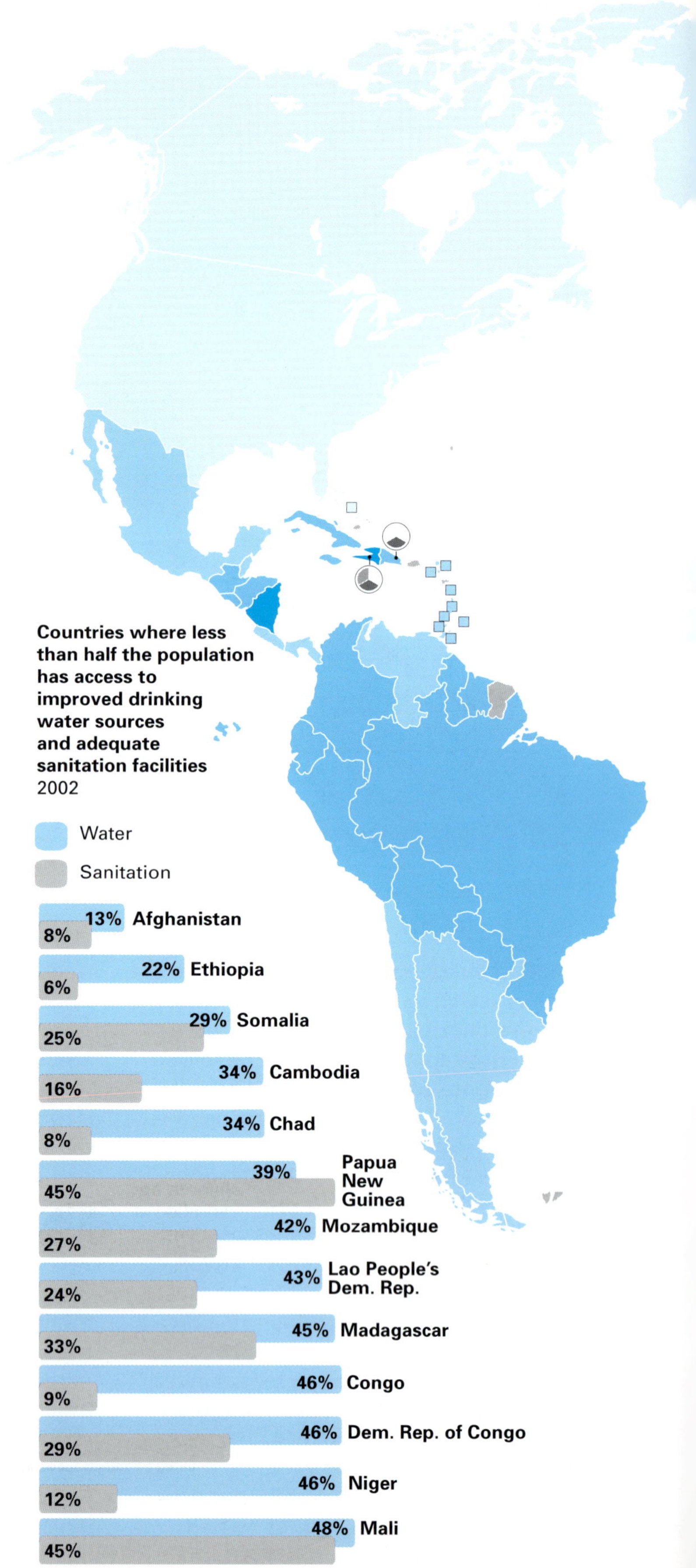

Childhood Under Threat: Poverty

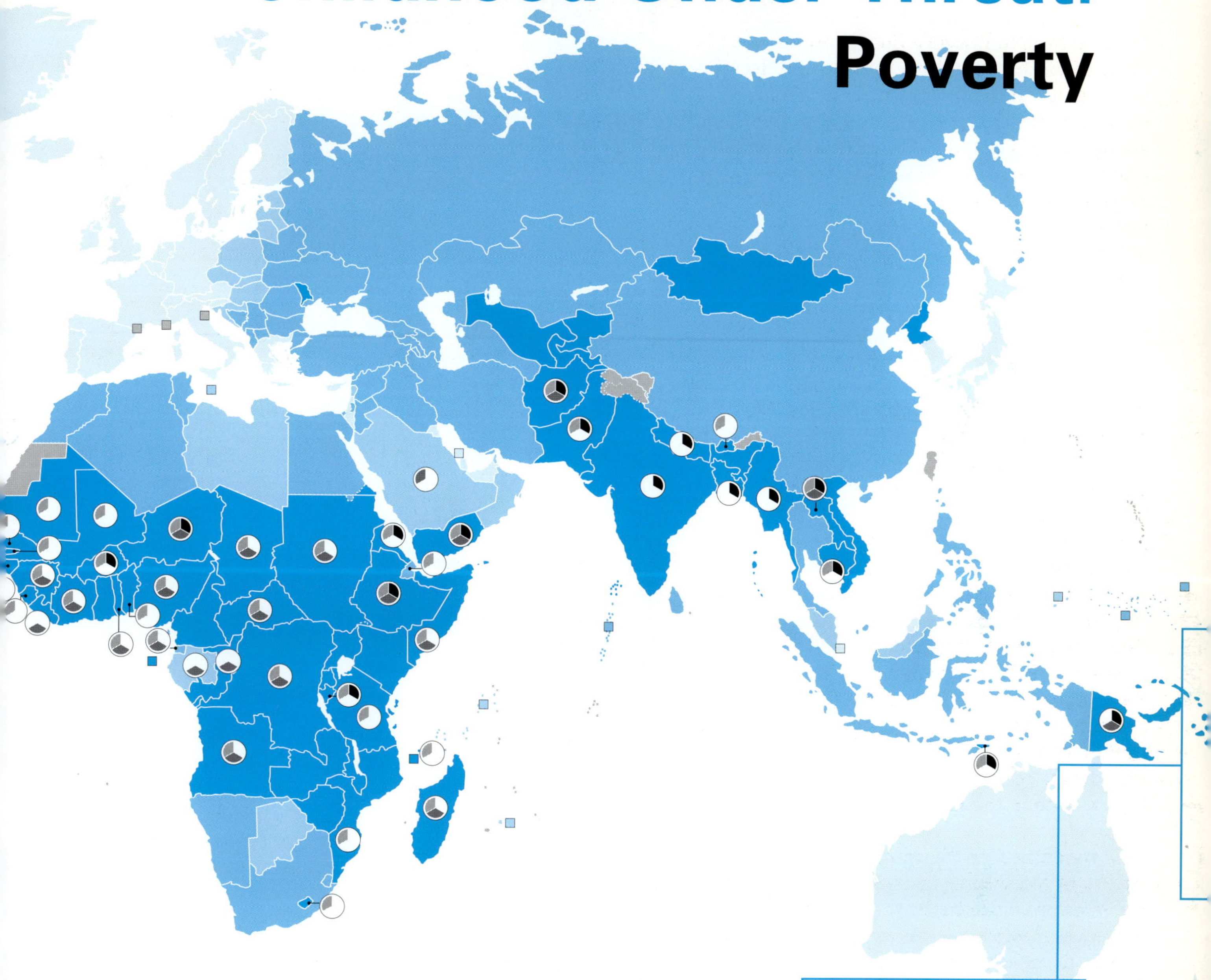

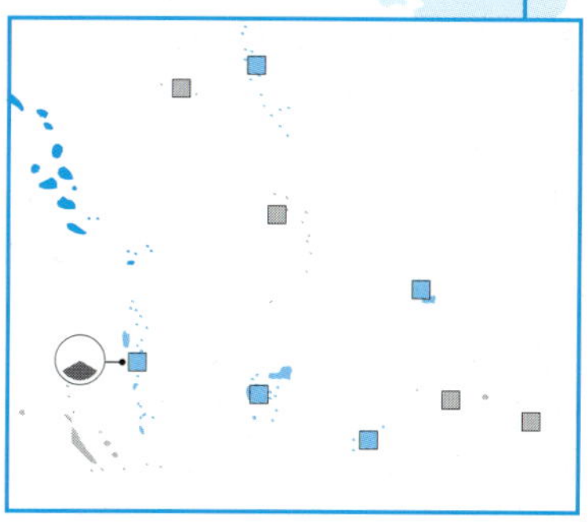

GNI per capita
2003

- Low income $765 or less
- Lower middle income $766–$3,035
- Upper middle income $3,036–$9,385
- Higher income $9,386 or more
- No data

Source: For income group classifications: World Bank.

Dimensions of Poverty

More than one third of children not enrolled in or attending primary school 1996–2003*

More than one third of under-fives moderately or severely underweight 1995–2003*

More than one third of one-year-olds not receiving DPT3 immunization 2003

* Data refer to the most recent year available during the period specified.

This map does not reflect a position by UNICEF on the legal status of any country or territory or the delimitation of any frontiers.

Dotted line represents approximately the Line of Control in Jammu and Kashmir agreed upon by India and Pakistan. The final status of Jammu and Kashmir has not yet been agreed upon by the parties.

3

Children Caught Up in Conflict

Children do not start wars, yet they are most vulnerable to its deadly effects. Children rarely grasp the complex causes of armed conflict, yet they are all too often forced to flee their homes, witness atrocities or even perpetrate war crimes themselves. Children are not responsible for war, yet it robs them of their childhood.

The unfolding tragedy in Darfur, Sudan, has provided further evidence that the world is not yet able to offer children the protection from armed conflict to which they are entitled. As of October 2004, more than 1.2 million Sudanese had been violently uprooted from their homes. Many were killed by armed militias, and those who survived by fleeing towards or across the border with Chad found themselves enveloped in a battle for survival of a different kind – against disease, inadequate shelter and poor nutrition. Camps set up to receive them were overwhelmed by the immensity of the humanitarian crisis. Resources were stretched to breaking point and a massive outbreak of disease constantly threatened, particularly for children weakened by the lack of food, adequate water and sanitation. Elsewhere in southern Sudan a conflict that had raged since 1983[1] between the government and the Sudanese People's Liberation Movement was close to resolution but the tragedy in Darfur has made progress in that peace process very difficult.

The changing nature of conflict

The situation in Sudan is a grim reminder of how the nature and complexity of warfare have changed in recent years. In the 14-year period after the cold war ended,

Summary

ISSUE: Children are always among the first affected by armed conflict. Even if they are not killed or injured, they can be orphaned, abducted and left with psychological and psychosocial distress from direct exposure to violence, dislocation, poverty or the loss of loved ones. Those who survive often find themselves enveloped in a battle for survival of a different kind – against disease, inadequate shelter, a lack of basic services and poor nutrition. Schools can also become caught up in violence, often with tragic consequences.

Children may be forcibly recruited into combat and servitude, experience sexual violence or exploitation, or be exposed to explosive remnants of war that kill and maim thousands each year. Girls are especially vulnerable to sexual violence, abuse, exploitation, and stigmatization during and after conflict situations. Many girls also experience war on the front lines.

ACTION: To protect children from armed conflict, a number of actions must be pursued:

- **Put children first, before and during conflict.** Countries must consider the impact on children before engaging in conflict or imposing sanctions, and must allow humanitarian agencies the scope to protect children and women during conflict.
- **End the recruitment of child soldiers.** Adoption and application of the Optional Protocol to the Convention on the Rights of the Child on the involvement of children in armed conflict must be stepped up.
- **Strengthen the protective environment** for children at every level. Encourage countries to ratify and apply – without reservation – treaties designed to protect children from the pernicious effects of conflict.
- **Eradicate the culture of impunity and strengthen accountability.** Perpetrators of genocide, war crimes – including the conscription of children under 15 – and crimes against humanity must be brought to justice.
- **Improve monitoring and reporting on child rights violations in conflict.** This must become a priority, especially the compilation of reliable data on children affected by or involved in armed conflict.
- **Expand demobilization and mine-awareness campaigns.** The sensitive reintegration into civil society of child combatants through a comprehensive support programme is vital. Greater attention must be paid to the reintegration of girl combatants. Mine-risk education should be included in school syllabi and in public health programmes.
- **Restarting education for children caught up in armed conflict as soon as possible** can inject stability and normalcy into their lives.
- **Prevent conflict** by addressing the underlying causes of violence and poverty, and investing more in mediation and conflict resolution.

Figure 3.1 Conflicts of high intensity, 1945–2003

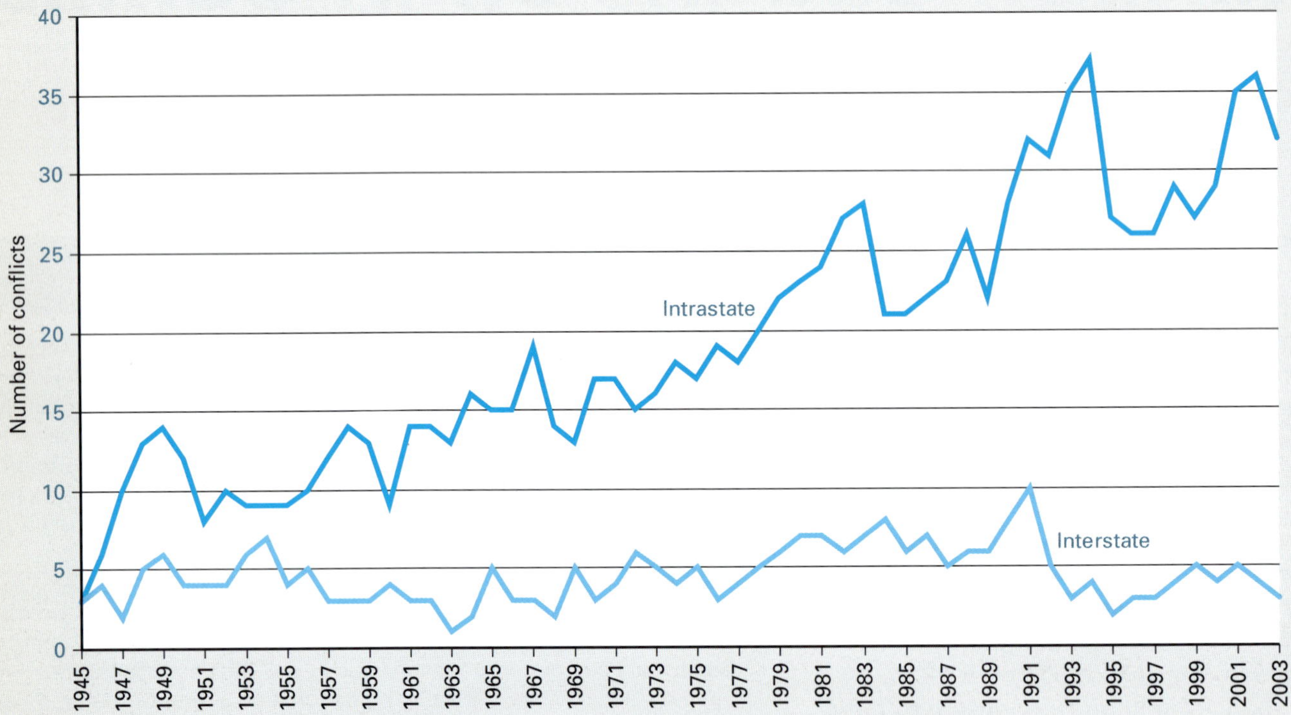

Source: Heidelberg Institute on International Conflict Research, *Conflict Barometer 2003.*

from 1990 to 2003, there were 59 different major armed conflicts in 48 locations – and only four of these involved war between nations.[2] There is now greater recognition that ethnically based conflict has increased – inevitably so, given that wars between nations have been largely replaced by more local, internecine forms of hostility.

The threat to civilians from conflict has grown enormously. An estimated 90 per cent of global conflict-related deaths since 1990 have been civilians, and 80 per cent of these have been of women and children.[3] In some cases, civilians are directly targeted; in others, they are indirect victims of stray bullets or explosive remnants of war. The nature of civil war dictates that fighting takes place where people live, rather than on a battleground. And if the roots of a conflict lie in ethnic hatred or resentment, all members of the 'despised' group become vulnerable, not just the combatants representing them.

By no means are all the victims of war killed by bullets or bombs; many suffer from the catastrophic impact of conflict on the health of an entire society. In a typical five-year war, the under-five mortality rate increases by 13 per cent and adult mortality increases even more. Even after a conflict is over, its repercussions undermine child survival. Recent research has shown that during the first five years of peace, the average under-five mortality rate remains 11 per cent higher than its corresponding level before the conflict.[4]

Many developing countries are locked in a vicious cycle in which poverty generates the desperation, fear and struggle for resources that can lead to conflict, which in turn gravely aggravates poverty. Of the world's 20 poorest countries, 16 have suf-

Figure 3.2 Where the major armed conflicts are

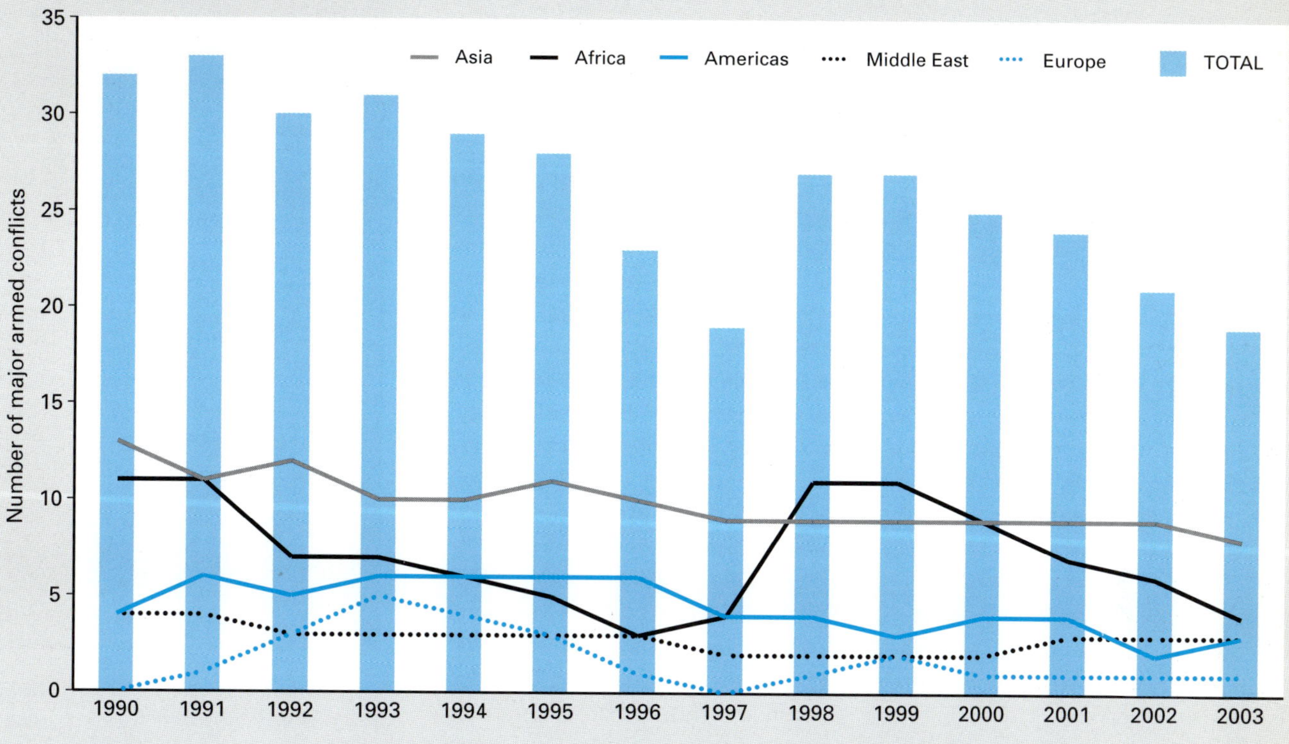

Source: Stockholm International Peace Research Institute, *SIPRI Yearbook 2004.*

fered a major civil war in the past 15 years.[5] Civil war typically triggers a prolonged reversal of economic and social development that often results in poverty continuing from one generation to the next.

The impact of conflict on childhood

Children are always among the first affected by conflict, whether directly or indirectly. Armed conflict alters their lives in many ways, and even if they are not killed or injured, they can be orphaned, abducted, raped or left with deep emotional scars and psychosocial trauma from direct exposure to violence, dislocation, poverty or the loss of loved ones.

The destruction wrought by war is likely to mean that children are deprived of key services such as education and health care. A child's education can be disrupted by the absence of teachers, or by an environment in which landmines and other explosive remnants of war jeopardize their safety. Schools can also become caught up in armed conflict, as was seen in September 2004 during the hostage crisis and subsequent calamitous battle in the Russian town of Beslan, which left more than 150 children and even greater numbers of adults dead. In Aceh, Indonesia, as part of the conflict between government forces and rebel groups, 460 schools were burned to the ground during May 2003 alone.[6] In Nepal, schools are regularly used as centres for propaganda and recruitment by the opposition to the government. Attacks on and abductions of teachers and students are frequent.

Children in combat

The exact number of children currently caught up in conflict as combatants is unknown, but it is likely to run into the

Girl soldiers: The untold story

Invisible soldiers

The use of children in combat went largely unacknowledged internationally until a consortium of humanitarian groups, the Coalition to Stop the Use of Child Soldiers, began systematically identifying girls and boys associated with fighting forces in every country caught up in armed conflict. There is now a greater awareness of the many children in this situation. Nonetheless, too often in international reports and initiatives, the generic terms 'child soldiers' or 'children' refer only to boys, even though girls were part of government, militia, paramilitary and/or armed opposition forces in 55 countries between 1990 and 2003 and were actively involved in armed conflict in 38 of those countries.

The focus has been on boys because they were viewed as soldiers in armed forces, while girls were seen mostly as the 'wives' or sexual slaves of adult combatants. Only now is it emerging that, in fact, girls' experiences are far more complex and include such diverse roles as active fighters, intelligence officers, spies, porters, medics and slave labourers.

Why is it important to talk about girl combatants separately from boys? Because their experiences are quite different from those of their male counterparts. Currently, international programmes addressing the needs of girls – where such programmes exist – are poorly informed. It is essential to document and understand the experiences of girl combatants in order to devise better responses during conflict, as well as in post-conflict activities such as demobilization and social reintegration.

Coercion, abduction and survival: How girls become involved in conflict

Studies indicate that girls are primary targets for abduction during armed conflict with the objective of forcing them to become warriors or sexual and domestic partners. Although precise figures are not available, it is clear that this type of abduction takes place worldwide. Over the past decade, girls have been kidnapped and forced into wartime service in at least 20 countries, including Angola, Burundi, Liberia, Mozambique, Rwanda, Sierra Leone and Uganda in sub-Saharan Africa; Colombia, El Salvador, Guatemala and Peru in Latin America; Cambodia, Myanmar, the Philippines, Sri Lanka and Timor-Leste in Asia; the former Federal Republic of Yugoslavia and Turkey in Europe.

Abduction is not the only cause of girls' participation in armed conflict. Girls are sometimes given into armed service by their parents as a form of 'tax payment', as happens in Colombia or Cambodia, or for other reasons. After the rape of his 13-year-old daughter, a Kosovo Albanian refugee father gave her to the Kosovo Liberation Army. "She can do to the Serbs what they have done to us," he said. "She will probably be killed, but that would be for the best. She would have no future anyway after what they did to her."

Some girls may also choose to become part of an armed group. However, their choice is largely a matter of survival. Given the high levels of physical and sexual abuse of girls in most current armed conflicts, taking up arms can be safer than waiting to be raped, injured or killed.

An adolescent girl stands in the doorway of a vocational training centre run by the Christian Brothers, a non-governmental organization that works with unaccompanied and abused children, children living or working on the streets, and former child soldiers, in the southern town of Bo, Sierra Leone.

And the supply systems of warring groups may be the only source of food, shelter and security available to children in war-affected areas. To call their enlistment voluntary is both misleading and erroneous.

There is a significant correlation between the abduction and forced recruitment of girls and their widespread and systematic sexual exploitation and abuse. Girls' overall lower social status makes them more vulnerable to assault than boys, and rape is a common occurrence, often resulting in sexually transmitted infections. In Sierra Leone, for example, health workers estimate that 70 to 90 per cent of rape survivors tested positive for sexually transmitted infections. Abductees were especially at risk because of repeated incidents of sexual violence.

Reintegration: Lack of appropriate interventions for girls

Post-conflict, girls may fall through the cracks, continually marginalized by disarmament, demobilization and reintegration programmes at all levels. Relatively few girls go through such programmes. Instead, many spontaneously return to their communities and never receive formal assistance, leaving them with a host of unresolved psychosocial and physical issues. The specific needs of girl soldiers during these processes are usually not addressed, largely because:

- The number of girl soldiers is routinely underestimated.
- Women and girls who enter or are abducted into the armed forces are not considered 'real soldiers'.
- Many of these girls are mistakenly classified as women because they are over 17 by the time of disarmament, demobilization and reintegration and often have children of their own.
- The current emphasis is on attracting armed males to areas for disarmament and demobilization.

Moreover, young women who were girls when they were abducted or forcibly recruited and who return with 'war babies' may be stigmatized and rejected by their families and communities because of the shame attached to rape and to giving birth to babies fathered by the girls' captors. Few girls are tested or treated for sexually transmitted infections, increasing the risk of HIV infection and transmission within their families and communities.

The existing international legal framework – including the Convention on the Elimination of All Forms of Discrimination against Women and UN Security Council resolution 1325 on Women and peace and security – calls upon states to condemn and eliminate violence against women. In addition, the Convention on the Rights of the Child and its Optional Protocol on the involvement of children in armed conflict are among the foremost international legal standards to stop the recruitment and abduction of girls and boys into armed conflict. However, protection and support for female survivors of violence during conflict situations in general, and for girl soldiers in particular, is still woefully inadequate.

What is needed, as an initial step, is greater recognition that the vast majority of girl soldiers have suffered severe violations of their human rights and have witnessed and, in some cases, participated, in acts of extreme violence. Although they show a tremendous ability to cope in spite of their experiences, their resilience should not be mistaken for empowerment. Girls overwhelmingly cite access to education, which helps them envision a broader and brighter future, and training in skills that will enable them to support themselves and their families as true sources of empowerment. A holistic approach involving leaders, parents, relatives and neighbours is critical: Girls and young women who return to their communities need the support of adults who will have a positive influence over them. They need to see that, although they have changed, they have a place, a future and a meaningful contribution to make in their communities.

See References, page 101.

Figure 3.3 Main causes of food emergencies, 1986–2003

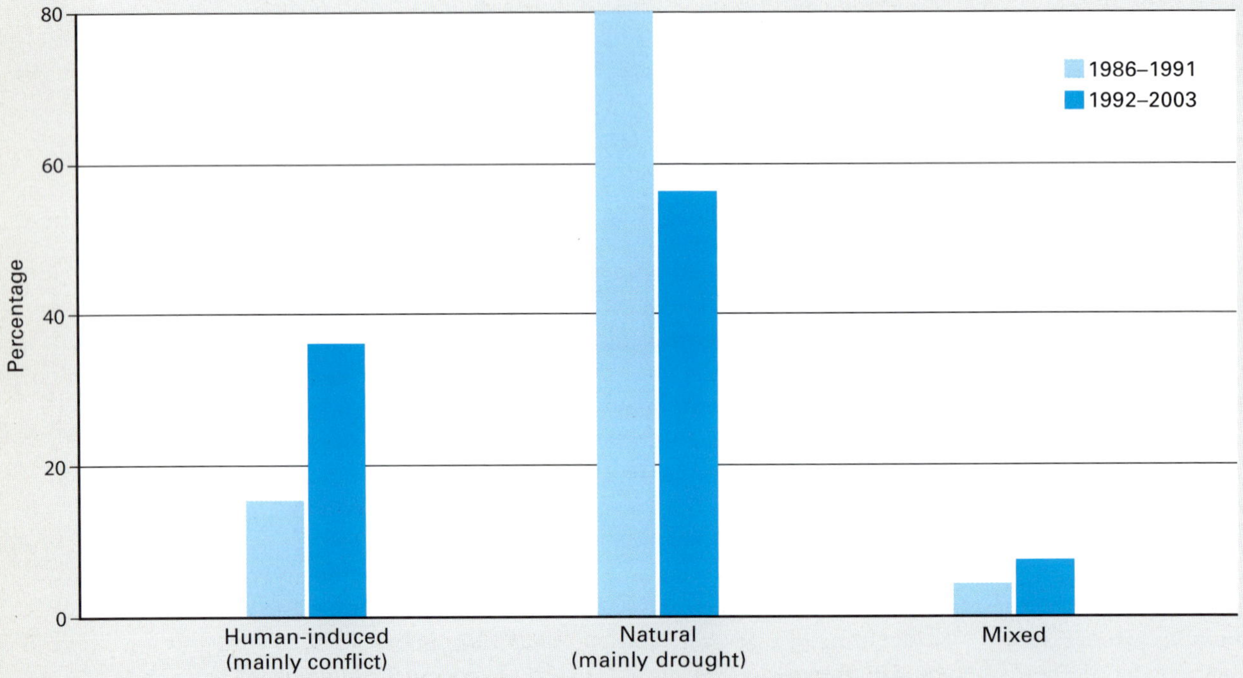

Source: Food and Agriculture Organization of the United Nations, *The State of Food Insecurity in the World 2003,* p. 14.

hundreds of thousands.[7] Children are conscripted, kidnapped or pressured into joining armed groups. Not all of them take part in combat, though the proliferation of lightweight weapons has made it possible for even children under 10 to become effective killers. Children are also forced into sexual slavery and to become labourers, cooks or servants, messengers or spies. Girls are particularly liable to be sexually exploited, whether by one commander or a whole troop. Many will also join boys on the front line *(see Panel: Girl soldiers: The untold story, page 42).*

Armed groups and, in some cases, government forces use children because they often prove easier than adults to condition into fearless killing and unthinking obedience. For all such children, whether they are forcibly recruited, join in order to escape poverty or hunger, or enlist to actively support a cause, the first loss is their childhood.

Africa and Asia have the highest numbers of children involved in conflict as combatants. And the trend in using children in conflict is not diminishing: During 2003, there was a surge in the recruitment of children in Côte d'Ivoire, the Democratic Republic of the Congo and Liberia. In the Democratic Republic of the Congo, in particular, there have been widespread reports of atrocities, rape and beatings involving children. Thousands of children in northern Uganda have been abducted by the rebel group Lord's Resistance Army and forced into combat and servitude. Thousands more flee their homes and villages each night to seek refuge in towns where they can avoid attack or abduction *(see Panel: Uganda's 'night commuter' children, page 48).* In Myanmar, there are still large numbers of children in the armed forces, while the number of children used by armed groups and urban militias in Colombia has increased to around 14,000 in recent years.[8]

Refugee and internally displaced children

A family life constitutes one of a child's fundamental rights. War has no respect for this: it drives people out of their homes as they flee battle zones or direct attack, leaving behind not only their property, but also their family and friends. During the 1990s, around 20 million children were forced by conflict or human rights violations to leave their homes.[9]

As they flee conflict, families may become separated. Children left alone are more likely to be sexually abused or recruited into combat. Deprived of a support network, they are also more vulnerable to hunger and disease. Some families manage to remain intact until they have found refuge, but the poor conditions in which many fleeing families find themselves increase children's vulnerability to malnutrition and illness.

When families leave their homes, it is usually seen as a temporary situation. All too often, however, the period of exile runs into years or even decades; in such cases, children may spend their whole childhood in camps. In southern Sudan and elsewhere, entire generations of children have never lived at home.

Of the 40 million people worldwide who have been forced to flee their homes, around one third are refugees who have been driven across national borders.[10] The other two thirds are internally displaced, a proportion that has been rising steadily in parallel with the increase in civil strife. It is much harder for the humanitarian community to assist internally displaced persons since national governments often view this as 'interference'. Yet the problems of the internally displaced can be as severe as those of refugees, including alienation from support systems, lack of identity papers and discrimination. Unlike refugees, who benefit from international legal protection, in many cases their legal status and care and protection provided by the internal authorities is weak.

Children suffering from sexual violence

Sexual violence is often a consciously deployed weapon of war. It can include rape, mutilation, exploitation and abuse. In the conflicts in Bosnia and Herzegovina, and Croatia in the early 1990s, it was a deliberate policy to rape teenage girls and women and force them to bear children, often referred to as the 'enemy's child'.[11] More recent conflicts in the Democratic Republic of the Congo, Liberia, Sierra Leone and Sudan have all involved the use of sexual violence. Adolescent girls are frequently singled out for their youth and relative defencelessness or because they are perceived to be less likely to be infected with HIV. Reports abound from conflict zones of girls being abducted and forced into sexual slavery by militias or rebel groups.

The rise in sexual violence that often accompanies conflict is not restricted to crimes committed by combatants. The chaos and disruption produced by war undermines the rule of law, leaving children – particularly those who have become separated from their families and communities – much more vulnerable to sexual violence or exploitation. Camps for displaced persons can be perilous places for children, where overcrowding, desperation and the weak application of the rule of law can expose them to sexual abuse. In addition, the poverty, hunger and insecurity generated by conflict can force children into prostitution: In Colombia, for example, girls as young as 12 are reported to have submitted sexually to armed groups in order to ensure their families' safety.[12]

All of these factors tend to increase the likelihood of HIV transmission in conflict zones, while the breakdown of school and health systems inhibits safeguards that could counter these risks. In addition, the hopelessness of life in a war-affected area can foster risky sexual behaviour among young people. A conflict in a region with low rates of HIV prevalence will not in itself produce an explosion in the infection rate. But the breakdown of social order and the sexual

Figure 3.4 Landmines: The global picture

A landmine costs as little as US$3 to produce. Clearing one landmine can cost up to US$1,000

200–215 million landmines are stockpiled in the arsenals of 78 countries

15,000–20,000 people are killed or injured by landmines each year

More than 300,000 people are living with landmine-related injuries worldwide

Landmine casualties are reported in 65 countries

Over 80 per cent of landmine victims are civilians

Nearly one third of these are children

Fewer than 10 per cent of landmine victims have access to appropriate medical care and rehabilitation services

Over 50

The number of mine-producing countries has dropped from over 50 in 1992, when the International Campaign to Ban Landmines began its work, to 15 by mid-2003

15

Sources: International Campaign to Ban Landmines, *Landmine Monitor Report 1999* and *Landmine Monitor Report 2003*; and the Landmine Survivors Network.

violence associated with conflict always increase the spread of HIV. When war erupts in an area already affected by HIV/AIDS, as in Rwanda during the 1990s and in the eastern region of the Democratic Republic of the Congo the effect is catastrophic.

Explosive remnants of war

Even after a conflict is over, children are often threatened by what it leaves behind. Explosive remnants of war, including abandoned explosives and weapons, landmines and unexploded ordnance, kill and maim thousands of children each year. Explosive remnants of war can prevent access to fields, wells, clinics or schools for whole communities, causing deprivation long after hostilities have ceased. Families may be condemned to live in temporary settlements because of the continuing presence of mines in their communities.

Landmines alone claim between 15,000 and 20,000 new victims each year.[13] Nearly two thirds of the 65 countries that suffered new mine casualties between 2002 and 2003 had not experienced active conflict in that period.[14] A study by Human Rights Watch found that the use of cluster munitions by coalition forces in populated areas of Iraq was one of the major causes of civilian casualties in 2003.[15]

Most victims of explosive remnants of war are men, often farmers. But children are also at risk: they tend to be curious about strange objects, and may be attracted to the colourful designs of some butterfly mines and cluster bombs. In addition, many children are responsible for herding animals and fetching water, which involve traversing large tracts of countryside that may include mined areas; they are also less likely than adults to understand signs marking minefields.

Protecting children affected by armed conflict

Since the United Nations General Assembly first requested that a comprehensive study on the impact of armed conflict on children be undertaken,[16] the plight of children affected by armed conflict has gained greater visibility, both in the international community and at the national and local levels in many countries.

Substantial efforts have been made to meet the challenges that conflict poses for children. The report on the obstacles encountered in protecting children from conflict, published by Graça Machel in 1996,[17] increased the attention given to war-affected children's issues throughout the international community. As a result, the Secretary-General appointed a Special Representative for Children and Armed Conflict to promote the protection, rights and well-being of children at every phase of conflict, and the UN Security Council has taken an increasingly active interest in receiving annual updates on the issue, incorporating child-specific considerations into its deliberations, and hearing the direct testimonies of affected children.

While this increased attention to the problems of children in conflict has generally resulted in important advances to better protect them, many of the problems identified in 1996 are even graver today – and new challenges have emerged to test the world's resolve to protect its children.

The Anti-War Agenda

Nine years ago, UNICEF set out a 10-point Anti-War Agenda, launched in *The State of the World's Children 1996 (see Panel: The Anti-War Agenda, 1996, page 50).*[18] Appalled by the plight of children in conflict situations that contradicted "not just every normal human concern for their welfare but also the professed beliefs and legal obligations of those responsible," the organization laid down a series of challenges that insisted on the rights of children. The remainder of this chapter examines the progress made on the agenda since 1996 and outlines the challenges that lie ahead in each area, which are still as relevant today as they were nine years ago.

Child soldiers and rehabilitation

Progress: Today there is a growing consensus against the use of children as soldiers. In 1999 the 'Worst Forms of Child Labour Convention' was unanimously adopted by the 174 Member States of the International Labour Organization and became the first specific legal recognition of the forced or compulsory recruitment of children for use in armed conflict as a form of child labour. It was also the first convention to set a minimum age of 18 years for recruitment and participation in armed conflict.

Adopted at the UN General Assembly on 25 May 2000, the Optional Protocol to the Convention on the Rights of the Child on the involvement of children in armed conflict raises the minimum age for direct participation in hostilities from 15 to 18 years, forbids the forced recruitment of any child under 18, and urges governments to raise the minimum age for voluntary recruitment. In the case of non-state-armed groups, the treaty prohibits all recruitment – voluntary or coercive – of children.

The adoption and entry into force in 2002 of the Optional Protocol is the result of an ongoing global campaign to end the recruitment and use of child soldiers. The effort involves governments, UN agencies and non-governmental organizations, with the Coalition to Stop the Use of Child Soldiers playing a leading role. It reflects a significant advance in protecting children from the pernicious effects of conflict, but it is only one step towards ending the human rights abuses suffered by the thousands of child combatants. As of September 2004, the Optional Protocol had been ratified by 82 States; work is ongoing to ensure that it is adopted by the remaining States parties.[19]

In November 2001, the UN Security Council took the unprecedented step of asking the Secretary-General to publish

Uganda's 'night commuter' children

The idea of childhood as a protected time of healthy growth has been effectively obliterated in northern Uganda. For children living there, the 18-year conflict has meant a continued reign of terror perpetrated by the rebel group Lord's Resistance Army. The rebels, most of whom are child combatants, usually attack at dusk. They surround small civilian settlements and camps for internally displaced persons, and then move in to steal food and abduct children and adults to swell their ranks. Children are especially vulnerable to these violent attacks and are often forced to kill their parents or other children. Those who are abducted by the army – an estimated 10,000 to 12,000 children since the escalation of the conflict in June 2002 – are used as soldiers and porters; girls are used in sexual slavery.

Dozens of children and adults seek refuge at a UNICEF-supported shelter run by the non-governmental organization Rural Focus Uganda, in the town of Gulu. They are among the tens of thousands of 'night commuters' across Uganda who leave their homes each night, fearing forced abduction or attack by the rebel group Lord's Resistance Army.

Children who are abducted in northern Uganda have often been forced to march to camps in neighbouring southern Sudan. Many thousands are thought to have died from disease or starvation on the way. As part of their initiation into rebel life, they have been made to participate in brutal acts of violence, often being forced to beat or hack to death fellow child captives who have attempted to escape. Those who do survive are forced to engage in combat against the Ugandan army and the Sudan People's Liberation Army. More recently, following the Ugandan army's destruction of several Lord's Resistance Army bases in southern Sudan and the intensification of the conflict since mid-2002, many abductees are now taken directly to Lord's Resistance Army units inside Uganda, where they may still face equally brutish treatment.

By October 2004, tens of thousands of children in the Gulu, Kitgum and Pader Districts of Uganda were fleeing their homes and villages each night to urban centres and the centres of larger camps for internally displaced persons, fearing attacks and abductions by the Lord's Resistance Army. These children, known as 'night commuters', also sleep in temporary shelters, empty churches, hospital compounds, verandas, bus stations or dusty doorways. They return home each morning. Some are, in fact twice displaced: first forced to leave their homes as a result of the conflict and then uprooted from their place of refuge by the rebels' incursions. Night commuting also takes place in camps for internally displaced persons, where children whose huts are on the periphery will sleep near public-service buildings in the centre of the camp for shelter. A lack of security prevents monitoring of the camps at night.

Night commuters – many of whom are without the protection of parents or organized shelter sites – face the threat of physical abuse, sexual exploitation and gender-based violence, including rape. Girls are subjected to sexual harassment and abuse along transit routes and in the sleeping spaces in town centres. The children are increasingly exposed to the risks of contracting HIV and other sexually transmitted infections, and of early pregnancy, as many are left with no choice but to become involved in 'survival sex' in exchange for food or money.

Material assistance and basic services are inadequate or non-existent in the shelters used by the night commuters. Since 2003, UNICEF, in cooperation with partners such as Noah's Ark and AVSI (Associazione Volontari per il Servizio Internazionale), has provided basic shelter, blankets and access to sanitation facilities to 12,000 night commuter children in the towns of Gulu, Kitgum and Kalongo. The shelter is provided in a relatively safe environment within a walled campground. As the phenomenon continues to grow with the conflict, UNICEF and its partners are increasing their assistance. However, they remain cautious in the level of assistance provided in each of these centres, to ensure that children only come to shelters for reasons of security. Accordingly, the shelter sites have all agreed that only basic overnight materials and facilities will be provided.

The people of northern Uganda, in particular children, have suffered from the impact of conflict for a generation. By May 2004, the number of Ugandans displaced by fighting in that part of the country had trebled to approximately 1.6 million, 80 per cent of whom are children and women. HIV/AIDS is spreading in the north at an alarming rate. Basic literacy is in decline. In the district of Gulu, where 90 per cent of the population has been forced from their homes by the conflict, less than 20 per cent of the population has access to effective health care.

The Ugandan Government and the Lord's Resistance Army, with the cooperation and support of the international community, must strive for a peaceful resolution of the conflict. Until a lasting solution is achieved, the Government is responsible for protecting its citizens, especially the most vulnerable. Donors, the UN system and other humanitarian organizations must urgently step up their assistance to ameliorate the plight of the night commuters.

Return to Saint Mary's: Ten abductees manage to escape the Lord's Resistance Army

In 1996, rebels from the Lord's Resistance Army raided Saint Mary's, one of Uganda's top boarding schools, abducting 139 girls. Although the rebels released most of the girls soon after the raid, they kept 30 of them captive. The abductees were beaten, tortured, forced to become 'wives' to rebel commanders and taught to kill.

Eight years later, Saint Mary's has not forgotten those girls. Every evening after class, the students pray for them, and a remembrance ceremony is held each year on October 10th, the anniversary of the abduction. In 2004, the school had some cause for celebration: ten of the girls abducted in 1996 have escaped. One of them is Charlotte Awino, who is now 22. Her mother, Angeline Atyam, had become a vocal activist for her daughter's return. She bonded with other parents of abducted girls and campaigned tirelessly to bring their plight to the attention of the international community. Her activism led her to appeal directly to international leaders, including former United States President Bill Clinton and the United Nations Secretary-General, Kofi A. Annan, for help in gaining their release.

Her activism also came to the attention of the Lord's Resistance Army, which offered to release Charlotte if Angeline stopped speaking out. It was an agonizing decision, but Angeline refused to be silenced until all the children were released. In the summer of 2004, Charlotte managed to escape with her son, who she conceived after being raped by a top commander.

While Charlotte is now reunited with her mother, Angeline is still an active advocate for the release of the Saint Mary's girls that remain in captivity – although some are believed to have been killed, around six have not yet been released – as well as all the other children who have been abducted by the Lord's Resistance Army.

The Anti-War Agenda, 1996

ISSUE	RECOMMENDATION
Prevention	The world must no longer wait for the outbreak of hostilities before it pays heed. Much more deliberate effort should be made to address the underlying causes of violence and to invest more resources in mediation and conflict resolution.
Girls and women	In the midst of conflict, specific community-based measures are necessary to monitor the situation and needs of girls and women, and especially to ensure their security because of the terrible threat of sexual violence and rape. Traumatized girls and women urgently need education and counselling. Because in times of conflict women's economic burdens are greater, access to skills training, credit and other resources must be secured. Education, women's rights legislation, and actions to strengthen women's decision-making roles in their families and communities are all needed, both before and after conflicts.
Child soldiers	UNICEF believes that the minimum age of recruitment into the military should be 18 years. At present, under the Convention on the Rights of the Child, it is 15 years. The change could be achieved through the adoption of an Optional Protocol to the Convention. Beyond that, there is a great need to concentrate on rehabilitating child soldiers to prevent them from drifting into a life of further violence, crime and hopelessness.
Landmines	No international law specifically bans the production, use, stockpiling, sale and export of anti-personnel mines. It is now time for such a law. UNICEF joins many other organizations in concluding that this is the only way to stop the endless suffering of children and other civilians. UNICEF will not deal with companies manufacturing or selling landmines.
War crimes	Recent years have seen the most barbaric acts of violence against children and other civilians. These must be denounced as they are revealed. International war crimes tribunals must have both the support and the resources to bring perpetrators to justice.
Children as zones of peace	This idea should be pursued more vigorously. The gains from establishing such zones may be fragile and temporary. Nevertheless, zones of peace have become an important part of international diplomacy – capable of prising open vital areas of humanitarian space in even the most tangled conflicts. As such, UNICEF intends to pursue the possibility that zones of peace be raised to a tenet of international humanitarian law.
Sanctions	Economic sanctions are imposed on the assumption that the long-term benefits of pressure on errant regimes outweigh the immediate cost to children. This may not be the case. There should be a 'child impact assessment' at the point at which any set of sanctions is applied, and constant monitoring thereafter to gauge impact.
Emergency relief	In situations of long-term conflict, aid should be seen as part of a process to help rebuild a society's capacity and promote development.
Rehabilitation	A much more deliberate effort needs to be made to demobilize both adult and child soldiers and rebuild communities so as to offer not just respite but also reconciliation. An important part of rehabilitation must be to address the psychosocial damage that children suffer.
Education for peace	Disputes may be inevitable, but violence is not. To prevent continued cycles of conflict, education must seek to promote peace and tolerance, not fuel hatred and suspicion.

Truth and reconciliation in Sierra Leone: Giving children a voice

The mandate of the Truth and Reconciliation Commission in **Sierra Leone** is unique in the way it pays special attention to the experiences of children affected by the conflict. The challenge has been to develop child-friendly procedures that ensure children's protection and help them feel as safe as possible when recounting their personal experiences of the horrors of war. Among the procedures developed are special hearings for children, closed sessions, a safe interviewing environment, protected identity for child witnesses, and training of staff in providing psychosocial support for children.

From the outset, children have been involved in the design of these procedures. In June 2001, UNICEF, in collaboration with the National Forum for Human Rights and the human rights arm of the UN mission in Sierra Leone, organized a meeting between child rights and child protection experts and a group of children, including former combatants who had been abducted by rebel forces, girls who had been forced into sexual relations with rebel commanders, and child amputees. The children were accompanied by their social workers, who provided support at difficult moments and confirmed that telling their stories would help the healing process. They recommended that children be permitted to express themselves in a variety of ways – through oral declarations, signs and actions, drawings and written statements. They cautioned, however, that children in Sierra Leonean society are taught to keep silent, and that in some cases they might be afraid to tell the truth or reluctant to speak up in order to protect friends or family. They suggested that the Truth and Reconciliation Commission try to overcome these challenges by using family discussions, by creating an environment of respect for children's voices, and by forming youth clubs to sensitize children about issues affecting them.

The commission began its public hearings in April 2003 and held closed hearings at district level for testimonies from children and women. Girls met individually with female commissioners and boys with male ones. Child protection organizations that carried out follow-up visits reported that the children's participation in the commission helped them come to terms with their experiences; some expressed a sense of relief and pride in their contribution. From June 2003, the commission held public hearings on children's experiences during the war. Many children testified, although some who were victims of the war did so by video so as to protect their identity. Recommendations from children were included in the commission's final report in 2004, and a child-friendly version of the report, the first of its kind anywhere in the world, was produced. More than 100 children from three national children's networks participated in its drafting.

a list of those parties to armed conflict that continue to use children as armed combatants. The list was first published in November 2002 and updated a year later. Another milestone was passed in July 2002, when the Rome Statute of the International Criminal Court entered into force, making the conscription, enlistment or use of children under 15 in hostilities a war crime.

One of the most significant developments in recent years has been the increasing use of truth and reconciliation commissions in post-conflict situations. These commissions can enable children to testify about their experiences and to participate in national healing processes *(see Panel: Truth and reconciliation in Sierra Leone, above)*. Psychosocial support for children who have endured trauma is an important part of UNICEF's integrated response to emergencies.

Challenges: Despite the progress noted above, the scope of the child combatant problem is still not well understood, and hard data to support many of the qualitative assumptions made thus far are lacking. The adoption of international legislation banning the recruitment of child soldiers, while necessary, will not by itself ensure an end to recruitment. Although a number of concrete commitments have been obtained from parties to armed conflicts to prevent the recruitment of children, challenges

A young boy stands amid the rubble of what used to be the Safe Play Area in Rafah, Occupied Palestinian Territory.

remain to the application of international standards such as the Optional Protocol.

New challenges have also emerged. The abductions of children by parties to conflict have significantly increased in recent years[20] and will require further attention if effective prevention methods are to be developed. In addition, a protective environment needs to be developed for demobilized child soldiers that prevents their re-recruitment and ensures successful reintegration into their families and communities.

Campaigning against the exploitation of children as combatants on the global stage must be supported by the sensitive reintegration into civil society of children who participated in armed conflict at the grass-roots level. Former child combatants are likely to have been denied a formal education and may face difficulties in returning home, especially if they have been forced to take part in violence against their families, friends and neighbours. In addition, communities and families need to be briefed and prepared for their return, and psychosocial and health care need to be provided. The provision of education, including literacy, life skills and income-generating skills, enable returnees to secure a livelihood after being demobilized. Yet these reintegration components have received less financial support than disarmament and demobilization efforts, an imbalance that can lead to frustration and further violence.

Girls and women

Progress: Great strides have been made in recognizing the unique impact that armed conflict has on girls and women. On 31 October 2000, the UN Security Council unanimously adopted resolution 1325 on Women and peace and security. The resolution marked the first time the Security Council had addressed the disproportionate impact of armed conflict on women. It recognizes the contributions – often undervalued – that women make to conflict prevention, peacekeeping, conflict resolution and peace-building, and stresses the importance of their equal participation as active agents in peace and security. Also in 2000, the Windhoek Declaration and the Namibia Plan of Action on Mainstreaming a Gender Perspective in Multidimensional Peace Support Operations was adopted at a seminar sponsored by the UN. The declaration called for the principles of gender equality to permeate UN peacekeeping operations in order to ensure the participation of women and men as equal partners and beneficiaries in all aspects of the peace process – from peacekeeping and reconciliation to peace-building.

Challenges: Despite these achievements, the rights of women and girls still receive

Reintegrating child soldiers: Initiatives across Africa and Asia

Reintegration initiatives by UNICEF and several non-governmental organizations are helping to ease the transition of child soldiers from combatants to civilians. While most of these programmes are currently operating in Africa, there are also projects in Asia.

Afghanistan: A demobilization programme has assisted 2,203 children in eight provinces since its launch in February 2004. Of the children who have been demobilized, more than 1,700 have been assessed for reintegration programmes. The demobilization programme is expected to expand to include six provinces in central Afghanistan and five provinces in the north before the end of 2004.

Burundi: A reintegration package has been standardized across all 17 of the country's provinces. It includes support for the families who will care for former child soldiers, whether they are biological relatives or foster parents; enrolling all demobilized children in appropriate educational courses; and launching projects suitable for youth participation, such as apprenticeships, small businesses and sports.

Democratic Republic of the Congo: Former child soldiers have been received by the Kimwenza Transit and Orientation Centre since December 2001. The demobilized children are given psychosocial and medical care, basic education and help with tracing their families. Older children receive vocational training and are helped to live semi-independently in shared rooms. They also receive a small allowance for food and are encouraged to develop self-sufficiency through income-generating activities.

Liberia: Demobilization of child soldiers recommenced in April 2004 and will continue for a year. Extensive awareness campaigns were conducted by UNICEF and the UN mission in Liberia to prepare children for demobilization and re-integration, and to prepare families and communities for their return. Child protection agencies are using common standards of care to ensure that children are able to recover from their conflict experiences.

Somalia: Where children are recruited by all the factions involved in the persistent fighting, UNICEF has supported the demobilization of former child soldiers through the Elman Peace Centre in Mogadishu. Over a six-month period, children benefit from four days per week of vocational training – including electrical installation, driving, office administration and computing – as well as two days per week of counselling and training in conflict resolution.

Sudan: Child soldiers have been demobilized in both northern and southern Sudan. A special task force has demobilized 12,000 child soldiers who were allied to the rebel Sudan People's Liberation Movement since it began in late 2001. The demobilization and reintegration of children from government forces and allied militia is also vital.

insufficient attention in post-conflict situations. Many reconstruction efforts do not specifically focus on women or undergo a gender-budget analysis, which compares spending in different sectors, such as the level of funding reserved for the military as compared to the financing assigned to education initiatives. For example, women-specific projects accounted for only 0.07 per cent of the $1.7 billion UN-sponsored 2002 reconstruction plan in Afghanistan.[21]

When it comes to protecting women and girls in conflict situations from rape and sexual violence, the most that can be claimed is that international agencies are more aware of the need for such protection. The problem is as serious as it has ever been. In the Democratic Republic of the Congo, hundreds of thousands of women are believed to have been raped since 1998. More recently, in Darfur, Sudan, militias have routinely engaged in rape and sexual assault, and the assaults have continued around the camps for displaced persons as women have ventured out in search of water and firewood.

The burden of protecting girls and women from rape in wartime rests squarely on the shoulders of governments, many of which regard incidents of rape in a conflict situation as almost inevitable. They are not. Rape is a crime for which perpetrators must be held accountable. The Rome Statute of the International Criminal Court defines rape and other grave sexual violence as war crimes. But much more needs to be done to ensure that perpetrators are brought to justice.

Landmines

Progress: The call for international legislation to ban the production and merchandising of anti-personnel mines has been heeded. A worldwide advocacy campaign, led by the International Campaign to Ban Landmines and involving more than 1,000 non-governmental organizations, resulted in the 1997 adoption of a treaty banning their use – and won campaigners the 1997 Nobel Peace Prize. The Convention on the Prohibition of the Use, Stockpiling, Production and Transfer of Anti-Personnel Mines and on their Destruction (the 'Mine Ban Treaty') entered into force in March 1999; by September 2004, 143 countries had formally agreed to be bound by the treaty. Its successful implementation demonstrates what international treaties can achieve when supported by careful monitoring and reporting of abuses.

Another positive step was the adoption in late 2003 of Protocol V to the 'Convention on Certain Conventional Weapons', which requires parties to a conflict to clear up explosive remnants of war, provide warnings to civilians about their dangerous nature and assist casualties. As increasing numbers of countries accept the moral necessity of banning weapons with such indiscriminate and pernicious effects, the number of reported incidents of landmine use continues to decline: 13 governments deployed them in 2000-2001, 9 in 2001-2002, and 6 in 2002-2003.

Challenges: The challenge now is to maintain this steady improvement while sustaining pressure on those governments that have not yet endorsed the Mine Ban Treaty. The non-signatories include three of the five members of the UN Security Council. Meanwhile, there is an urgent need for mine-risk education. This does not simply mean teaching people basic mine-recognition skills, including how to recognize warning signs. Increasingly mine-risk education involves uncovering, through detailed qualitative surveys, the main factors that contribute to landmine accidents such as poverty, displacement and social exclusion. Since the late 1990s, communities have been increasingly encouraged to determine what the local priorities in risk education about landmines should be. Mine-risk education is also increasingly integrated into school syllabi and in public health programmes. Improving data collection will not only result in better advocacy but also in more effective programmes to help and protect affected children.

War crimes

Progress: The establishment of the International Criminal Court as a permanent international tribunal that can bring individuals to justice for genocide, war crimes and crimes against humanity has been a profoundly important step forward in recent years. The 1998 Rome Statute, the basis of the Court's establishment, makes it clear that intentional attacks on a civilian population (including children), attacks on schools and the conscription of children under 15 all constitute war crimes.[22]

The ad hoc special courts and tribunals set up to consider particular conflicts – like the tribunal in Arusha, United Republic of Tanzania, considering the genocide in Rwanda – also help eradicate the culture of impunity. The landmark ruling by the Special Court for Sierra Leone in June 2004 – that the recruitment or use of children under 15 in hostilities is a war crime under customary international law – may result in the first-ever conviction for the conscription of children as armed combatants. The decision came in response to an assertion by one of the accused that he was immune from prosecution on the grounds that conscription of children under age 15 had not been established as a war crime until after the inception of the Special Court's jurisdiction, which dates back to 1996. The challenge now lies in making the historic significance of this decision widely known.

Challenges: Accountability mechanisms can take many forms, including truth and reconciliation commissions such as those in post-apartheid South Africa, or Sierra Leone, national courts, and traditional dispute resolution procedures, such as the gacaca court system in Rwanda. Accountability contributes to the process of healing and helps children understand that they are not to blame for what has happened to them and their society. It calls attention to violations of children's rights and records atrocities committed against them, both of which are vital to understanding the broader context of what happens to children affected by conflict. Accountability can also help break the cycle of violence, restore confidence in democracy and the rule of law, increase the chances of success during a peace process, and strengthen the legitimacy and authority of a new government.

Most children experience war crimes, crimes against humanity and genocide as victims or witnesses. However, some children are also recruited and made complicit in those crimes, as has been the case in recent years in Liberia, Rwanda, Sierra Leone and other countries. Forcing children to commit atrocities during an armed conflict is itself a war crime: it causes severe psychological harm and violates their rights. Child perpetrators should be considered victims of criminal policies for which adults are primarily responsible. International judicial mechanisms should focus on prosecuting the political and military groups that are responsible for planning and ordering the commission of such egregious crimes.

However, in order to restore respect for the rule of law in post-conflict societies, children who may have participated in serious crimes should undergo an appropriate form of accountability, conducted in a way that respects their rights and takes into consideration their age and maturity. This may involve the child's testifying to a truth and reconciliation commission or taking part in traditional healing and reconciliation processes. According to the Convention on the Rights of the Child, the key objective is to promote the reintegration of child perpetrators into society.

Any judicial proceedings for children should be in the context of juvenile and restorative justice to ensure the child's physical, psychological and social recovery. These proceedings should involve judges, lawyers, police and social workers who have benefited from child rights training.

Sanctions

Progress: Concern about the impact of sanctions on children and other vulnerable members of the population is increasingly widespread and has resulted in attempts to develop sanctions that are much more carefully targeted to avoid harming these groups.

The UN is empowered to impose economic and other sanctions on Member States by Article 41 of its Charter. In the 1990s, the Security Council imposed sanctions on Eritrea, Ethiopia, Haiti, Iraq, Liberia, the Libyan Arab Jamahiriya, Rwanda, Sierra Leone, Somalia, Sudan and the former Yugoslavia – and on the Taliban in Afghanistan and the National Union for the Total Independence of Angola (UNITA) in Angola.

Of these, the most comprehensive sanctions were imposed on Haiti, Iraq and the former Yugoslavia. And in each of these countries the impact of the measures on children, the poor and the elderly caused such grave concern that the ethical validity of sanctions was called into question.

The negative effects of sanctions inevitably fall most heavily on the most vulnerable members of the population. Healthy adults can generally endure long periods of deprivation but children have far fewer resources to call upon and may suffer irreparable harm.

The 1991 sanctions imposed on Haiti, for example, had a devastating impact on children. A survey conducted in 1994-1995 found that 7.8 per cent of children under five suffered from acute malnutrition, compared with 3.4 per cent in 1990. School enrolment fell from 83 per cent in 1990 to 57 per cent in 1994, and the number of children living on the street doubled over the same period.[23]

Evidence like this from Haiti, together with the plight of children in Iraq (where the under-five mortality rate more than doubled during the sanctions period), persuaded the UN that sanctions must be much more carefully deployed in the future. It has become clear that sanctions imposed under Article 41 of the UN Charter are likely to conflict with the organization's responsibility under Article 55 to promote higher standards of living and improve social progress, health and education.

In 1999, the UN Security Council adopted resolution 1261, which addresses the issue of children caught up in armed conflict. In a clause to one of the resolution's articles, the council pledged to consider the impact on children whenever it adopted sanctions under Article 41. In April 2000, it set up a working group to review UN sanctions policy and recommend ways of making sanctions more targeted. In recent years,

UNICEF's core commitments to children in conflict and unstable situations

INITIAL RESPONSE

In the **first six to eight weeks** following the outbreak of a crisis, UNICEF will work with partners to meet the following core commitments for children in emergencies:

- **Within established mechanisms, assess, monitor, report on, advocate and communicate on the situation of children and women:** Conduct a rapid assessment of the situation of children and women, establish initial monitoring systems – including for severe or systematic abuse, violence and exploitation – and report through the appropriate mechanisms.
- **Provide measles vaccination, vitamin A, essential drugs and nutritional supplements:** Vaccinate all children between six months and 14 years of age against measles and provide vitamin A supplementation as required. Provide emergency health kits, post-rape care kits where necessary, oral rehydration mix, basic health kits, fortified nutritional products and micronutrient supplements. Provide other emergency supplies such as blankets and tarpaulins.
- **Provide child and maternal feeding and nutritional monitoring:** Support infant and young child feeding, and therapeutic and supplementary feeding programmes, with the World Food Programme and non-governmental organization partners. Introduce nutritional monitoring and surveillance.
- **Provide safe drinking water, sanitation and hygiene:** Provide emergency water supply and purification, basic family water kits, safe disposal of faeces and hygiene education.
- **Assist in preventing the separation of families and facilitate the identification, registration and medical screening of children if they are separated** from their families. Ensure family-tracing systems are put in place, provide care and protection, and prevent sexual abuse and exploitation of children and women.
- **Initiate the resumption of schooling** and other learning opportunities for children: Set up temporary learning spaces, reopen schools and start reintegrating teachers and children, with a focus on girls, and organize recreational activities.

To fulfil these initial emergency response commitments, UNICEF will cooperate with national governmental and non-governmental bodies and other international partners, with an emphasis on community capacity-building from the onset of conflict.

sanctions imposed on UNITA in Angola, and on Liberia and Sierra Leone, have been restricted to banning trade in arms and diamonds, as well as travel by senior government officials, and their impact and effectiveness have been carefully assessed.

Challenges: The UN hopes that these targeted or 'smart' sanctions will restore the international community's confidence in measures that stop short of using military force but exert far greater pressure on errant Member States than mere verbal warnings or exhortations.

Children as 'zones of peace'

Progress and challenges: The aspiration to incorporate the idea of children as 'zones of peace' into international law has not been realized. The notion has, however, continued to prove useful and to save lives in some conflict situations. In Sri Lanka, for example, over half a million children in the conflict-ridden north-east were immunized against polio during a UNICEF-supported Sub-National Immunization Day in October 2003. Since 1995, the Government and the Liberation Tigers of Tamil Eelam have annually observed such 'days of tranquillity': cease-fire days in which children across the country have been immunized.[24]

A significant recent development has been the specific mention in UN Security Council mandates to UN peacekeeping missions of the need to protect women and children. It is also increasingly common for such missions – in Afghanistan, the Democratic Republic of the Congo and

LONGER TERM

Beyond the initial response, country offices may address other elements of the Core Commitments for Children in Emergencies. It is particularly important to consider the transition to national ownership and leadership and to support the building of national systems.

- **Monitoring the situation of, and advocating for, children:** Ensure that information on the situation of children and violations of their rights is collected and kept up to date. Make this information available to relevant partners, child rights advocates, the public and the media, as appropriate. Advocate on behalf of children.
- **Survival:** Expand support to immunization and preventive health services (i.e. provide essential health supplies and services to prevent mortality related to diarrhoea, pneumonia, malaria and tetanus among children, pregnant and lactating women, including emergency obstetric care services). Support infant and young child feeding, including breastfeeding and complementary feeding, and, when necessary, support therapeutic and supplementary feeding programmes. Establish, improve and expand safe water and sanitation facilities and promote safe hygiene practices.
- **Organizing child protection:** Continue support to identify and register unaccompanied and orphaned children, and strengthen communities to provide for their protection and care. Establish child-friendly spaces for children and women and provide psychosocial support. Monitor, report on and advocate against abuse and exploitation of children, including recruitment of child soldiers and other exploitative forms of child labour. Initiate work on the release and reintegration of child combatants. Promote activities that prevent and respond to sexual violence against children and women. Take the lead in the organization of mine-risk education.
- **Resuming primary education services:** Re-establish, and/or sustain primary education, as well as community services (such as water supply and sanitation) within schools.
- **Preventing HIV/AIDS:** Provide access to relevant information on HIV/AIDS. In collaboration with relevant partners, facilitate young people's access to comprehensive HIV-prevention services, including treatment for sexually transmitted infections.

See References, page 101.

Sierra Leone, among others – to appoint one or more child protection advisers.

In Angola, Colombia and Sri Lanka, among other conflict-ridden states, the idea of schools as zones of peace – safe havens from the violence plaguing their countries – has been actively promoted. Schools must be places of safety for children in every respect, where they are protected by adults they can trust. This is among the first prerequisites of the global push for universal primary education, one of the Millennium Development Goals. If this sense of safety is lost – as it was, tragically, when children died in an armed engagement at a school in western Nepal in October 2003 – the sanctity of childhood itself is impugned.

Emergency relief

Progress and challenges: Today, emergencies are more complex than ever before and their numbers are rising. The expertise of humanitarian workers – and their sensitivity to the needs of the people they are aiding – has unquestionably increased. But while progress has been made in providing relief, the long-term rebuilding process has been endangered by the targeting of aid workers, the underfunding of vital aid projects and the inability of humanitarian workers to reach many areas.

The problem in Somalia, for example, as in other nations caught up in civil strife, has been compounded by the underfunding of humanitarian programmes and the deliberate murders of aid workers. This has led to heightened restrictions for humanitarian agencies and, consequently, increased deprivation for those most in need. Worldwide, over 200 UN civilian staff lost their lives to violence between January 1992 and March 2002. Hundreds more have been taken hostage, raped or assaulted.

Humanitarian agencies must continually adapt, responding to emerging or abating crises. In 2000, UNICEF formulated a set of core commitments to govern its initial response in protecting and caring for children and women in conflict and unstable situations. Since then, the organization has continued to develop its policy and practice in relation to the array of challenges that conflict poses for children. These include initiatives to assist unaccompanied and internally displaced children, to provide education in emergencies, and to demobilize and reintegrate children actively involved in armed conflict. The core commitments were revised and expanded in 2004 *(see Panel: UNICEF's core commitments to children in conflict and unstable situations, page 56)*.

Education

Progress and challenges: Peace education is the process of promoting the knowledge, skills, attitudes and values that will enable children, youth and adults to prevent conflict and violence, both overt and structural; to resolve conflict peacefully; and to create conditions conducive to peace, whether at an interpersonal, intergroup, national or international level.

Peace education has a place in all societies – not only in countries undergoing armed conflict or emergencies. Because lasting behaviour change in children and adults only occurs over time, effective peace education is necessarily a long-term process. While often based in schools and other learning environments, peace education should ideally involve the entire community.

One area in which the past decade has seen significant progress is the use of education in emergency situations. In the past, education was not seen as a frontline service during emergencies – its provision was often deferred until the situation had stabilized. This is no longer true: Education is increasingly seen as one of the first essentials in an emergency. Schools can provide physical protection for children, and education can itself inject stability and normalcy into their lives. In Afghanistan, Iraq, Liberia, and in Darfur,

Back to school: Safeguarding education during complex emergencies

An emergency can sometimes unlock doors, allowing agencies to address areas of children's rights that had previously been ignored. The most prominent example of this was in **Afghanistan** during 2002, when more than 3 million children were successfully enrolled in school after years of warfare and educational neglect – the first time education had been made the top priority for a country recovering from conflict. Since then, UNICEF has also organized major back-to-school campaigns in Angola, Liberia and the Occupied Palestinian Territory.

Angola: In addition to a major back-to-school campaign, UNICEF has launched child-friendly spaces for children affected by the war – specially designated areas in which children receive an education and psychosocial assistance. These spaces provide much-needed stability for children who may never have seen their home village or town before, as they were born while their parents were refugees from the civil war. The challenge remains to increase donor funding so that additional child-friendly spaces can b provided for war-affected childrer .

Liberia: The back-to-school initiative in Liberia follows a decade of war and aims to reach an estimated 1 million children. The initiative does not only provide education; basic services, including health care, water and sanitation, are also being channeled through the new schools. UNICEF has supplied over 7,000 school supply kits and is training and supporting 20,000 teachers and preparing suitable curricula. The United Nations Development Programme and United Nations Office for Project Services are rehabilitating some schools, while the World Food Programme is supporting school feeding projects and food-for-work plans for teachers.

Occupied Palestinian Territory: Over the past two years, the decline in the well-being of children in the Occupied Palestinian Territory has been rapid and profound. This is directly linked to the violence and mobility restrictions children experience daily, including death and injury to family and friends, damage to property, and frustration and poverty as a consequence of stifling closures, curfews and home confinement. The back-to-school campaign helped 1 million Palestinian children attend school and remain there. Close to 1,300 schools were, however, disrupted by curfews, sieges and closures, and UNICEF has responded by supporting alternative education projects in the most vulnerable areas.

Papua New Guinea: Another example of how education can restore a sense of normalcy to children caught up in armed conflict is in Bougainville, where nine 'no-go zones' had been controlled by rebels fighting for secession. Aware that the rights of children in these areas were being denied, UNICEF called a round-table meeting in 2002 involving ex-combatants, village chiefs, women's groups and other stakeholders to stress the importance of children receiving a basic education. Three no-go zones were targeted and permission obtained from rebel commanders to implement programmes. Teachers were allowed to undertake two weeks' intensive training before returning to the zones. The programme was sufficiently successful that initially sceptical parents requested it be extended to three additional no-go zones during 2003. To date, only one no-go zone still remains in Bougainville, but these initiatives laid a firm foundation for the education system to recover.

Sudan, UNICEF has made it a priority to get children into school – in many cases for the first time in their lives – as well as to provide safe drinking water, nutrition and basic health care.

In collaboration with other UN organizations such as the Office of the UN High Commissioner for Refugees and the World Food Programme, as well as with non-governmental organizations within the inter-agency Emergency Education Network, UNICEF aims to create a safe environment for children in which they can learn, play and receive psychosocial support, and where mothers can spend private time with infants or receive counselling. In a wider conflict zone the goal is

Dangerous assignment: Going to school despite ongoing violence in Iraq

Every year, during the early summer months, Iraqi children take an exam that determines whether they will pass to the next grade or stay behind. This year-end exam is therefore the single most important event of the school year.

Like everything else in Iraq these days, education has been heavily disrupted. The damage caused by war and the ensuing looting and burning have devastated an already dilapidated education system. Continuing insecurity – daily bombings, kidnappings and muggings – has kept attendance rates erratic and relatively low, especially for girls. In addition, the looting of schools has left students and teachers with few learning or teaching materials. Intense heat and no more than a couple of hours of electricity each day in most areas make studying at home and in the classroom difficult.

As a result of these adverse conditions, the year-end exams for 2003 were to be cancelled. This would have meant that millions of Iraqi children would have effectively lost an entire year of schooling and would have been required to repeat the same grade.

Recognizing the value placed by Iraqi parents and society on these exams, UNICEF, with support from the US Agency for International Development, the Governments of Denmark, Italy, the Republic of Korea, Sweden, and the Italian Committee for UNICEF, supported the Iraqi Ministry of Education in planning and implementing these exams. Fifteen million exam booklets, and essential supplies and equipment were procured and distributed, and a social mobilization campaign was launched to inform parents and communities that the exams would take place. Finally, in early July 2003, 5.5 million Iraqi children were able to take their year-end exam. Girls, many of whom were not attending school because of security concerns, were especially encouraged to take the test and outperformed boys at every level.

While overall school attendance rates stood at 60 per cent immediately after the fall of the regime of President Saddam Hussein in early April 2003, 96 to 99.8 per cent of Iraqi children attending primary, intermediate and secondary schools showed up for the end-of-the-year exam. This was a major achievement, for the children and their families, as well as for the new Ministry of Education, which was severely incapacitated during the war. It has helped restore confidence among students and parents in the education system and greatly facilitated the return of students to schools.

The year-end exams were part of UNICEF's Back-to-School campaign for the 2003/2004 school year, which constituted the largest logistical operation in the history of the organization. It involved the production and distribution of over 68,000 school-in-a-box kits and the printing and distribution of 46 million textbooks. In addition, 220 schools damaged by the war have been rehabilitated and work is ongoing in another 25.

The situation in Iraq remains extremely volatile. More than 100 children were reported killed in Fallujah and Basra as a result of the clashes between Iraqis and coalition forces – some of them on their way to school. Still, in June 2004 students flocked to schools throughout the country to take their year-end exams. At the Bilad Al-Arab High School for Girls in Baghdad, there was no electricity and everyone was suffering from the intense heat. Khalid Salman was waiting outside the school building with his wife, while their daughter, Yusra, took the test.

"There are security guards here to protect the students but we are still frightened," he said. "In the past, we didn't accompany our children to school because it was safe and no one dared harm them. I'm hopeful that the situation will improve."

Sahira Ali, who brought her sixth-grade daughter Rusul to take the exam at the Al-Kahira High School for Girls, described her fears as she waited outside the school gates. "Since I got to the school we heard several explosions, and on our way here there was an abduction followed by a police investigation, which delayed our arrival," she said.

Rana Rasheed, a sixth-grader at Al-Kahira High School, said her teachers were unable to complete the curriculum for the year because of ongoing disturbances and lack of security. "Today I arrived at school late because of traffic jams, and then there was another delay because the security guards had to search the school to make sure that nobody had placed explosives inside," she said. "Our movement is extremely restricted. When we walk in the street we are vigilant and apprehensive, and we are suspicious of any person who looks in our direction. Electricity is rare and studying for exams in this hot weather is an ordeal. We sweat in the exam hall with no fans running over our heads."

Yet neither the oppressive heat nor the constant fear of violence have managed to make Iraq's children and their parents give up on education. For the children, going to school has become a daily calculated risk, one they hope will bring a better future for themselves and their country.

to reopen schools, rebuild infrastructure or launch back-to-school campaigns *(see Panel: Back to school, page 59).*

The participation of older children and adolescents in times of crisis and conflict is imperative. If they are left without opportunities to envision and contribute to a better future, their youthful optimism is frustrated under the extreme conditions of war. Addressing their rights to participation is therefore not negotiable: it is an imperative.

Prevention

Progress: In 1996, there were 22 major armed conflicts worldwide. In 2003, there were 19 such conflicts, the second-lowest annual number since 1990. Yet it is difficult to claim that there has been significant progress in mediating and resolving conflict. For example, today there are 25 million people in 52 countries who are internally displaced by violence and persecution, broadly the same number as in the mid-1990s.

There have been some notable achievements over the past nine years. The long-standing conflict in Angola, still active in 1996, has finally been laid to rest. Huge efforts have been made to bring resolution to conflicts in Burundi, Liberia and Sierra Leone. Yet for every step forward – the ongoing peace process in Sudan after two decades of war between the Government and the Sudanese People's Liberation Movement, for example – there seems to be a step backward, as a new conflict erupts elsewhere or, in the case of Darfur, in a different area of the same country. Far from seeming safer, the world at the beginning of the 21st century appears more riven by conflict and fear – and its dominant political discourse to be one of war.

Challenges: UNICEF and its partner agencies are dedicating a large proportion of their resources to addressing the social and economic inequalities that can lead to violence. By emphasizing outreach to vulnerable groups, including girls, rural

Participation in emergency situations: Children lead the way

Against all odds, children in communities torn apart by war have led the way in creative initiatives to participate and improve their lives.

Indonesia: In Maluku, the Christian-Muslim conflict between 1999 and 2002 cost the lives of thousands and left an estimated 1.4 million people internally displaced. Communities continue to be riven by religious intolerance, but since 2002 children have played a leading role in peace-building processes and acted as positive role models in their families and communities. In close collaboration with UNICEF and partners, a Muslim-Christian coalition of child-focused non-governmental organizations launched a campaign that resulted in the creation of a participatory Children's Parliament, which was held in Ambon in July 2000. This was not only the first children's parliament ever convened in Indonesia but also the first major event that successfully crossed the Muslim-Christian divide.

In February 2002, at an event that made national news, young people representing all local religious and ethnic groups visited the governor's office as a follow-up to Valentine's Day, performing songs and distributing red paper flowers that included peace messages. Initial fears that the children's cross-community collaboration might spark violence proved groundless and the growing momentum of the initiative has proved a stabilizing force, serving to strengthen dialogue between the groups. Young people have found it easier than adults to cross the cultural and religious divide and have thus become genuine leaders in the peace-building process.

Occupied Palestinian Territory: Children's municipal councils have been set up in Gaza City, Jenin, Jericho and Rafah to give young people an opportunity to plan and implement activities that will help improve and rebuild community life. Of the 155 young council representatives, more than half are girls. They meet to decide on priorities, plan and implement small-scale community projects and organize campaigns to raise awareness on children's rights and related issues. Such initiatives can provide a much-needed alternative to violence and provide children and adolescents with the skills they need to build peace.

Russian Federation: In the North Caucasus, children are actively involved in the design of the Mine Risk Education programme implemented by the State Chechen Drama Theatre in Grozny. They decide on the best ways to conduct mine-risk education presentations in their communities and determine which messages are the most appropriate. They are trained to write the script and stage drama presentations, and then they have the opportunity to put their skills into practice.

In Chechnya and Ingushetia, UNICEF supports a programme on Child Friendly Schooling implemented by the International Rescue Committee, whereby pupils in every school elect a president and a government and are given the opportunity to participate in the planning of activities for the academic year. They are also involved in parent/teacher meetings, editing the school newspaper and maintaining discipline among their peers.

communities and the poor, these programmes combat marginalization, defuse tensions and promote effective social integration. UNICEF's role in lobbying governments to pursue equitable development policies has expanded over the past decade and is helping to equip communities with the tools they need to resolve issues peaceably.

If ever there were children needing their right to protection fulfilled it is those caught up in armed conflict, from those forcibly recruited as soldiers to those who see their homes and communities destroyed. But the world also needs to protect millions of children in the future from the damage to their childhood that conflict inflicts. The only sure way of doing so is for the international community to take more urgent and serious steps towards preventing war and resolving existing conflicts.

The way forward

If we are to safeguard children from the brutality of armed conflicts, a number of actions must be pursued, and the international community must demonstrate the political and economic will required to implement them.

- Put children first, before and during conflicts.
- End the recruitment of child soldiers.
- Strengthen the protective environment for children at every level, from the family right through to the level of national and international legislation.
- Eradicate the culture of impunity, and strengthen accountability.
- Prevent conflict by addressing the underlying causes of violence and investing more resources in mediation and conflict resolution.
- Make monitoring and reporting on child rights violations in conflict zones a priority, including gathering reliable data on children who are actively involved in armed conflict and other war-affected children.
- Expand demobilization and mine-awareness campaigns.
- Restart education for children caught up in armed conflict as soon as possible.
- Enhance humanitarian agencies' capacity to respond to conflicts by developing early warning systems and better preparedness.
- Combat poverty and HIV/AIDS, which interact with conflict to magnify the negative impact on childhood.

Wars Roll Back Progress For Children

Developing countries are often locked in a vicious cycle in which poverty generates the desperation and fear that can lead to conflict, threatening the rights of vast numbers of children.

Armed conflict maims and kills children and those who protect them. It destroys the homes and schools that were built to nurture them. It separates children from their families, increases their risk of exploitation and abuse, and exposes them to violence that can result in psychological and psychosocial trauma for years to come. In a number of countries, children are forced to take part in combat or to become servants, messengers or spies.

The threat of violence can drive entire communities from their homes, creating large populations of refugees and internally displaced persons who are vulnerable to malnutrition and diseases, including HIV/AIDS. All too often, the period of exile runs into years or even decades. Generations are growing up in camps where overcrowding, poor sanitation and the weak application of the rule of law make conditions particularly hazardous for children.

The effects of armed conflict extend far beyond the battlefield. Damage to infrastructure can disrupt routine immunization activities or impede access for vaccinators – making children in conflict zones disproportionately vulnerable to death from preventable diseases. Explosive remnants of war often remain embedded in the landscape of war-affected countries, endangering children's lives and rendering much of their environment unsafe. And by draining much-needed funds from national budgets and depriving families of their livelihoods, wars roll back development, deepen poverty and entrench the social disparities that blight every aspect of childhood.

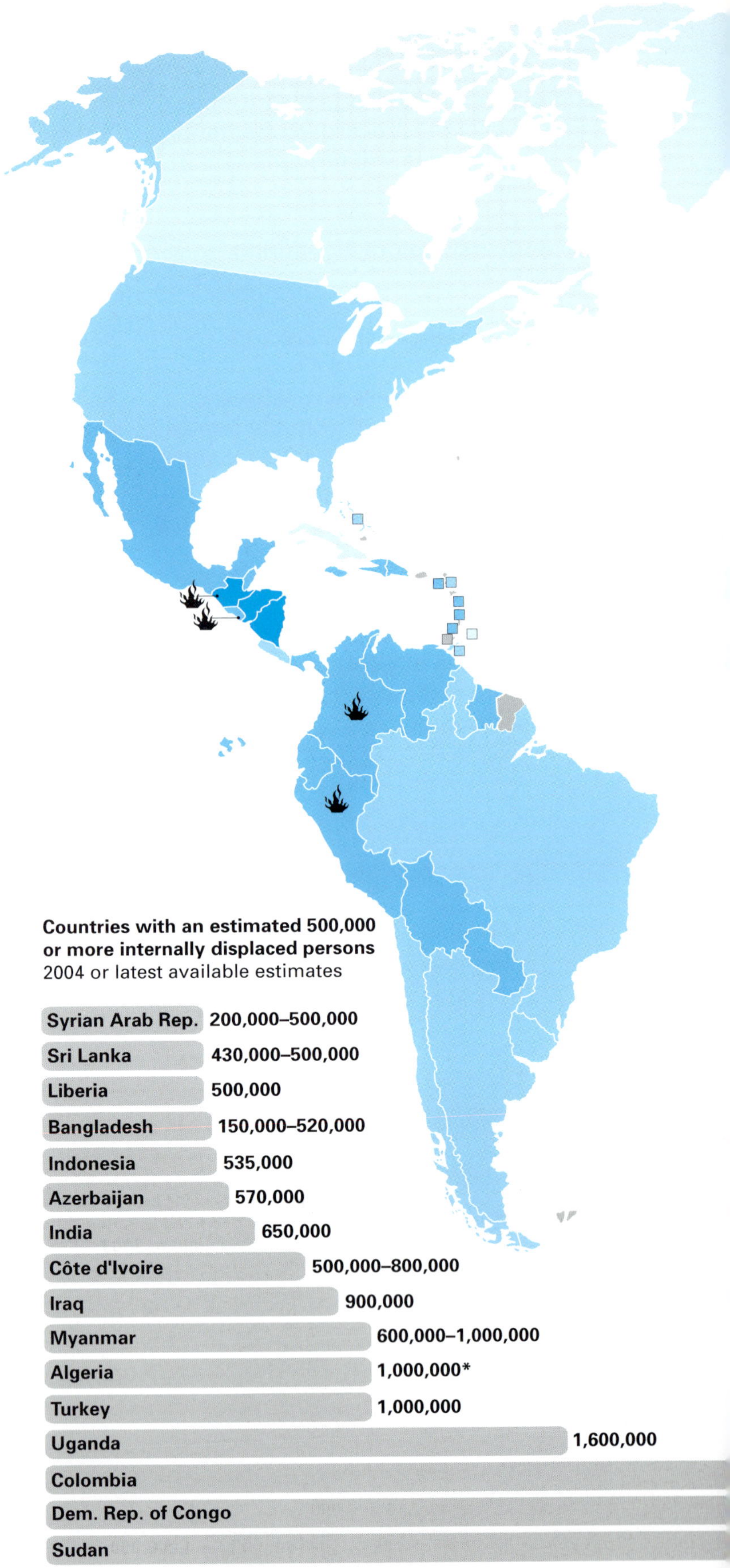

* Estimated number of persons displaced 1992–2004
** Estimated number of persons displaced 1985–2004

Childhood Under Threat: Conflict

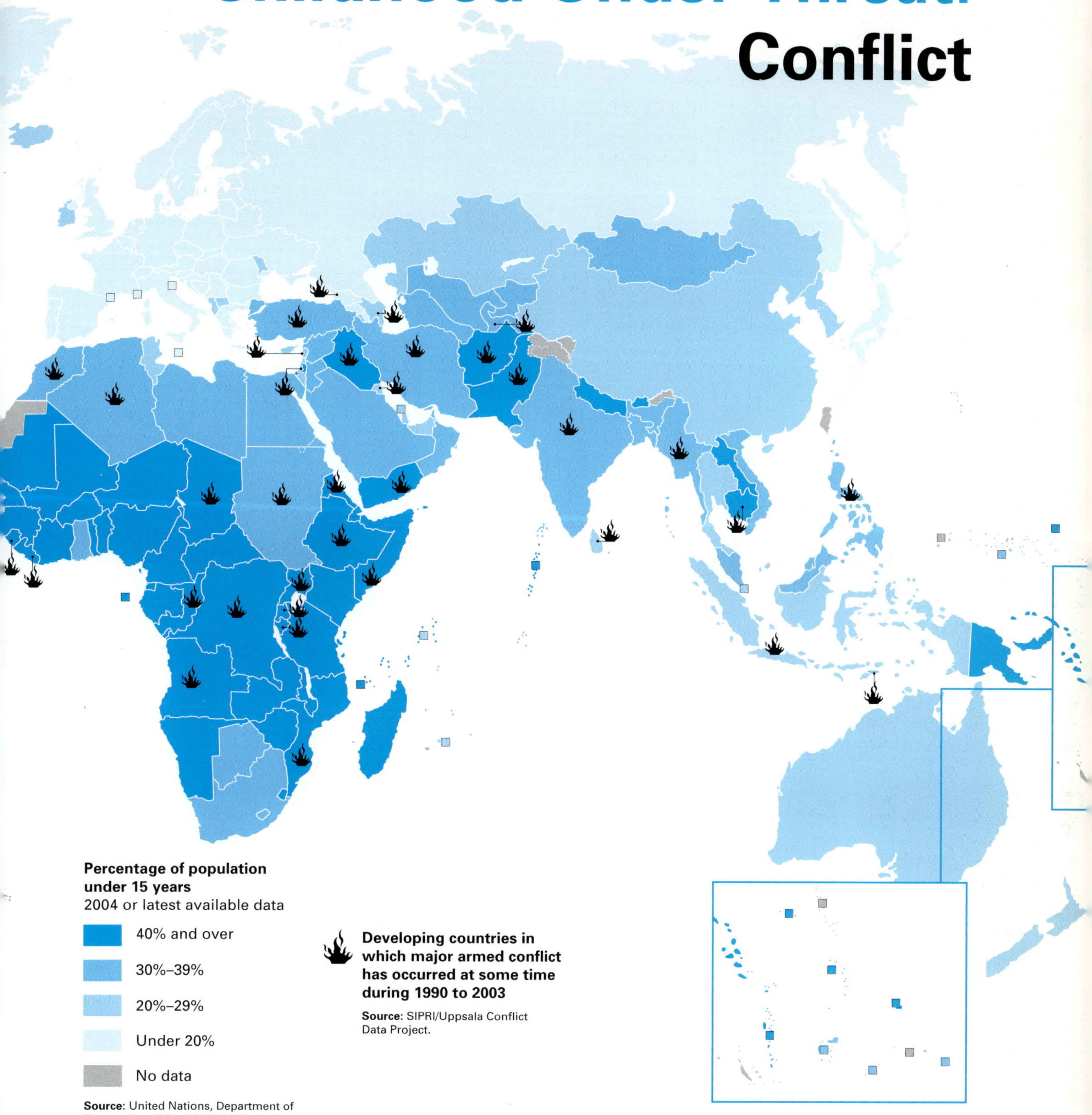

Source: United Nations, Department of Economic and Social Affairs/Statistics Division.

Source: SIPRI/Uppsala Conflict Data Project.

This map does not reflect a position by UNICEF on the legal status of any country or territory or the delimitation of any frontiers.

Dotted line represents approximately the Line of Control in Jammu and Kashmir agreed upon by India and Pakistan. The final status of Jammu and Kashmir has not yet been agreed upon by the parties.

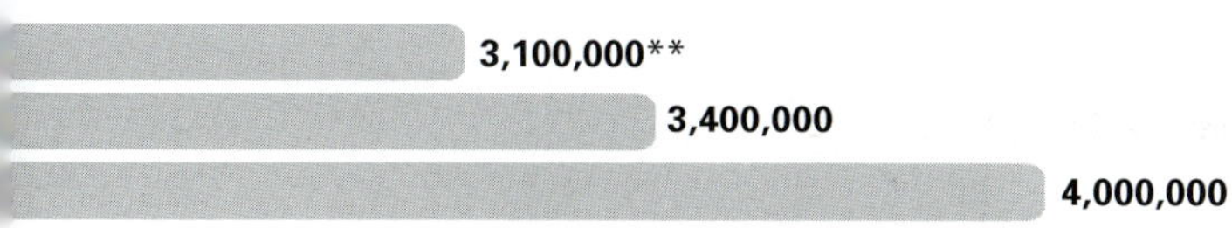

Source: Global IDP Project, Norwegian Refugee Council.

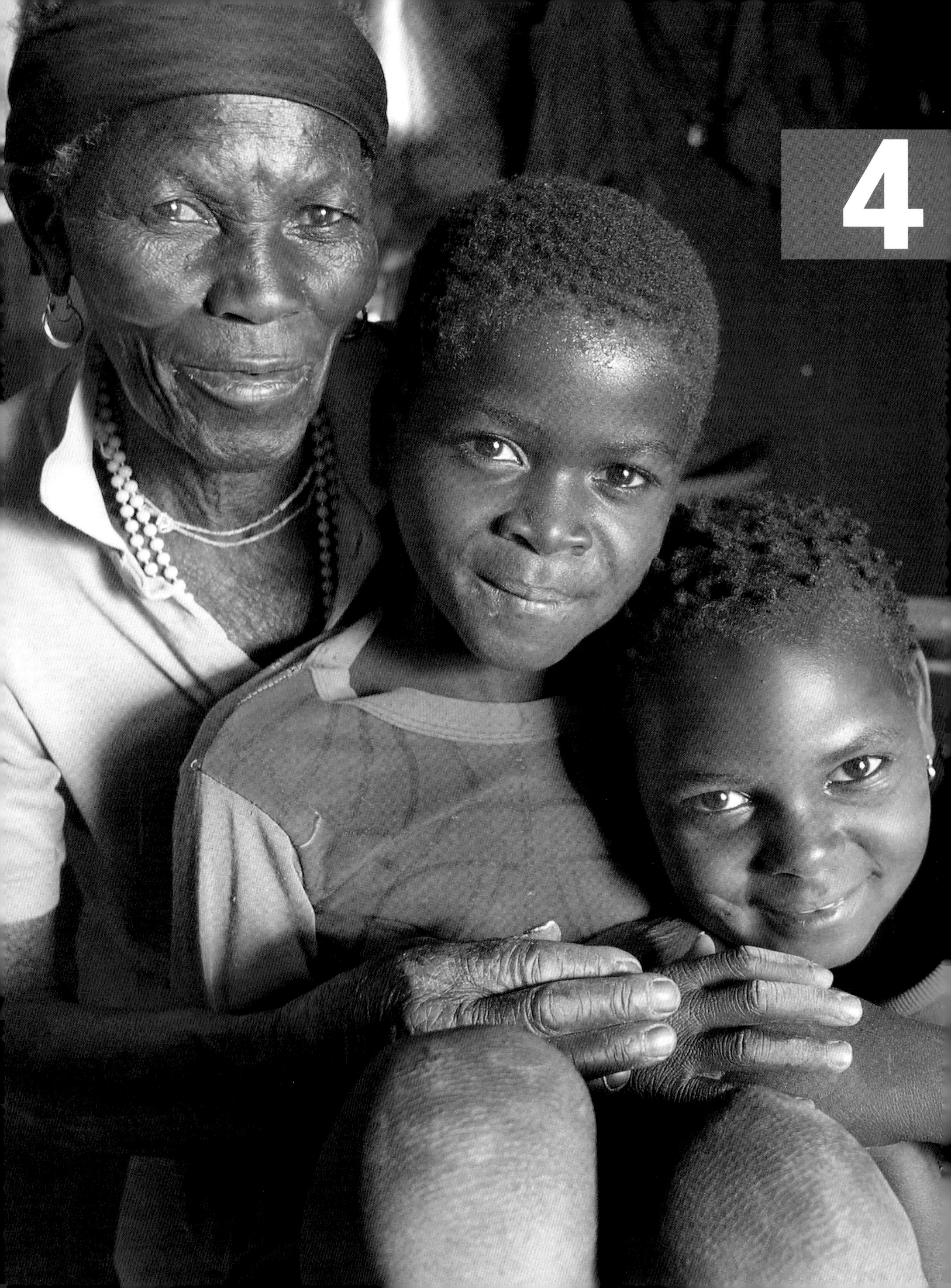

4

Children Orphaned or Made Vulnerable by HIV/AIDS

Children do not need to have HIV/AIDS to be devastated by it. When HIV/AIDS enters a household by infecting one or both parents, the very fabric of a child's life falls apart. The statistics are numbing: By 2003, 15 million children under the age of 18 had been orphaned by HIV/AIDS; just two years earlier, the figure stood at 11.5 million.[1] Eight out of 10 of these children live in sub-Saharan Africa. It is estimated that in 2010, over 18 million African children under the age of 18 will have lost one or both parents to HIV/AIDS, and the number of double orphans – children whose mother and father have died – will increase by about 2 million over the same period.[2] Millions more live in households with sick and dying family members. Although they are not yet orphaned, these children also suffer the pernicious effects of HIV/AIDS.

Summary

ISSUE: HIV/AIDS is tearing at the very fabric of childhood. Around 15 million children under the age of 18 had been orphaned by the pandemic by the end of 2003. Eight out of 10 of these children live in sub-Saharan Africa. Unless action is taken, swiftly and decisively, to stem the tidal wave of infection and loss, it is estimated that by 2010 over 18 million African children will have lost one or both parents to HIV/AIDS.

The loss of a parent implies more than just the disappearance of a caregiver. It pervades every aspect of a child's life: their emotional well-being, physical security, mental development and overall health. It deprives them of the right to live in a family environment. It implies that part of a child's safety net against violence, abuse, exploitation, stigmatization and discrimination is lost, often further isolating them from others at a time when they need as much care and support as possible. In the most extreme cases, children can find themselves utterly devoid of family support and end up living on the street.

A child's right to an education is often jeopardized when caregivers become sick or die, since it propels children out of the classroom and into the adult roles of caring and providing for their families. So is the right to rest, play and recreation. As HIV/AIDS often exacerbates poverty, it places children at an increased risk of engaging in hazardous labour and of being exploited.

ACTION: Respecting the rights of children orphaned or made vulnerable by HIV/AIDS must be an international priority for the next two decades. In order to do this, action must be taken on several fronts:

- **Limit the spread of AIDS** through forthright national leadership, widespread public awareness and intensive prevention efforts.
- **Dedicate the funds needed** to support programmes for orphans and vulnerable children, which receive only a small share of total HIV/AIDS funding.
- **Prolong the lives of parents** and provide economic, psychosocial and other support.
- **Mobilize and support community-based responses** to provide both immediate and long-term support to vulnerable households.
- **Ensure access to essential services,** including education, health care and birth registration, to orphans and other vulnerable children.

The impact of HIV/AIDS on children

Unfulfilled rights lead to loss of childhood

As horrifying as these numbers are, they do not adequately reflect the toll that HIV/AIDS inflicts on childhood or the lives of children affected by the pandemic. They fail to describe how the virus deprives children of their rights. The illness or death of a mother or caregiver during a child's first year jeopardizes the fulfilment of that child's basic needs, such as access to adequate health care, sanitation and nutrition, often threatening their right to survival. HIV/AIDS also deprives children of the right to live in a family environment, which is crucial for the development of a positive self-identity and self-esteem. The disease increases the likelihood that

The global threat of HIV/AIDS

In Africa, the prevalence of HIV/AIDS exploded from fewer than 1 million cases in the early 1980s to approximately 25 million cases by the end of 2003.[a] Between 1990 and 2003, the number of children orphaned by the disease in sub-Saharan Africa increased from fewer than 1 million to more than 12 million.[b] Other regions now face a similarly bleak future unless urgent steps are taken to halt the spread of the pandemic.

Home to 60 per cent of the world's population, Asia is witnessing a rapidly escalating epidemic. An estimated 7.4 million people are living with HIV in the region, and 1.1 million people were newly infected in 2003 alone. China, Indonesia and Viet Nam have seen sharp increases in the number of infections. The HIV/AIDS epidemic in Asia remains largely concentrated among injecting drug users, men who have sex with men, sex workers, clients of sex workers and their immediate sexual partners. Effective prevention coverage among these groups is inadequate, in large part because of stigma and discrimination. Asian countries that have chosen to openly address high-risk behaviour, such as Cambodia and Thailand, have been significantly more successful in reducing infection rates. Nonetheless, prevalence rates still remain disturbingly high in both countries; Cambodia has the highest HIV prevalence rate (2.6 per cent) in Asia.[c]

Eastern Europe and Central Asia are also facing a growing epidemic that is largely fuelled by intravenous drug use. Between 1995 and 1998, the former socialist economies of Eastern Europe and Central Asia experienced a sixfold increase in the HIV infection rate.[d] About 1.3 million people in the region are living with HIV today, compared with some 160,000 in 1995. Estonia, Latvia, the Russian Federation and Ukraine are the worst-affected countries, but HIV prevalence also continues to spread in Belarus, Kazakhstan and the Republic of Moldova.

The face of the epidemic in Eastern Europe and Central Asia is changing along with the numbers. More than 80 per cent of cases in the region today are among people under the age of 30. Women account for an increasing share of new infections across the globe – a trend clearly in evidence in the Russian Federation, where one in three new infections in 2003 occurred in women, up from one in four just two years earlier.

Latin America has so far escaped a generalized HIV epidemic, but there is no room for complacency. According to the most recent report on the epidemic from UNAIDS, conditions appear ripe for the virus to spread more widely in several countries. In Brazil, the most populous country in the region, infection levels above 60 per cent have been reported among injecting drug users in some areas. In the Caribbean, the virus is already spreading among the general population: Haiti, the worst-affected country, suffers from an adult prevalence rate of around 5.6 per cent.

For those who are entrusted with the task of fighting the HIV/AIDS pandemic, one of the most pressing challenges is the scarcity of reliable data. By 2002, only 36 per cent of low- and middle-income countries had a fully implemented surveillance system in place. In North Africa and the Middle East, for instance, much of the available information is based solely on case reporting. These estimates suggest that around 480,000 people are living with HIV in the region, but the lack of surveys among populations at high risk, such as sex workers, injecting drug users and men who have sex with men, suggests that potential epidemics among these groups may be overlooked.

The experience of the past 25 years should be a sobering reminder of the importance of acting quickly to contain incipient epidemics. Unless effective interventions are put in place immediately, mortality rates will continue to escalate – AIDS is already the leading cause of death worldwide for people aged 15 to 49 – and the crisis of children orphaned or made vulnerable by HIV/AIDS will no longer be confined to sub-Saharan Africa.[e]

Figure 4.1 Newly diagnosed HIV infections in Eastern Europe and Central Asia, 1993–2003

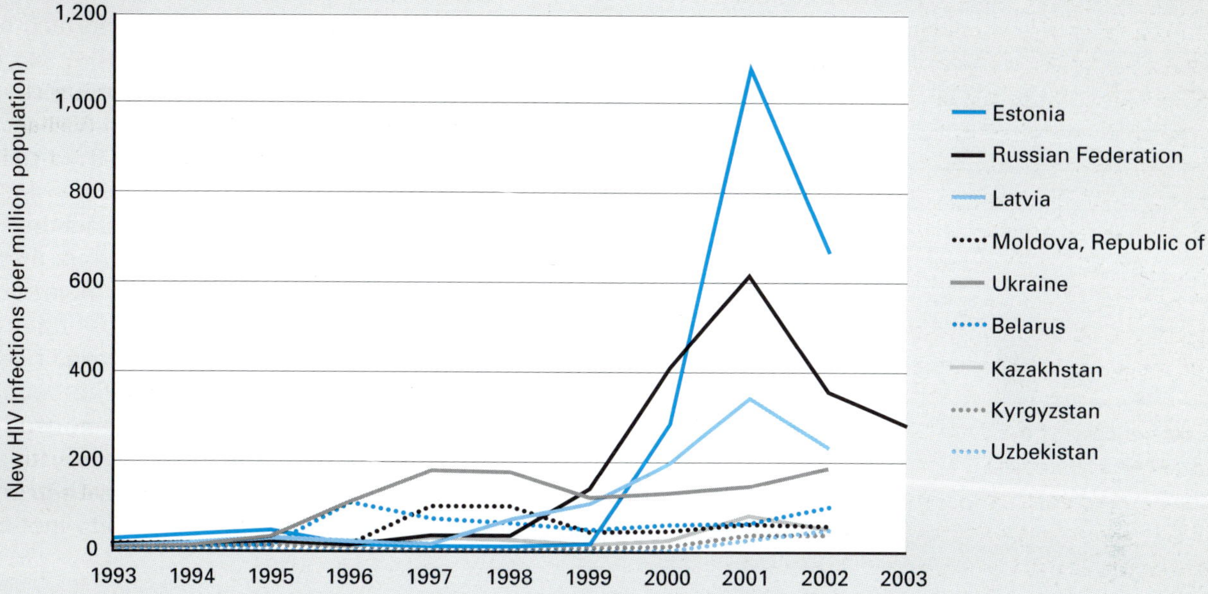

Sources: European Centre for the Epidemiological Monitoring of AIDS, *HIV Surveillance in Europe: Mid-year report 2003,* No. 69, Institut de Veille Sanitaire, Saint-Maurice, 2003; AIDS Foundation East-West.

children will be institutionalized, live on the street or be subjected to child labour.

The death of caregivers, coupled with the stigma attached to HIV/AIDS, can put children at risk of discrimination, further isolating them from others at a time when they are most vulnerable and need as much care and support as possible. Children orphaned and made vulnerable by HIV/AIDS are often exposed to violence, abuse and exploitation. There are also false assumptions applied to this group, including that they are themselves infected.

When caregivers become sick or die, a child's right to an education is often jeopardized as they are pulled out of the classroom and into the adult role of caring and providing for their families. Families are affected long before a parent dies, since from the time adults first fall ill they may not be able to work. A study in eastern Zimbabwe concluded that there were significant losses of income and capital associated with terminal illness.[3] Further pressure is exerted on these often meagre incomes by increased health-care costs and, eventually, by funeral costs. In the same study, these amounted to around half of the average per capita income.[4] Because of these financial pressures, many children whose families are affected by HIV/AIDS, especially girls, are forced to drop out of school in order to work or care for their families, and they face an increased risk of engaging in hazardous labour and of being otherwise exploited. Children working to support their families do so at the expense not only of their education but also of rest, play and recreation. They lose out on the opportunity to participate in their community, religion, cultural activities and sports. The loss of these rights means that, in effect, many children orphaned or made vulnerable by HIV/AIDS miss out on their childhood.

Figure 4.2 Children orphaned by AIDS in sub-Saharan Africa

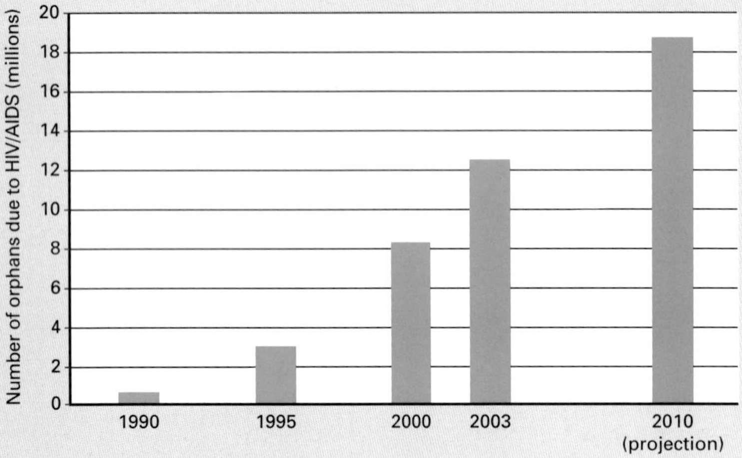

Source: UNAIDS, UNICEF and USAID, *Children on the Brink 2004.*

Families and communities are feeling the strain

In sub-Saharan Africa, most children who have lost one or both parents have been cared for within the extended family, an intricate and resilient system that has traditionally been quick to respond and still takes responsibility for around 90 per cent of orphans in the region.[5] But the tidal wave of loss that the HIV/AIDS pandemic has occasioned has severely stretched this safety net, particularly in the most-affected countries: Botswana, Lesotho, Swaziland and Zimbabwe. Households that have taken in orphans – whether these children are relatives or not – are likely to become poorer as a result because the household income will have to sustain more dependents. In Uganda, households with orphans had 77 per cent of the per capita income

The 'feminization' of HIV/AIDS

At the outset of the HIV/AIDS pandemic in the early 1980s, men greatly outnumbered women among those who were HIV-positive. Since then, the proportion of women with HIV has risen steadily; today, nearly half of those who are HIV-positive are women or girls. The pandemic's 'feminization' is most apparent in sub-Saharan Africa, where close to 60 per cent of those who are HIV-positive are female; among young people aged 15-24 in the region, females account for 75 per cent of the infected population.

Poverty and gender inequality are the driving forces behind the fact that the spread and impact of the HIV/AIDS pandemic disproportionately affect women. Faced with economic hardship, women and girls become more vulnerable to prostitution and trafficking in which they have little power to negotiate safe sex. They may also succumb to the lure of transactional sex, entering into relationships with older or wealthier men in exchange for money, goods and other basic services. This transactional sex greatly increases their risk of contracting HIV.

Violence against women, deeply embedded in some of the countries most affected by HIV/AIDS, as well as social taboos that foster a culture of silence around sex and the risk of HIV transmission, increase the risk of women and girls becoming infected with HIV. In addition, women are more physically susceptible to HIV infection than men: Male-to-female transmission during sex is about twice as likely as female-to-male transmission.

Higher rates of HIV/AIDS among women have changed the pattern of orphaning in sub-Saharan Africa, with maternal orphans due to HIV/AIDS now outnumbering paternal orphans due to HIV/AIDS. In the most-affected countries in sub-Saharan Africa, 60 per cent of all orphans have lost their mother, compared with 40 per cent in Asia and Latin America and the Caribbean. Although the implications of a child losing her or his mother as compared to her or his father are still not fully understood, recent household surveys show that in the countries of southern Africa, maternal orphans are especially likely to be 'virtual' double orphans, as it is common for the father to live elsewhere.

Besides forming the majority of those infected, women and girls bear the brunt of the pandemic in other ways. In many countries women are the carers and guardians of family life. When a family member becomes ill, it is the women in the family who take care of them. This burden of care is far-reaching and not age-specific. In families where assistance is needed to tend for sick relatives or to compensate

of those without.[6] Despite the undeniable stress placed on the extended family network, it is important to emphasize that retaining some sort of family life is extremely important for children who have lost one or both parents to HIV/AIDS. If preserving the family is the best option for orphaned children, then the family's capacity to care for and protect these children must urgently be strengthened.

Women take on the greater burden of care

When HIV/AIDS affects a family, women – particularly elderly women, as well as girls and young women – take on by far the greater burden of care. The strain is beginning to show. Two thirds of caregivers in households surveyed in a recent study in South Africa were female, with almost a quarter of them over the age of 60.[7] Female-headed households generally assume more of the care for orphans than those headed by males, often compounding their own poverty *(see Panel: The 'feminization' of HIV/AIDS, page 70).*

Children are increasingly forced to head households

Too often children or adolescents are forced to assume the burden of caring for sick parents or for their younger siblings. The proportion of households officially headed by children is still small – less than 1 per cent in most countries – but this vastly underestimates the scale of the problem. Though a household in which the lone parent is sick may still formally be headed by that parent, in practice the burden of care and responsibility may have already passed to the children. Similarly, even

for a loss of income, girls tend to be the first to be withdrawn from school. This not only deals a devastating blow to their education, it also prevents them from obtaining vital information about HIV/AIDS prevention and transmission, and therefore increases the risk that they will become infected. Older women also shoulder the burden of care as their adult children fall ill, and often die, from HIV/AIDS. And as the pandemic claims more lives, it is these women who, increasingly often, are left to take care of children orphaned by HIV/AIDS.

When the main income provider falls ill or dies, the remaining caregivers have to contend with additional work and diminished incomes and assets. Women are often responsible for providing the family's food and shelter, and may not be able to manage on their meagre earnings. As a result, some are driven to transactional sex in exchange for food and other essential goods. As HIV/AIDS claims the lives of their husbands, fathers and brothers, women, especially those in cultures where property rights devolve along the male line, also face losing the family land and property. In some cases, women may be dispossessed of these assets upon disclosing their HIV status to their spouse.

Women can also be primary targets of the stigma that is attached to HIV/AIDS. Women are often the first to be tested for HIV and blamed for introducing the disease into the household or community, even though their male partners may have been the true source of the infection. There is growing evidence that HIV/AIDS can incite violence as women face retribution for their HIV-positive status. The fear of such violence causes some women and girls to avoid getting tested or seeking treatment if infected. Lower rates of employment among women also mean that they may encounter difficulties in obtaining private medical insurance or paying for treatment.

Given that gender inequality is one of the main causes of the dramatic increase in the number of women infected by HIV/AIDS, gender-sensitive approaches are key when designing prevention programmes. Women need to have access to the knowledge and tools that will help them protect themselves from becoming infected. Women should constitute at least half of the millions in developing countries expected to gain access to antiretroviral therapy in the coming years. Communities need to overcome barriers to women being tested, including the risk of violence they may face if they are found to be HIV-positive.

See References, page 101.

Three HIV-positive children watch a skit at a UNICEF-supported home for children orphaned or abandoned because of AIDS in the city of Kalinigrad, Russian Federation. Currently receiving antiretroviral treatment, the children are unlikely to be adopted because of the continuing stigma associated with HIV/AIDS.

Figure 4.3 Grandparents are increasingly shouldering the burden of care for orphans*

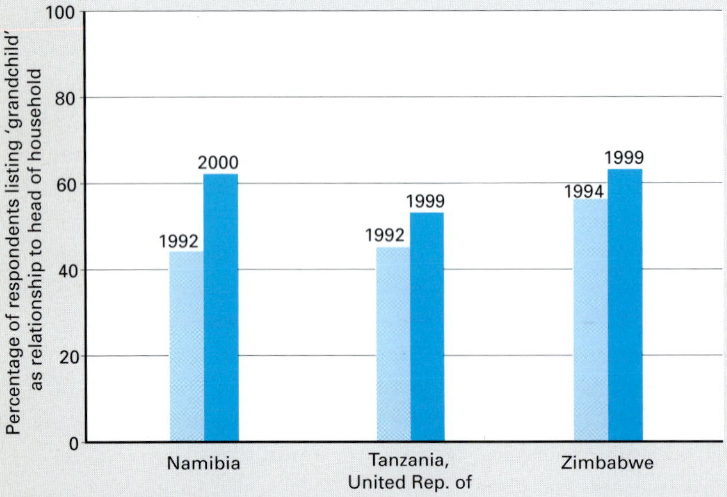

*Selected countries

Source: Demographic and Health Surveys, 1992-2000.

where children have been taken in by grandparents or other relatives, they may be required to work in order to help sustain the family.

Running a household inevitably jeopardizes a child's education

In many cases, assuming this burden of care results in children dropping out of school. Forgoing their education does not just limit the chances that they will be able to create a better future for themselves and their families, it also means they will not receive important, often life-saving information on how to avoid HIV infection or access treatment for HIV/AIDS.

HIV/AIDS is depriving children of their rights and deepening child poverty

The loss of a parent pervades every aspect of a child's life: their emotional well-being, physical security, mental development and overall health. Food consumption in an AIDS-affected household can drop by as much as 40 per cent, leaving children at higher risk of malnutrition and stunting.[8] In Cambodia, a recent joint study by the Khmer HIV/AIDS NGO Alliance and Family Health International found that about one in five children in AIDS-affected families had been forced to start working in the previous six months to support their family. One in three had to provide care for family members and take on major household tasks. Others were forced to drop out of school, or were sent away from home. These experiences exposed children to high levels of stigma and psychosocial stress, with girls found to be more vulnerable than boys.[9]

The breakdown of the protective environment

Children orphaned or made vulnerable by HIV/AIDS are more exposed to exploitation, abuse and violence

With the death of a parent, children lose part of their safety net. Without the protection of the family environment, they risk

Figure 4.4 **Sub-Saharan Africa, epicentre of the HIV/AIDS pandemic, is the only region where orphan numbers are increasing**

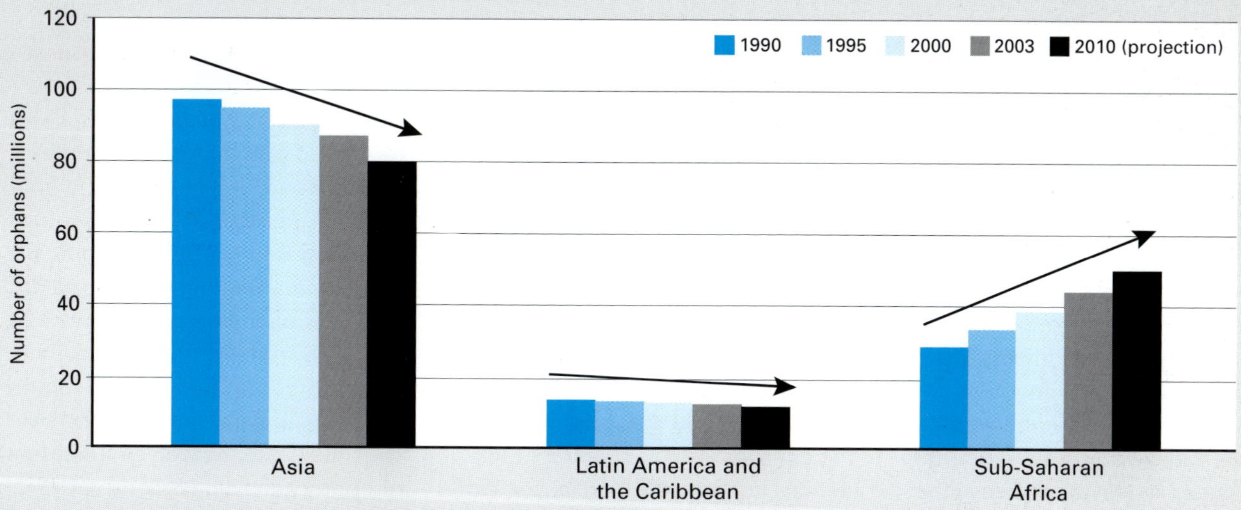

Source: UNAIDS, UNICEF and USAID, *Children on the Brink 2004.*

Figure 4.5 **Challenges facing children and families affected by HIV and AIDS**

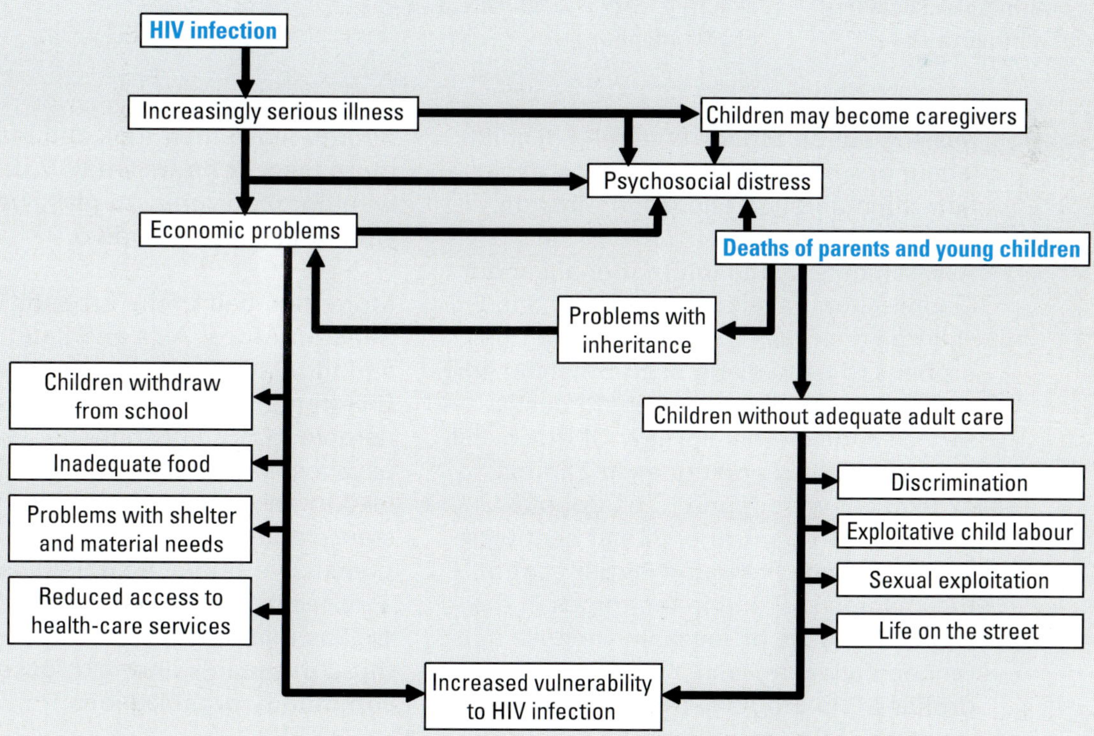

Source: Williamson, J., *A Family is for Life* (draft), USAID and the Synergy Project, Washington, D.C., 2004.

Children with HIV/AIDS

Every day, about 1,700 children become infected with HIV. There are an estimated 2.1 million children worldwide under age 15 currently living with HIV. In 2003, about 630,000 children under the age of 15 became infected.

While adolescents become infected with HIV primarily through unprotected sexual activity, infants are infected through their mothers. Preventing HIV infection in women of reproductive age is therefore the most effective way to decrease the number of young children infected with HIV. In the absence of prophylaxis, estimated rates of mother-to-child HIV transmission in developing countries range from 25 to 45 per cent. Approximately two thirds of these infections occur during pregnancy, labour or delivery, and the others occur during breastfeeding. Prevention of mother-to-child transmission (PMTCT) programmes that provide antiretroviral drug prophylaxis to pregnant women and to newborns at birth can reduce the risk of transmission by half.

In countries with concentrated epidemics among men having sex with men, men and women who engage in commercial sex or injecting drug users, risky behaviour mostly starts during adolescence. Boys are especially affected in these epidemics. In countries with concentrated epidemics among commercial sex workers and in those with HIV epidemics among the general population, adolescent girls face a disproportionate risk of HIV infection. In some of these most-affected countries, the ratio of infected girls to boys is 5 to 1. Young people living outside a family setting – on the street, for example – are also at increased risk of HIV infection.

Including HIV-positive children in scaled-up care and treatment programmes is critical. Brazil has successfully implemented antiretroviral treatment for children and adolescents as part of its national treatment policy. A number of other countries, including South Africa, Uganda and Zambia, are beginning to enrol large numbers of children living with HIV/AIDS in their programmes. Such programmes should include routine child health care, nutrition and psychosocial care, as well as treatment of opportunistic infections and HIV/AIDS. In addition, programmes that address HIV/AIDS and its secondary conditions need to be integrated into routine primary health-care services because the HIV status of most children is unknown and their health needs are generally addressed through these services.

See References, page 101.

missing out on school, engaging in child labour or suffering abuse, violence, exploitation, stigmatization and discrimination.

Assessments by the International Labour Organization have found that orphaned children are much more likely than non-orphans to be working in commercial agriculture, as street vendors, in domestic service and commercial sex. Of those children working as prostitutes in Zambia, 47 per cent were found to be double orphans, while a further 24 per cent were single orphans.[10] Around 38 per cent of the children working in the mines in the United Republic of Tanzania – whose ages ranged between 7 and 17 years old – were orphans.[11] In Ethiopia, more than three quarters of the child domestic labourers interviewed in Addis Ababa were orphaned, 80 per cent of them had no right to leave their jobs and many worked more than 11 hours a day, 7 days a week, with no opportunity to play, watch television or listen to the radio.[12]

More than half of the orphans in sub-Saharan Africa, Asia and Latin America and the Caribbean are adolescents. Children in this age group are more vulnerable to HIV infection, not least because psychosocial and economic distress can lead to risky sexual behaviour and substance abuse. As a result, they need comprehensive sexual health education and services to reduce the risk of infection, as well as relationships with caring adults through schools and faith-based or community organizations.[13]

For all of these children, the psychosocial impact can be as grave as the physical.

Even in societies where HIV/AIDS is commonplace, children in households affected by the disease or who are living with HIV/AIDS themselves may still be stigmatized. They may end up being mistreated or disregarded by their foster household, or may have to endure separation from their siblings as well as the loss of their parents.

Strategies to support children orphaned or made vulnerable by HIV/AIDS

An integrated agenda for action

The issues surrounding children orphaned or made vulnerable by HIV/AIDS have been highlighted at two Special Sessions of the UN General Assembly: one on HIV/AIDS in June 2001 and the other on Children in May 2002. The United Nations and its partner organizations have endorsed a framework of action to provide guidance to donor nations and the governments of affected countries on how to respond to the urgent needs of children affected by HIV/AIDS. Specific goals to be achieved by 2005 include developing national strategies to deal with orphans and other vulnerable children, ensuring non-discrimination, mobilizing resources, and building international cooperation.[14]

Clearly the highest priority of all is to limit the spread of HIV/AIDS and therefore reduce the number of children being deprived of their parents. Despite the grim advance of the disease worldwide, there are significant national successes in turning back the tide of the pandemic that can serve as models. Forthright national leadership, widespread public awareness and intensive prevention efforts, for instance, have made Uganda the pre-eminent example of sustained achievement, while comprehensive action in Thailand averted some 5 million HIV infections during the 1990s.[15]

Keeping adults alive is critical. To this end, the World Health Organization, UNAIDS,

Figure 4.6 Access to antiretrovirals, by region, as of end-2003

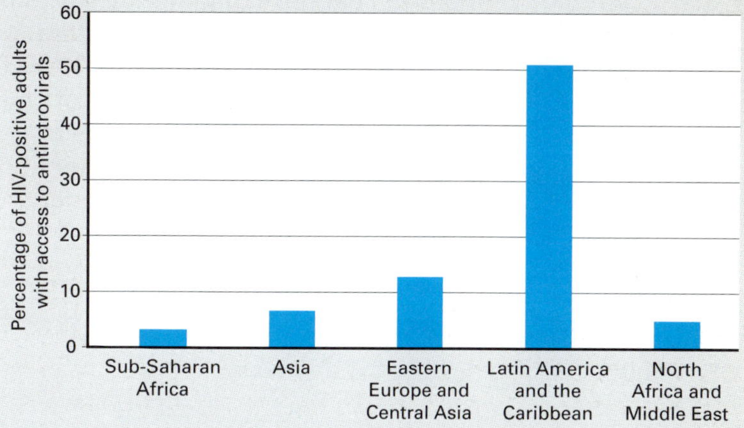

Source: UNAIDS/WHO, 2004.

UNICEF and other partners are supporting the '3 by 5 Initiative', which aims to ensure that 3 million people have access to antiretroviral treatment by the end of 2005. Antiretrovirals are also key to programmes to prevent mother-to-child transmission of HIV/AIDS (PMTCT): Providing antiretroviral prophylaxis to pregnant women and to babies at birth can reduce the risk of transmission by half.[16] UNICEF is currently supporting such programmes in 70 countries, five of which now have national coverage – Belarus, Botswana, Georgia, Kyrgyzstan and Ukraine.[17] Brazil has successfully implemented antiretroviral treatment for children and adolescents as an integral part of its national treatment policy.[18] In addition, UNICEF is working with the Mailman School of Public Health at Columbia University, New York, and others to roll out 'PMTCT Plus', an initiative to not only prevent infection in newborns but also treat mothers and families living with HIV.

Any reduction in HIV prevalence can take as much as a decade to translate into lower AIDS-related death rates among parents because of the long time lag between infection and death. Consequently, orphan numbers will continue to rise even in countries where inroads are being made against HIV infection. In Uganda, for instance, HIV prevalence peaked in the late 1980s at 14 per cent and by 2001 had shrunk to 5 per cent, yet the number of children orphaned by HIV/AIDS continued to rise until they accounted for 14.6 per cent of all children in 2001.[19] With this in mind, respecting the rights of children orphaned or made vulnerable by HIV/AIDS must remain an international priority for at least the next two decades.

Recognizing the urgent need to address the growing number of children orphaned or made vulnerable by HIV/AIDS and meet the goals committed to by the international community, in March 2004 the UNAIDS committee of co-sponsoring organizations formulated a comprehensive strategy for action on the following five fronts:

- Strengthen the capacity of families to protect and care for children by

Antiretroviral treatment: Prolonging the lives of adults and children living with HIV/AIDS

More than 20 million people have died of AIDS over the past two decades. If antiretroviral therapy had been available to them, most would probably still be alive today.[a]

Antiretroviral medicines work by blocking HIV from replicating and functioning inside the body. While the medicines are not a cure for AIDS, they have brought extraordinary hope to people infected and have transformed AIDS into a chronic but manageable disease. The World Health Organization and UNAIDS estimate that at least 6 million people worldwide suffer from advanced HIV infection and are in urgent need of antiretroviral therapy. In affluent nations, where treatment has been available since the mid-1990s, there has been a 70 per cent decline in AIDS-related deaths since the introduction of the medications and comprehensive AIDS management.[b]

The outlook is very different in the developing world. By late 2003, antiretroviral therapy was available to only 7 per cent of those in need of immediate treatment.[c] Although the cost of antiretroviral therapy has plunged over the past decade, falling from $10,000–$15,000 a year in the 1990s to as low as $300 for some generic combinations today,[d] it is still prohibitively high for the vast majority of patients in some of the most-affected countries. In Malawi, for example, 14.2 per cent of adults are infected with HIV, but the average adult earns only $170 in an entire year. For children living with HIV, the global situation is even worse: Price reductions in antiretrovirals have not been reflected in lower costs for paediatric treatment. Moreover, many children die undiagnosed.

In response to both the despair created by the epidemic and the remarkable promise of antiretroviral therapy, the World Health Organization, UNAIDS, UNICEF and other partners launched an ambitious new plan, the 3 by 5 Initiative, in 2003. The initiative aims to provide antiretroviral treatment to 3 million people in developing and transitional countries by 2005. It will complement the work of government donors, international agencies and faith-based groups, together with the efforts of pharmaceutical companies, to reduce the prices of medicines and increase access to treatment in developing countries.

The initiative focuses on developing simplified treatments and easy-to-use tests and medicine packs. Because it is imperative that patients adhere to treatment regimens to avoid the emergence of drug-resistant strains, tens of thousands of health workers are being trained to support monitoring and delivery systems. Counselling programmes and follow-up evaluations help ensure that an integrated package of services is provided to each participant.

The 3 by 5 Initiative has the potential to revolutionize health care in developing nations. The strategy will encourage testing by offering people treatment if they are found to be HIV-positive. This will increase the number of people who are aware of their HIV status – leading to safer practices and enhanced prevention efforts. Antiretroviral therapy lowers the incidence of opportunistic infections, easing burdens on public health facilities and releasing funds to care for other patients. And because the initiative is working to bolster the capacity of health-care systems to provide a wide variety of services, one of its most significant legacies will be a stronger health-care infrastructure.

prolonging the lives of parents and providing them with economic, psychosocial and other support.

- Mobilize and support community-based responses to provide both immediate and long-term support to vulnerable households.
- Ensure access for orphans and other vulnerable children to essential services, including education, health care and birth registration.
- Ensure that governments protect the most vulnerable children through improved policy and legislation and by channelling resources to communities.
- Raise awareness at all levels through advocacy and social mobilization to

Antiretroviral therapy has demonstrated that HIV/AIDS is not a death sentence. The medications combat stigma and discrimination by enabling people with the virus to work, socialize and participate. The 3 by 5 Initiative builds on this opportunity by encouraging community support and commitments from key stakeholders.

Recognizing that many health-care facilities in Africa are administrated by faith-based organizations, the president of the All Africa Conference of Churches, the Right Reverend Nyansanko Ni-Nku, vowed in June 2004 to fight stigma and support the 3 by 5 Initiative. "We will make treatment available at mission hospitals, clinics, dispensaries and health posts," he promised. "We will make our congregations and health facilities havens of compassion."[e]

The drive to provide universal access to antiretrovirals is grounded in concrete evidence. A recent study in Cameroon found that a simplified, fixed-dose combination of generic antiretrovirals costing just $20 per month is highly effective. Studies have shown that adherence rates in poorer nations can be even greater than those in developed countries: The trial in Cameroon, for instance, revealed compliance levels of 99 per cent.[f] In Brazil, one of the only developing countries to make antiretrovirals widely available, the average survival time for AIDS patients used to be less than six months. It is now close to five years.[g] The World Bank has said there is no evidence to show that viral resistance or non-adherence to drug regimens are bigger problems in developing countries than in industrialized countries.[h]

If the effort is successful, widespread antiretroviral treatment will do much more than simply keep patients alive. Unlike many diseases, HIV/AIDS tends to attack young adults, annihilating what is known as 'human capital' – the accumulated life experiences, skills, knowledge and insights that an adult builds over his or her lifetime – and severing the transmission of knowledge from one generation to the next. Antiretroviral treatment renews patients' ability to care for their relatives and contribute to their communities, healing broken families as well as individuals.

The international community has shown unprecedented commitment to the victims of HIV/AIDS in its provision of over $20 billion for the effort to combat the epidemic. Groundbreaking agreements among the Global Fund to Fight AIDS, Tuberculosis and Malaria, the World Bank, UNICEF and the Clinton Foundation are making it possible for developing countries to purchase high-quality medicines and tests at heavily discounted prices. Yet many funding needs remain unmet, and progress has not been swift enough. As the clock ticks towards 2005, only 400,000 of the 6 million people who need medications are being treated.

Antiretroviral medications are not the ultimate cure for AIDS. Drug resistance, side effects and finding appropriate distribution systems continue to be a concern, just as they are in the industrialized world. But without treatment, over 5 million more people will soon die – prematurely, painfully, and at great cost to their families, communities and human development worldwide.

create a supportive environment for all children affected by HIV/AIDS.

Strengthening families

The extended family is, and should remain, the key source of support for children orphaned by HIV/AIDS. When deprived of the opportunity to grow up in a supportive family environment, children receive less stimulation, individual attention and love and are ill prepared for life and healthy social interaction. Children who grow up outside families, whether living on the street or in institutions, often face discrimination and may feel unloved or excluded. In the worst cases, children who lose contact with their families can suffer physical or psychological abuse.

Among the approaches that can be adopted to strengthen the ability of families and communities to care for orphaned children are:

- Fostering the economic well-being of households caring for orphans, for example by ensuring they are reached by social safety nets as well as poverty-reduction initiatives, including seed funding for small businesses and methods to improve farming efficiency.

Going to school and thinking about the future: Not an easy feat in Mozambique

Celina* possesses a calm dignity. She holds her head high, her hair is neatly braided, her large eyes look directly at you when she speaks. She rarely smiles, but when she does, her smile is beautiful.

It has been two days since the family of six has eaten, but when Celina is given money by an aid worker to go to the market to buy basic food items, her aunt panics.

Twelve-year-old Celina is looking after her aunt, Margarida Araujo, and her three-year-old cousin, Paulo. Celina's three other siblings are not at home that afternoon.

The aunt's hollow eyes look scared. Her breathing quickens. Her face grimaces with pain. Her emaciated body covered by a grubby old sheet, she is too weak to speak. She can only lie there on an old mat, in front of their family's crumbling mud hut and look as Celina disappears through the overgrown weeds.

Her aunt is not the only one upset. Paulo, who had been sitting on Celina's tiny lap, is screaming hysterically at being left behind.

But Celina has no choice; food is critical now for the survival of the family. The children are all hungry and Margarida is dying from AIDS-related illnesses, including tuberculosis, as well as from severe malnutrition. "I haven't taken my TB tablets for five days, because I'm too hungry," she says in a faint voice. "The pills have strong side effects if taken without food," she adds, with tears rolling down her cheeks.

Margarida is only 20 years old, but she has not had much of a youth herself. She dropped out of school when she was 15 to look after her own parents, who she says were ill for a long time before they died.

Margarida was married, but she has no children of her own. The children living with her are the offspring of her three sisters, all of whom died of AIDS. Three years ago, when Margarida herself became sick, her husband abandoned her.

Margarida and the children live in a tiny mud hut, a 15-minute walk from the main road and reachable only by foot along dense pathways. Inside, it is dank and empty, and when it rains water leaks from the roof. The family's only belongings are some old rusty pots and a few ragged clothes.

The family receives weekly visits from activists belonging to KEWA (which means "to listen" in the local language, Chuabo), a non-profit association of people living with HIV/AIDS in Mozambique's central province of Zambézia. This is part of a UNICEF-supported project for organizations of people living with HIV/AIDS. The aim is to ensure that the rights of each orphan in the 15 districts in five provinces that UNICEF has identified as priorities are protected, including the right to an

- Offering children and their caregivers psychosocial counselling and support.
- Improving caregivers' childcare skills, especially in the area of early childhood development, and making community-based childcare available.
- Helping parents prepare their own wills and identify future careers for their children.
- Enabling parents to live longer, better and in greater dignity.
- Enhancing young people's life skills, including knowledge of how to avoid HIV infection.

The United Nations Secretary-General's Task Force on Women, Girls and HIV/AIDS in Southern Africa recognized in its 2004 report the particular burden placed upon older female caregivers. It recommends that governments and their development partners provide social grants or other financial support to these women whenever possible.[20] To this end, Swaziland submitted a proposal to the Global Fund to Fight AIDS, Tuberculosis and Malaria to provide stipends to women caring for orphans and

education, to health care and to birth registration.

KEWA activists visit Margarida and her family and other orphaned children. They now reach some 2,400 children in Zambézia Province. Zambézia was once known as the breadbasket of Mozambique, but 16 years of civil war, deteriorating infrastructure, widespread poverty and unpredictable weather, combined with the devastating impact of HIV/AIDS, have kept most people at subsistence level and plunged many others into absolute poverty.

The HIV/AIDS epidemic has pushed families like the Araujos over the edge. According to UNAIDS, 12.2 per cent of Mozambique's population between 15 and 49 years old lived with HIV/AIDS in 2003. However, government projections placed the number of HIV-infected Mozambicans in 2004 at 14.9 per cent. When those infected with the virus develop AIDS, like Margarida, they no longer have the strength to farm and are forced to sell what little they have for food. About 470,000 children have lost one or both parents to HIV/AIDS.

With UNICEF's support, Anita Martinho, a KEWA activist, has distributed school materials to many of the school-age orphans throughout the province, including Celina and her 13-year-old brother, Marcelino. The eldest niece, 14-year-old Sylvia, dropped out of school when she became pregnant. Now, with her eight-month-old baby strapped to her back, she does odd jobs to survive.

Celina does not want to drop out of school. Apart from an education, every day she also gets a meal in school provided by the World Food Programme. Her brother is at a different school where there is no supplementary feeding. However, Celina says, "some days I can't attend classes because I have to take care of my aunty. She is now too ill to walk to the hospital."

Celina bathes her aunt and assists her with her daily needs. She also handles the daily chores of fetching water and firewood, and cooking – if they are fortunate enough to have any food to cook.

What are her hopes for the future – What are her dreams? – Celina's eyes are blank as she responds flatly, "I don't think about anything."

**All names have been changed.*

Since this story was first reported in March 2004, Margarida Araujo has died and the children were left homeless until Anita Martinho invited them to live with her.

© UNICEF/HQ97-0085/Jeremy Horner

At the Sem Pringpuangkeo Foundation for children orphaned by AIDS in Chiang Mai, Thailand.

vulnerable children. Additionally, securing assets and property rights for women and girls is key to addressing the economic hardship they face because of HIV/AIDS.

Mobilizing community responses

When extended families cannot take responsibility for orphaned children, the next option should ideally be the local community. Fostering and adoption are alternatives that allow a child to remain in a family setting, and the greatest continuity and security is provided if such options are available within the child's own village or district. Foster families, whether spontaneously formed or formally arranged, need and deserve to be supported in their role by the wider community as well as through government services.

Community-based responses need to be mobilized and reinforced to ensure that the local community becomes a source of strength and support to orphaned children. Among the strategies that can help are:

- Sensitizing local leaders – including religious authorities, teachers and other prominent citizens – to the impact of HIV/AIDS on vulnerable children, mobilizing their support and encouraging them to counter the risks of abuse and exploitation.

- Fostering dialogue on HIV/AIDS within communities in order to dispel myths, combat ignorance and maximize the chances that people will respond to affected children's needs with compassion. Children and adolescents can play a key role, exploring opportunities for discussion and community education in schools, religious gatherings and youth clubs.

- Organizing cooperative support for affected households. This can involve home visits, community day-care programmes or childcare to give caregivers some respite. The support can also be material, for example, assisting vulnerable households through pooled funds.

- Ensuring that community responses are appropriate to children's ages and stages of development.

Increasing access to services

Orphans and other vulnerable children often have the least access to essential services, yet they are among those with the greatest need. Ensuring that they gain access to those services requires commitment and action at all levels, from the community right up to national governments. Among the key areas are:

- **Schooling.** Schools can offer children a safe environment, with built-in support, supervision and socialization. The best way to maximize the enrolment and attendance of orphans and other vulnerable children is to abolish school fees. In addition, removing the requirement to buy a uniform, introducing school-feeding programmes and ensuring access to life skills education to reduce the risks of HIV infection can also have a major impact.

The Global Campaign for Orphans and Children made Vulnerable by HIV/AIDS

There is an urgent need to massively scale up the protection and assistance given to orphans and children made vulnerable by HIV/AIDS and to mobilize the partnerships and resources necessary to do so. The Global Campaign for Orphans and Children made Vulnerable by HIV/AIDS, led by UNICEF, its National Committees and other partners, aims to reach an additional 10 million orphans and vulnerable children by 2010 with the essential services of education, nutrition, health care and counselling, providing them with household items and teaching them income-generating skills. This will require the concerted efforts of all major partners.

The campaign is based on five broad tenets: providing assistance for orphans aged 0-4 years; providing assistance and support for orphans aged 5-18 years; supporting child-headed households; keeping parents alive; and educating children and young people on how to protect themselves against HIV/AIDS. Although the campaign will be global, it will also have a strong focus on the most-affected countries in sub-Saharan Africa, the region most affected by and least able to respond to the HIV/AIDS pandemic.

- **Psychosocial support.** Losing a parent is a traumatic experience, and children need immediate support as they deal with the host of new difficulties and challenges. In the longer term, their new caregivers may also need such help.

- **Health services.** Children orphaned by HIV/AIDS are likely to be more vulnerable in terms of both health and nutrition. It is therefore paramount to ensure they have access to essential health services in early childhood such as immunization, vitamin A supplementation and growth monitoring. For adolescents, education and health services focused on HIV prevention and sexual and reproductive health are particularly vital. Treatment for HIV-positive youth is also an emerging necessity.

- **Safe water and sanitation.** Extended pipelines and new boreholes can help increase access to safe water. Those living with HIV/AIDS need clean water in order to avoid opportunistic infections such as skin diseases. Caregivers need to be informed about proper hygiene and food handling. Lack of access to safe water, especially in sub-Saharan Africa, means that women and girls have to spend long hours fetching it from wells that are often miles away, adding to their work burden and compromising their safety.

- **Justice systems.** Strong and independent legal systems, with judges who are educated about key child protection issues, are vital in protecting orphans and other vulnerable children from abuse, discrimination and property loss.

- **Birth registration.** All children need to be registered at birth to ensure that their rights are not denied, yet in sub-Saharan Africa in 2000, more than two in three births were not registered. Vulnerable children need official evidence of their identity to ensure they have access to public services and welfare.

Ensuring government protection

Children are cared for primarily within families, but overall responsibility for ensuring their protection and well-being also resides with the national government. Governments must ensure that their laws are in line with current international standards, and that they allocate the resources and take the initiatives required to maximize children's protection. They are responsible for ensuring that the justice system both protects children and understands their rights. They need to make a coherent link between emergency responses – such as providing swift and effective support to families – and longer-term development plans. People living with HIV/AIDS should be actively involved in developing and implementing policies. Among the main areas to be addressed are discrimination, foster care, inheritance rights, abuse and child labour.

Raising awareness

Even after two decades of HIV/AIDS awareness, efforts to deal with the impact of the disease are still hampered by fear, ignorance and denial at all levels. Children orphaned or made vulnerable by the disease continue to pay a heavy price as a result, not only because the deaths of their parents might have been prevented in a more open and informed social climate, but also because of their own stigmatization and abuse.

In countries where strong political leadership has fostered openness and wide-ranging responses to the HIV/AIDS pandemic, such as Brazil, Senegal, Thailand and Uganda, there has been notable progress and new impetus in the fight against the disease. The greatest headway is made when young people are given all the information and encouragement they need to protect themselves and can participate in planning and implementing the programmes that support them.

Resources for providing support to orphans and other children made

Members of the Vitoria Youth Football Team during practice in Salvador, Brazil. The team benefits from a complementary education programme for at-risk boys and young men.

vulnerable by HIV/AIDS have increased in recent years, not least through the establishment of the Global Fund to Fight AIDS, Tuberculosis and Malaria and the start up in 2004 of the US President's Emergency Plan for AIDS Relief. Nonetheless, funding for programmes for orphans and vulnerable children remains far below the level required to adequately protect and support this group.

© UNICEF/HQ-00-0440/Alejandro Balaguer

An enormous gap remains between what has been done and what still needs to be done to protect the rights and address the needs of orphans and vulnerable children. At the end of 2003, for example, only 17 countries with generalized HIV/AIDS epidemics reported having a national policy for orphans and vulnerable children to guide strategic decision-making and resource allocation.[21] Closing the gap is possible, but it will require the combined efforts of all those able to respond – governments, donors, non-governmental organizations, faith-based organizations, the private sector and the thousands of community groups already struggling on the front line of response.

The way forward

HIV/AIDS is one of the greatest threats to childhood in the world today. But the lines of response to the plight of orphans and vulnerable children are clear – provided the international community has the political and economic will to pursue them:

- Strengthen the protective environment for children at every level, from the family right through to the level of national and international legislation.
- Dedicate the funds needed to support programmes for orphans and vulnerable children, which currently receive only a small proportion of overall HIV/AIDS funding.
- Scale up projects for orphans and vulnerable children.
- Keep adults alive by increasing access to antiretroviral therapy and raising awareness of HIV/AIDS.
- Prevent new infections among children by applying and scaling up proven techniques and interventions.
- Eliminate school fees and other barriers to education.
- Combat poverty and conflict, which interact with HIV/AIDS to magnify the negative impact on childhood.

The Young Face of HIV/AIDS

While most of the nearly 38 million people living with HIV/AIDS are adults, the pandemic is increasingly recognized to have devastating repercussions for childhood. Over 2 million children under the age of 15 are already infected with HIV. Fifty per cent of HIV-positive infants die before they reach the age of two.

Childhood is at risk as soon as HIV/AIDS enters the household. By 2003, 15 million children – 80 per cent of them in sub-Saharan Africa – had been orphaned by the disease. The rise in infection rates among women in the region means that a growing proportion of the children orphaned because of HIV/AIDS have lost their mothers. Countless more have been deprived of their relatives, teachers and health workers. Many children have become caregivers themselves, increasing the likelihood that they will not receive an education, have access to health care, or be safeguarded from exploitation and abuse.

The pandemic has contributed to higher poverty levels, an increased incidence of child labour and dramatically shortened lifespans. In Botswana, for instance, over 37 per cent of adults are infected with HIV – and a child born there in 2003 could expect to live just 39 years, down from 65 years in 1990. In the most-affected countries, HIV/AIDS is eliminating the protective environment that is the right of every child and the first responsibility of adults to children.

Region	Life expectancy 2003
Sub-Saharan Africa	46
Middle East and North Africa	67
South Asia	63
East Asia and Pacific	69
Latin America and Caribbean	70
CEE/CIS	70
Industrialized countries	78
Developing countries	62
Least developed countries	49
World	63

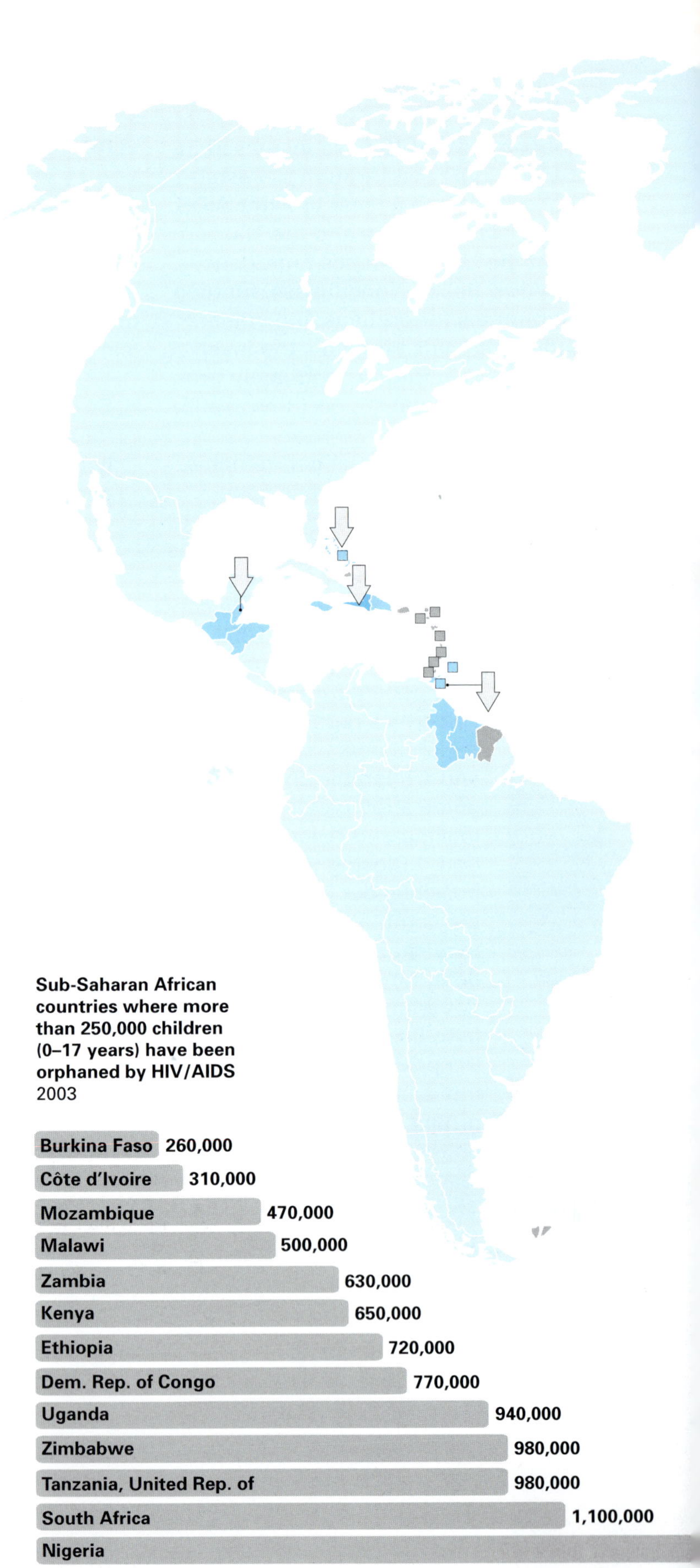

Source: UNAIDS, UNICEF, USAID, *Children on the Brink 2004*.

Childhood Under Threat: HIV/AIDS

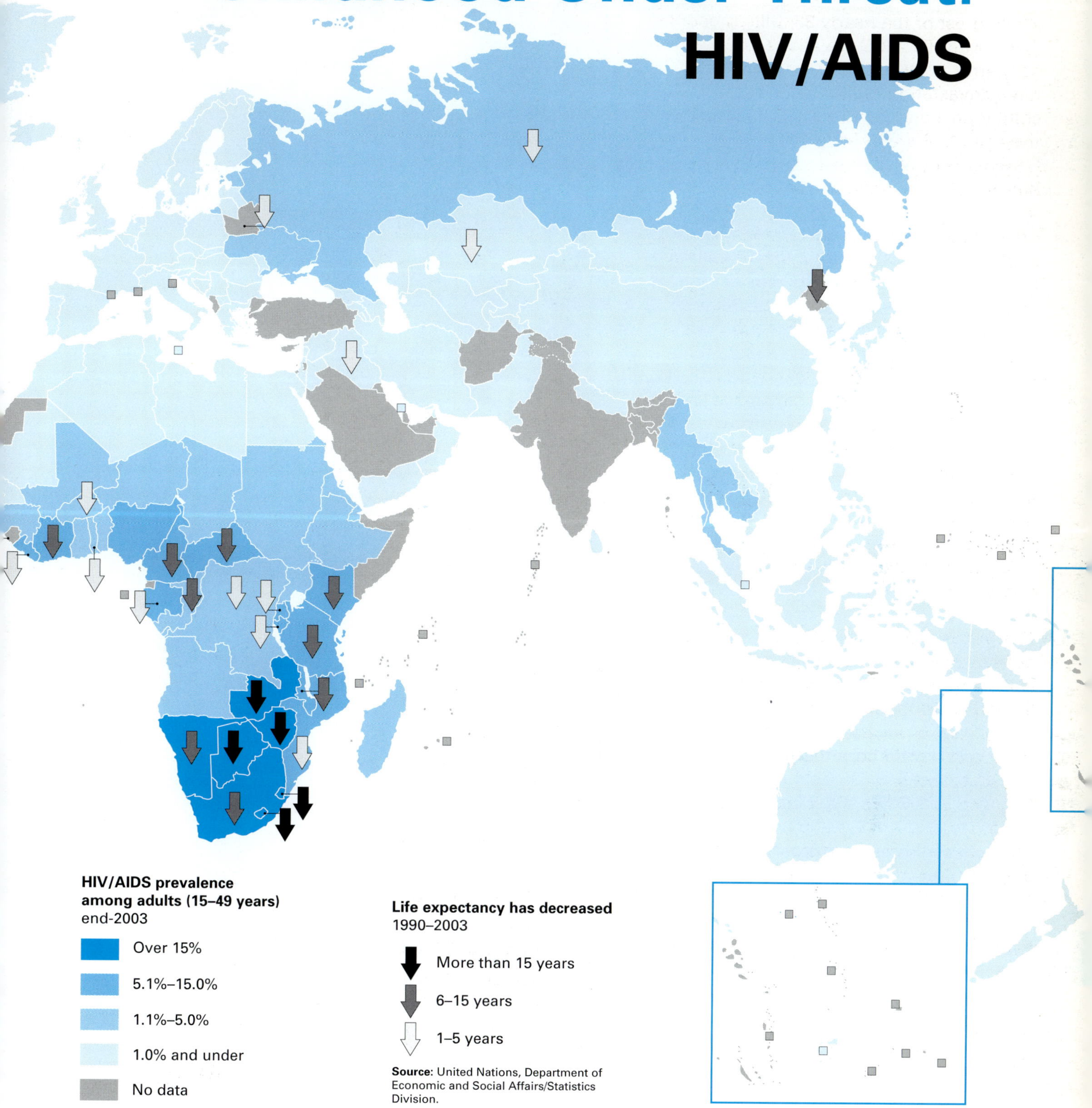

HIV/AIDS prevalence among adults (15–49 years) end-2003

- Over 15%
- 5.1%–15.0%
- 1.1%–5.0%
- 1.0% and under
- No data

Life expectancy has decreased 1990–2003

- More than 15 years
- 6–15 years
- 1–5 years

Source: United Nations, Department of Economic and Social Affairs/Statistics Division.

1,800,000

This map does not reflect a position by UNICEF on the legal status of any country or territory or the delimitation of any frontiers.

Dotted line represents approximately the Line of Control in Jammu and Kashmir agreed upon by India and Pakistan. The final status of Jammu and Kashmir has not yet been agreed upon by the parties.

5

A Childhood for Every Child

Fifteen years have elapsed since the world embraced the terms of childhood as laid down in the Convention on the Rights of the Child. In the intervening years, children's rights have been vigorously championed by many, UNICEF among them. Never before have children's rights been so high on the public agenda; never before have children's voices been heard as clearly and distinctly by the international community as they were during the United Nations General Assembly Special Session on Children in 2002.

A broken promise

Yet for hundreds of millions of children, the promise of childhood that undergirds the Convention already appears broken as poverty, conflict and HIV/AIDS threaten their lives and well-being. Though a childhood of love, care and protection, in a family environment, with ample scope to survive, grow, develop and participate is the right of every child, millions do not experience it. When they become parents, their own children also risk having their rights denied as the threats to childhood, particularly the ones highlighted in this report, replicate themselves from generation to generation. This is already evident in the lives of millions of youth – those aged 15 to 24 – who have grown up since the Convention was adopted and who are still living amid penury, conflict, violence, exploitation and disease. To take but one example, more than 140 million youth were illiterate in 2000, over 60 per cent of them young women.[1]

It is hard to avoid the conclusion that we, the adults of the world, have failed these young people and are failing the children

Summary

ISSUE: For hundreds of millions of children the promise of childhood laid down in the Convention on the Rights of the Child already appears broken. They do not inherit their right to a childhood of love, care and protection, in a family environment, encouraged to reach their full potential. When they become parents, their own children risk having their rights denied as the threats to childhood, particularly poverty, armed conflict and HIV/AIDS, replicate themselves from one generation to the next.

It does not have to be this way. We have an unparalleled opportunity to fulfil the rights of children. The intent is there, as evidenced by the near-universal ratification of the Convention, and the endorsement of other international and national instruments related to children's rights and well-being. The resources – knowledge, money, technology, strategies and people – are available in abundance. The targets are clear: Achievement of the Millennium Development Goals and the broad aims of 'A World Fit for Children', would do much to make the world a better place for children.

ACTION: UNICEF believes that the rights of all children everywhere can be fulfilled, if only the world demonstrates the **will** to enact its promises. Everyone can make a contribution.

- **The world must reaffirm and recommit to its moral and legal responsibilities to children.** For governments and donors, the message is unambiguous: Keep your commitments to children. Children's rights must be given the highest priority.
- **Each nation must apply a human rights-based approach to social and economic development.** Placing rights at the heart of human development strategies allows countries to prioritize goods and services essential for children and to construct a protective environment.
- **Governments must adopt socially responsible policies, keeping children specifically in mind.** Pursuing measures with children specifically in mind is the most effective route to reduce poverty and lower HIV prevalence. A key starting point would be to abolish school fees, which will encourage poor families to enrol their children in school.
- **Donors and governments must invest additional funds in children.** The resources are available to fund a global transformation of childhood, through both increased official development assistance and improvements in the quality of national public finances.
- **Everyone must fulfil their obligations to children.** Many possibilities exist for participation in activities that benefit children: All that is required is the willingness to get involved and stay engaged.

Childhood is the foundation of the world's future. Many are already contributing, at all levels and in innovative ways, to ensuring that every child enjoys their right to a childhood. Many more must follow their example.

"In violating our children's rights by denying them the essentials they need and deserve, we harm them and ourselves, permitting and encouraging the seeds of poverty, alienation and despair to take root."

Carol Bellamy, Executive Director, UNICEF

of today. But this does not have to be the case. We have an unparalleled opportunity to fulfil the rights of children. The **intent** is there, as evidenced by the near-universal ratification of the Convention and the endorsement of other international and national instruments related to children's rights and well-being. The resources – knowledge, money, technology, people – are available in abundance: by any aggregate measure, the world is richer than it has ever been. The targets are clear: Achievement of the Millennium Development Goals, and fulfilment of the broad aims embodied in 'A World Fit for Children', though not a panacea for all childhood's woes, would do much to make the world a better place for children. Decades of human development research have fine-tuned our strategies: We now know, for example, that for development gains to be sustainable, the participation of all parties – including children and young people – is essential.

Where change will come from

Previous chapters have outlined ways in which the threats to childhood posed by poverty, armed conflict and HIV/AIDS can be lessened, or even eliminated. There is hope as well as discouragement in the fact that all three of these areas are so interconnected. While poverty fuels conflict, which in turn creates more poverty in a destructive spiral – and both render people much more vulnerable to HIV/AIDS – the flipside of this coin is that a serious assault on poverty will also reduce both conflict and HIV/AIDS.

And there is the optimism that infuses both the Universal Declaration of Human Rights and the Convention on the Rights of the Child. If every family, community and government lived by the principles and worked to realize the standards established by the Convention, which preceded all other current commitments to children by over a decade, the Millennium Development Goals would be met and 'A World Fit for Children' would become a reality.

Will we create a world fit for children in which every child enjoys a childhood? Will the promise of the Convention ever be fulfilled? Sceptical voices murmur "No," pointing to the broken promises of the past to support their view that too little will be done. Their point of view is understandable: Time and time again the world has clearly failed to live up to its commitments to children. But UNICEF does not share their opinion. From its inception, the organization has held the conviction that the rights of all children everywhere can be fulfilled, if only the world demonstrates the **will** required to enact its promises.

A question of will

The notion of will is pivotal to creating a world fit for children. It is will that translates intentions into action. The will of one woman, Eglantyne Jebb, inspired her to launch the Save the Children Fund in 1919, in response to the misery of thousands of children in Europe. The will of the international community led to the creation of UNICEF in 1946 to look after the needs of children in post-war Europe. That will has helped save millions of lives as UNICEF has expanded its work into every developing nation where children's lives are at risk.

Not all of us will have the opportunity to launch a children's fund or to save the lives of millions of children. But we all have a part to play in ensuring that every child enjoys a childhood. Children's rights are human rights, the rights that we all share. The fulfilment of rights implies responsibilities. It is the duty of each and every one of us – not just parents, guardians and relatives, educators and governments – to guarantee that the terms of childhood laid out in the Convention, which our governments have endorsed on our behalf, are upheld for every child. States and societies, communities and families, individuals and international agencies and, most importantly, children and young people themselves – are all duty-bound to fulfil children's rights.

Each can make a different contribution, depending on their capacities and resources.

Fulfilling children's rights: Our collective responsibility

Children's rights, human development and moral considerations are increasingly intertwined. In a world that brings us televised or Internet images of suffering from the other side of the planet, we are as capable of being moved by the pain of someone 5,000 kilometres away as we are by that of someone next door. In this sense, we are increasingly becoming a global community in which we can no longer partition off our ethical responsibility along local or even national lines.

No image is more likely to speak to us across continents, from beyond oceans, than that of a child in distress. A girl abducted from her village and forced into sexual slavery by a gang of armed rebels: the very idea is unbearable. It moves us to justified anger, to a desire to do whatever we can to ensure that it does not happen again. The difficulty is to have the same response to – and the same sense of responsibility towards – all the hundreds of thousands of children who we do not see or read about, except as bald statistics: those, for example, who die for want of a simple hydrating formula that could counteract the ravages of diarrhoea; those who die from diseases that are preventable either by inexpensive vaccinations or increased access to basic health-care services; those who are orphaned by HIV/AIDS, without family or the comfort of even one caring adult.

Although some of these threats to children have existed since the dawn of recorded history, in a very real sense we live in a new world. Since 1990, we have committed ourselves, through the Convention on the Rights of the Child and its two Optional Protocols, the Millennium Declaration and its associated goals, 'A World Fit for Children' and other international, regional and national initiatives, to a conception of childhood that is profound in its implications and will stand for decades, even for centuries to come. It gives us a clearer vision than ever before of what a safe, healthy, active childhood should look like.

In a crowded class at Chadza Primary School in LiLongwe, Malawi, a young girl volunteers an answer during an English lesson. The school is involved in the African child-to-child survey, which works to boost the attendance of out-of-school children.

The world must reaffirm and recommit to its moral and legal responsibilities to children

For governments, the message is unambiguous: Keep your commitments to your nation's children. Despite numerous treaties and pledges, despite the UN Special Session on Children, there is simply not enough being done to realize children's rights: They **must** be given the highest priority. A key starting point for many nations will be to make progress in the health and development of their children a priority. At present, it is estimated that approximately one third of the global burden of disease is borne by children.

Without greater attention to providing basic health care and education services for children, it is clear that most of the Millennium Development Goals will not be met in full by 2015.

Of all the MDGs, it is widely acknowledged that progress has been slowest on reducing under-five mortality. This goal can be achieved: It is estimated that two thirds of the almost 11 million under-five deaths that occur each year could be averted if children would receive appropriate home care and if simple curative treatments for the common childhood illnesses were available. The interventions to prevent child deaths, such as immunization, exclusive breastfeeding and oral rehydration therapy, are well known and tested, and can be scaled up even in resource-poor settings. Achieving the MDG for child survival is therefore a clear case of will, for while the financial investment will be fairly modest, massive efforts will be required in social mobilization and the development of innovative strategies for delivering the interventions.

Reaching every child with a basic package of essential, proven interventions will

Child trafficking *by H.M. Queen Silvia of Sweden*

Trafficking in children, an affront to human rights and human dignity, has reached epidemic proportions and is escalating out of control. The evidence is all too clear: Millions of children are trafficked for exploitation into sweatshops, into domestic work, to work on farms, for adoption, as child soldiers and, most perniciously, into the commercial sex industry, now a global multibillion-dollar business. These children are not only ruthlessly exploited, they are also deprived of a childhood and denied a future.

Thanks to an initiative taken by ECPAT (End Child Prostitution, Child Pornography and Trafficking of Children for Sexual Purposes) and hosted by the Swedish Government, the First World Congress against Commercial Sexual Exploitation of Children was organized in Stockholm in August 1996. Representatives of 122 governments, non-governmental organizations, UN agencies and the private sector came together to address this crisis. I was asked to be the patron of this gathering, and since then I have closely monitored the issue of commercial sexual exploitation and trafficking in children and the measures being brought to bear around the world to combat this problem.

As part of my own commitment to help make the world a safe place for children, I founded the World Childhood Foundation, which provides funding to projects all over the world, especially those that seek to rescue and rehabilitate sexually abused and exploited children. Through our work, I have met many children and young mothers who, on a daily basis, personify this epidemic. Too many children suffer in poverty, live in institutions, are ill and have parents who abuse drugs. They are, in turn, often abused themselves and used in ways that we are reluctant to talk about let alone confront. But we have to, because the reality of the situation is so much more powerful than the words that describe it.

I have learned this first-hand. For example, in my travels to the Russian Federation I met young mothers struggling in a harsh economic environment and with no safety net. In Brazil, I have seen children in small villages who go to school for only a few hours each day because they are required to work long hours to help their family survive, exposing them to dangers that no child should have to bear. These are the very conditions that produce the breeding grounds for trafficking – targets who succumb to the false promise of a better life elsewhere.

Trafficking is made possible by a breakdown in the protective environment. When social, political or economic conflicts are accompanied by poor legal and justice systems, deepening poverty as well as a lack of educational or economic opportunities for children and their families – not to mention the growing demand from the industrialized world for exploitive sex – children are left much more vulnerable to the prey of traffickers.

Illegal trafficking in human beings has become a global trade. Its success represents a signal failure on the part of the world community, which ought to be working to ensure that every child has the opportunity to grow up in safety and with dignity.

demand cooperation between governments, bilateral and multilateral agencies, non-governmental organizations, health professionals, professional associations and the private sector. Such a collaboration, including governments, UNICEF, the World Health Organization, and many others, has recently been formed under the auspices of the Child Survival Partnership to respond to the health crisis facing children and help countries scale up their interventions rapidly. The partnership provides a forum for coordinated action to enable governments and partners to agree on consistent approaches to child survival interventions and to ensure concerted efforts towards their implementation.

The Child Survival Partnership is not a fund-holding or fund-disbursing organization. It is an advocacy initiative for the increased mobilization of resources and support for child survival programmes by participating countries and organizations to meet a specific objective: attain the fourth Millennium Development Goal. The interventions it recommends and encourages will require substantial additional funding, however, from national, bilateral and multilateral sources, as will other initiatives

Yet much can be done to stop trafficking. We need to acknowledge our failures to date and launch a fresh initiative to create a protective environment for children. The following are a few actions that can be taken:

- **Raise awareness:** Law enforcement officials need to be trained on how to investigate trafficking rings; border guards need to be trained on how to identify traffickers and their victims; and adults and children need to learn more about the risks of trafficking.

- **Enforce laws:** We must all work to ensure that strong laws are in place to punish perpetrators and protect victims. But they also need to be strictly enforced. Those who trade in children and those who buy children must be punished. Far too often, trafficked children are treated as criminals, while those who ruthlessly exploit them go free. Frameworks to punish perpetrators and protect victims are laid out in the Optional Protocol to the Convention on the Rights of the Child on the sale of children, child prostitution and child pornography; the International Labour Organization's Convention 182 on the Worst Forms of Child Labour; and the Protocol to Prevent, Suppress and Punish Trafficking in Persons, Especially Women and Children, supplementing the United Nations Convention against Transnational Organized Crime. These must be ratified into law and implemented.

- **Challenge discriminatory practices and attitudes** that make young girls in particular vulnerable to trafficking.

- **Consider expanding the practice of providing temporary permits for protective residence** that allow a sexually exploited child to remain in the country to which she or he was trafficked, in order to obtain the testimonies necessary for pressing charges against the perpetrators.

- **Reintegrate victims of trafficking:** Children need to be reunited with their families wherever possible and provided with necessary services to help them recover, including the opportunity to return to school.

Working together, I know it is possible for us to end this assault on our children. Children, like the ones that I have met, demand no less from us. It is time to go beyond talk and to take all measures necessary to create a world where children are safe and secure.

It is surely a daunting task to confront such a massive, global force as these traffickers and sex buyers, but surely we must. And, if at any moment we feel the challenge overwhelming, we must remain steadfast, following Winston Churchill's exhortation in 1941 to children at Harrow School, United Kingdom, who were frightened by the horrors of World War II:

Never give in, never give in, never, never, never, never – in nothing, great or small, large or petty – never give in except to convictions of honour and good sense.

For all children to be happy is my vision. Please share it with me and make it come true.

designed to achieve the MDGs, and other rights-based and development targets.

Donors, therefore, are also pivotal actors in ensuring that every child has a childhood. Promises made to children at the Special Session and enshrined in 'A World Fit for Children' cannot be forgotten. Pledges made following the Monterrey Consensus in 2002 to increase official development assistance by around $18.5 billion a year until 2006 must also be realized. Though this may appear a substantial sum, in truth it is a minimal increment: A figure closer to $50 billion annually over the same period would be required to meet all of the Millennium Development Goals by 2015.[2] The quality of aid also requires enhancement through improved harmonization of donor policies with recipients' priorities. Investment in essential goods, services and infrastructure that directly satisfy children's rights is crucial: without it, none of the other international development agendas will be realized.

Each nation must apply a human rights-based approach to social and economic development

By 1994, four years after the Convention's inception, nearly 170 nations had accepted

The human rights-based approach to development: Examples from Latin America

In May 2003, the agencies of the United Nations issued a declaration affirming their commitment to the promotion and protection of human rights worldwide. The Statement of Common Understanding calls for human rights considerations to be integrated into all programmes: Policies should be designed with a view to empowerment, and the principles of equality, participation, inclusion and accountability should guide development strategies from their inception.

For the children whose rights to survival, health, education and protection are routinely violated, these are not abstract ideals. The human rights-based approach to development has helped policy makers to see injustices they may never have recognized before. It has directed attention and resources to those who are most vulnerable, and it has fostered programmes that address the causes, as well as the effects, of marginalization and social exclusion.

In Chile, for example, the human rights-based approach was the foundation for UNICEF's efforts to identify highly vulnerable children who were not benefiting from important educational reforms. Despite Chile's relatively high secondary enrolment rates – over 80 per cent in the late 1990s – research by UNICEF on the number of students who actually completed this phase of their education revealed that about one third of adolescents were not completing secondary school and that 70 per cent of school dropouts were from the poorest families.

The Chilean Government responded by launching the 'Secondary School for All' programme, which provides extra resources for selected schools and scholarships for students at high risk – enabling children to attend school instead of looking for work. To raise completion rates in rural areas, the government expanded its support to small, locally-managed schools that make it possible for teenagers to obtain a high-quality education without leaving their communities. At the same time, the Ministry of Education adopted policies to encourage participation by children and parents in the educational process.

By mid-2001, overall school enrolment had increased by more than 17 per cent above the 1990 level, and secondary school dropout rates had declined by almost one third. In 2003, a constitutional amendment was adopted that guarantees all children the right to 12 years of free education. These developments have set off a chain of reforms in other areas. Teachers now hold class discussions on child labour and help identify children whose academic performance suffers because of the number of hours they are working outside of school. By providing financial resources that assist poor families, Chile's new programmes help convince parents and youth that it is in their long-term interests to complete a secondary education – thus reducing the incidence of child labour and helping to redress social disparities.

the document as an internationally agreed standard for childhood. A decade has since passed and human rights have been elevated to the top of the international agenda. But few governments have been guided by human rights principles in all of their actions towards their citizens.

The human rights-based approach to development is relatively new *(see Panel: The human rights-based approach to development: Examples from Latin America, page 92)*. It is based on a long-term process of investing in people as citizens and actors in their nation's destiny as well as supporting their capacity to hold their government accountable for its promises. Placing rights at the heart of human development strategies allows countries to give attention to those children and vulnerable members of society living at its margins; to prioritize goods and services essential for children's survival, health and education; and to construct a protective environment to safeguard children from the rights violations that cannot easily be quantified: abuse, exploitation, violence, conflict, bonded labour, stigmatization and discrimination.

Applying new concepts such as the human rights-based approach to development and

The human rights-based approach has also influenced national economic policies. In Ecuador, the macroeconomic crisis of the late 1990s prompted UNICEF to analyse the national budget. The study showed that spending on social programmes was plummeting: investments in education and health had dropped by nearly one half in three years, and indigenous communities were disproportionately affected by the cuts.

These findings led to an agreement that enabled UNICEF to track social and economic indicators using information gathered from the Ministry of Economy and Finance. The organization created a series of visual tools to make budget data accessible and easily comprehensible to Ecuadorians from all walks of life. Over time, the budget data became available online. As part of its agreement with the Ministry of Economy and Finance, UNICEF then embarked on an ambitious outreach effort, sharing the information with legislators, academics, business leaders, media representatives, and indigenous, religious and trade union groups.

UNICEF collaborated with government officials to develop programmes to mitigate the effects of the budget crisis on the most marginalized communities. School nutrition and early childhood programmes were expanded and educational subsidies for poor families were scaled up. The organization also provided input for a tax reform proposal that received extensive press coverage and was the topic of a national conference sponsored by the Ecuadorian Congress.

Economic recovery, greater attention to social programmes and improved tax revenue collection brought concrete gains. By 2002, the percentage of total government spending devoted to social programmes had risen to 23.2 per cent, surpassing the 1996 figure of 19.1 per cent, and government revenue from taxes had increased from 6.4 per cent to 13.7 per cent of gross domestic product. Perhaps most significantly, a broad consensus on the need for more equitable public spending policies emerged during the first few years of the initiative. Whereas few Ecuadorians had previously been aware of the disparities in the national budget, the leader of one of the country's largest indigenous groups noted that the scheme had "democratized budget information."

The examples in Chile and Ecuador illustrate how the human rights-based approach has led UNICEF to go beyond the utilitarian principle of the greatest good for the greatest number. By pushing for services to reach the 'last 10 per cent' of those in need, and by addressing the underlying causes of deprivation, the human rights-based approach encourages bottom-up economic growth that will ultimately pay greater dividends for all.

See References, page 102.

the protective environment is not only important for governments: donors and international agencies also have much to gain. Refinements in development thinking over the decades have broadened UNICEF's approaches to its own programmes. We now know, for example, that educating children caught up in armed conflict, which was previously not given a high priority among our core commitments to children in emergency situations, is actually vital for injecting stability into their lives *(see 'Education', Chapter 3, 'Children Caught up in Armed Conflict', page 58).*

The threats to, and opportunities for, childhood are not static: they evolve with the changing of the world. Each new generation faces fresh challenges: for instance, polio, long a leading cause of child deaths, has almost been eradicated, but a new threat – HIV/AIDS – has emerged. On the brighter side, the leap in information technology achieved in the 1990s has allowed several developing countries, India among them, to make great strides towards closing the technology gap with the industrialized nations. The utilization of information technology is almost certainly destined to drive economic development in most countries. But it is not without cost or concerns, including the danger posed to children by predators using the Internet, and the difficulty faced by parents in monitoring their children's use of the web.

There is no excuse for ignorance. It is the responsibility of both governments and

China's 'digital divide'

While much has been said about the potential of the Internet to encourage the free flow of information and ideas, the promise of the cyber age has so far been mostly a reality only for the affluent minority. As a result, the world has become divided into those who can go online and those who cannot. The impact of this phenomenon on the rights and aspirations of children is important today and likely to become even more significant tomorrow.

China provides an example of this global issue. Internet users in this country have soared from 620,000 in 1997 to more than 87 million today, a figure surpassed only by the United States.[a] The good news is that nearly 20 per cent of these users are children.[b] The not-so-good news is that China's six most developed administrative units make up more than 50 per cent of its Internet population, while its six poorest units account for less than 1 per cent.[c]

The Internet effectively bypasses the conventional Chinese mass media, which has traditionally been controlled by the State. Today, there are over 2,500 Chinese language chat rooms used predominantly by young people. Not surprisingly, the Chinese Government, while strongly committed to accelerated growth through the embracing of new technology, tends to view children's access to such technologies as a double-edged sword. This quandary is perfectly illustrated by the fact that, in 2004, local governments across China were ordered not to approve any Internet cafe operations in residential areas or within 200 metres of primary and high schools.[d]

Banning Internet cafes in close proximity to schools is partly based on the government's desire to protect young people from uncensored information, pornography and exploitation. Placing a major emphasis on public morality, the government has cracked down on these perils with particular vigour and declared Internet cafes off limits for children under the age of 16.[e] This may have helped solve the problem of children being exposed to pornography and violent video games, but it also means that many are unable to benefit from the Internet since an estimated 80 per cent of 'netizens' in small and medium-sized cities are only able to access the Internet through cyber cafes.[f]

With its capacity to improve the quality of teaching and learning, Internet technology can provide China, and its remote communities in particular, with an educational and developmental springboard. Through the Internet, children can exercise their rights to self-expression. They can become a global constituency, engaging in active debates on the issues they face and bringing influence to bear on decision makers in their societies. UNICEF's experience has been that through active participation and the sharing of 'ideas that work', children

© UNICEF/Serbia and Montenegro/Zoran Jovanovic Maccak

Children in front of the old school building in the village of Manic in Barajevo, the poorest municipality in Belgrade, following a workshop on poverty and children in Serbia and Montenegro.

can themselves play an active role in building 'A World Fit For Children'.

UNICEF China's work with the China Children's Press and Publication Group over the past four years illustrates some of the potential uses of the Internet for development. Their website, launched in 2001, has become one of China's top websites for children and youth, with some 120,000 registered users. The site has up to 1 million hits daily, with some 7,000 to 8,000 messages posted by children every day on its various discussion forums.

In partnership with UNICEF, the site opened an anti-smoking forum in 2002 that generated data through an online survey. Nearly 7,000 questionnaires were completed and returned by children during the first three months, and the findings were later shared online. Thereafter, 200,000 children accepted the site's invitation to develop their own messages and graphics for an anti-smoking campaign that was also run in the organization's print and broadcast media.

During the SARS epidemic of 2003, when schoolchildren were sent home, the website helped keep children in touch with one another. It also provided reassurance and information about how to protect oneself and one's family from SARS. The open discussion generated by the forum revealed high levels of stress and anxiety, which experts were able to address through online counselling.

While boys often spend much of their time on the Internet playing games, two thirds of all online participants in the discussion forums are girls. Their use of the medium to contact peers and share experiences has special significance in a single-child society where domestic chores and fears for their safety often prevent girls from having as many social contacts outside the home as boys.

With the aim of bridging the digital divide between itself and the industrialized world, China has made great efforts to promote Internet growth. Tremendous progress has unquestionably been made in terms of information accumulation, database design and software development.[9] Furthermore, the number of Internet users continues to grow rapidly. The country needs to ensure, however, that its push to close the gap between itself and the industrialized world does not exacerbate its own internal disparities, for the risks are many now and will increase in the future. Children denied access to the Internet today may struggle later on to catch up with their privileged peers who have been immersed in such self-empowering forms of information and knowledge from an early age. If all China's children are to have a chance of experiencing the opportunities of the 21st century together, ways will need to be found to address this country's internal digital divide today.

A willing world can end child poverty *by Joseph E. Stiglitz*

In recent years, the issue of poverty in the developing world, and how to reduce it, has commanded a great deal of attention. There has been less recognition, however, of the problem of **poverty among children**, which is more pervasive and has pernicious long-term consequences. Poverty threatens children's lives: it is the main reason that the under-five mortality rate in sub-Saharan Africa, the least developed geographical region, is twice the world average and nearly 30 times higher than the average of the high-income Organisation for Economic Co-operation and Development (OECD) countries. Poverty, along with HIV/AIDS and armed conflict, shortens average life spans: A child born in 2003 in sub-Saharan Africa can only expect to live 46 years, compared with 78 years in the highest-income countries. Malnutrition, which is most prevalent in South Asia, not only stunts growth but also affects brain development, preventing children from blossoming to their full potential. It is also a contributory factor to many of the diseases that can result in child death or disability.

A lack of education also has severe and lifelong repercussions for children. Study after study confirms the high economic returns to both individuals and economies from investment in education. But more than simply material gain is at stake. Without an education, children will struggle to fulfil their potential, or to enjoy as rich and meaningful lives as they otherwise could have. In 2003, according to UNICEF estimates, over 121 million school-age children were out of school; this is more than the number in 1990. One in every three children in developing countries does not complete five years of primary education, which is the minimum period required for achieving basic literacy. These children will join the ranks of the 1 billion adults who cannot read or write. In high-income OECD countries, annual public expenditure on education per child is $7,372, nearly 200 times higher than the average for sub-Saharan Africa of just $38. The disparities in income between the industrialized countries and the least developed countries, already huge, will widen further unless investment in education in low-income countries increases markedly.

The fact that poverty among children is even a greater problem than poverty in general should come as no surprise: The poorest regions of the world are rich in children. Nearly 50 per cent of the population in the least developed countries is under the age of 18, compared with just 22 per cent in the high-income OECD countries.

What makes the poverty children experience so appalling is that it would cost very little to do something about it. While the cost of educating a child varies across countries, the average annual cost for developing countries is about $40 per student. The additional cost of achieving universal primary education by 2015 – the second Millennium Development Goal agreed to by 187 countries in September 2000 – is estimated at $9.1 billion annually.[a] Less than $100 billion will be required over the next 10 years to make this goal a reality. To put this number in perspective, global defence spending in 2003 amounted to over $956 billion. A 1 per cent reduction in annual global military spending – which would only shave a fraction off the 11 per cent spending increase that took place in 2003 alone – could provide primary education for all children around the world. A 10 per cent reduction in spending in a single year would cover all the expenses to eliminate global illiteracy for the next decade. The numbers make one thing clear: The world can afford to eliminate illiteracy.

The disparity in health is no less glaring, and again, the world can easily meet the expense of basic health care for the least developed countries if it is willing. The average yearly cost of servicing sub-Saharan Africa's external debt is roughly $80 per household, almost half the average amount ($173) that each family spends on health and education combined. The implication is obvious: Faster and deeper debt service relief for the poorest countries could free up additional resources for social expenditure that would go a long way to ameliorating poverty. UNICEF's projected cost for immunizing children for the whole of 2004 is about $187 million: This amounts roughly to 0.02 per cent of global military spending. If just 0.5 per cent of global military spending were diverted to immunization, every child in the world could be immunized for the next decade.

The responsibility to eradicate the poverty that children experience, which threatens their survival, health, education and potential, is global: Every country must do more to live up to this challenge. As this *State of the World's Children* report makes clear, every society should mobilize its resources to reduce the level of deprivation that children experience on a day-to-day basis. However, in this era of global economic interdependence, the more affluent economies have broader responsibilities; their spending priorities and policies not only affect the children in their own countries, but also have implications for children elsewhere.

Our self-interest is at stake: A world with such social injustice and despair provides a fertile breeding ground for terrorism. Democracy without education often falters. As an economist, it is easy to say that we are not allocating resources in ways that maximize our own long-term interests. Lack of resources is not, and cannot be, an excuse. But we should not view the eradication of poverty among children as simply a matter of self-interest. It is a question of what is morally right.

Nobel Laureate **Joseph E. Stiglitz** is recognized around the world as a leading economic educator. A former Chief Economist and Senior Vice-President of the World Bank, he has made major contributions to many branches of economics. Professor Stiglitz also helped to create a new branch of economics, the Economics of Information, pioneering pivotal concepts that have now become standard tools, not only of theorists, but also of policy analysts. He founded one of the leading economic journals, *The Journal of Economic Perspectives,* and has written several books, including the international bestseller *Globalization and Its Discontents,* which has been translated into more than 20 languages. A former professor at Yale and Stanford Universities in the United States, and All Souls College, Oxford, United Kingdom, he is now a University Professor at Columbia University in New York.

donors to be aware of how children are affected by poverty, discrimination, ignorance, labour and exploitation, life-threatening diseases and the environment. Accountability and knowledge provide a firm basis for action and must be incorporated into policies and programmes to bring about change.

Governments must adopt socially responsible policies, keeping children specifically in mind. For any government hoping to promote and protect human rights and achieve sustainable development, especially in the areas of poverty reduction and lowering HIV/AIDS prevalence, pursuing measures with children specifically in mind is the most effective route. Applying human rights principles to child policies will bring rich rewards. Educating and supporting citizens to participate in civic affairs will enhance their capacity to support their children's development and ensure the protection of their rights. Abolishing school fees will encourage poor families to enrol their children in school, as it has done in Kenya, Malawi, Uganda and the United Republic of Tanzania, allowing millions of children to enjoy their right to an education.

Mechanisms that increase the transparency and accountability of state services will help ensure that these are of the highest quality possible and the least wasteful of human and financial resources. Empowering and directing resources to marginalized groups will assist in strengthening the social fabric and reducing potential social discord, conflict and disintegration. Provision of social and protection services should be mandatory, not optional, and citizens should be encouraged to participate and fulfil their own duties to children and to society.

Donors and governments must invest additional funds in children. The resources are available to fund a global transformation of childhood, through both increased official development assistance and improvements in the quality of national public finances. Implementing national

© UNICEF/HQ01-0370/Roger LeMoyne

plans of action for children with a set of specific, time-bound and measurable targets and goals, as agreed to at the UN Special Session on Children, would go a long way towards meeting the agenda of 'A World Fit for Children'. The monitoring and analysis of national budgets from the perspective of their impact on children is a promising approach to promoting increased resource allocation for children and maximizing their effective use. Better targeting of education, health and social assistance services towards the poor, addressing government-related impediments to service quality and effectiveness, increasing community participation and scaling up on the basis of successful programmes would help meet the requirements of the Monterrey Consensus for developing countries – and must be matched by increased donor funding. Substantial additional resources could be freed up, for example, by diverting expenditure on weapons and other military equipment. If even a fraction of this expenditure were diverted to health or education, it would release millions – if not billions – of dollars.

Everyone must fulfil their obligations to children. Individuals, families, businesses and communities: all are duty-bound to make the Convention a reality by using their resources and capabilities to promote and protect children's rights. An array of possibilities exists for participation in activities that will benefit children, from sitting on school councils or volunteering as a youth counsellor, to sponsoring a local football team or expressing outrage at violations of children's rights to politicians and other leaders. All that is required is commitment and willingness to get involved and to stay engaged.

A global endeavour

Childhood is the foundation of the world's future. And though the future may look bleak now, we must not despair. Our optimism is rooted in history – the world has shown that it is capable of doing great things when it has the will to achieve them. Major feats have already been achieved. To take just one example, children are half as likely to die before the age of five today as they were 40 years ago, largely thanks to better access to health-care services and increased knowledge of the causes of child deaths. Expert opinion is that the Millennium Development Goals can still be achieved if both donor and recipient countries increase their efforts. Several countries are already putting in place the elements required to create a protective environment for children that will help meet the protection aims of 'A World Fit for Children'. Although idealistic in the context of past experience, these goals are realistic in the sense that the principal obstacle standing in their way is the lack of will and commitment to achieve them.

Many are already contributing, at all levels and in innovative ways, to ensuring that every child enjoys their right to a childhood. Many more must follow their example.

REFERENCES

CHAPTER 1

1 See the remarks of former United Nations General Assembly President Joseph N. Garba related to the adoption of the Convention on the Rights of the Child, *UN Chronicle*, March 1990.

2 Bel Geddes, Joan, *Childhood and Children: A compendium of customs, superstitions, theories, profiles, and facts*, Oryx Press, Phoenix, 1997, p. 2; and United Nations Children's Fund, *The State of the World's Children 1996*, Oxford University Press for UNICEF, New York, 1995, p. 14.

3 Bel Geddes, op. cit., pp. 6-7.

4 Santos Pais, Marta, 'A Human Rights Conceptual Framework for UNICEF', *Innocenti Essays No. 9*, UNICEF Innocenti Research Centre, Florence, 1999, p. 6.

5 United Nations Children's Fund, *Progress since the World Summit for Children: A statistical review*, UNICEF, New York, 2001.

6 World Health Organization, 'Polio eradication: Now more than ever, stop polio forever', 15 January 2004.

7 Calculated from the annual figure of 10.6 million under-five deaths for 2003.

8 United Nations Development Programme, *Human Development Report 2003*, Oxford University Press for UNDP, New York, 2003, p. 45. Between 1990 and 2003, conflicts killed as many as 3.6 million people. Of these, the report claims that civilians accounted for more than 90 per cent of deaths and injuries, and that at least half of civilian casualties were children. By extension, this implies that children accounted for around 45 per cent of deaths and injuries from armed conflict.

9 Joint United Nations Programme on HIV/AIDS, United Nations Children's Fund and the United States Agency for International Development, *Children on the Brink 2004: A joint report of new orphan estimates and a framework for action*, Population, Health and Nutrition Information Project for USAID, Washington, D.C., July 2004, p. 3.

CHAPTER 1 PANELS

The protective environment

Information supplied by Child Protection Section, Programme Division, UNICEF, New York, 2004.

Failure to achieve the Millennium Development Goals: Implications for childhood

The analysis in this panel is derived from several sources: Joint United Nations Programme on HIV/AIDS, United Nations Children's Fund and the United States Agency for International Development, *Children on the Brink 2004*, op. cit., pp. 14, 29; United Nations Children's Fund, *The State of the World's Children 2004*, UNICEF, New York, 2003, p. 31; United Nations Educational, Scientific and Cultural Organizaton, *Education for All Global Monitoring Report 2003/4*, UNESCO, Paris, 2003, p. 8; Oxfam International, 'Last Chance in Monterrey: Meeting the challenge of poverty reduction', Oxfam International, *Briefing Paper 17*, 13 March 2002; Gordon, David, et al., *Child poverty in the developing world*, The Policy Press, Bristol, October 2003; World Health Organization, United Nations Children's Fund and the United Nations Population Fund, *Maternal Mortality in 2000*, WHO, Geneva, 2000; World Bank and International Monetary Fund, *'Global Monitoring Report 2004: Policies and Actions for Achieving the Millennium Development Goals and Related Outcomes'*, World Bank, Washington, D.C., 2004, pp. 33-48.

Access to safe drinking water is estimated using the percentage of the population using improved drinking water sources as tracked by the Joint Monitoring Programme (JMP) for Water Supply and Sanitation, a collaboration between the World Health Organization and UNICEF since 1990. To resolve issues of definition, the JMP classifies both water supply sources and sanitation facilities as 'improved' or 'unimproved'. A different definition of safe water may result in a different view of progress towards the safe drinking water MDG: for example, the analysis in the World Bank/IMF *Global Monitoring Report 2004* implies that this goal is seriously off track.

CHAPTER 2

1 Derived from United Nations Children's Fund, 'A League Table of Child Poverty in Rich Nations', *Innocenti Report Card No. 1*, UNICEF Innocenti Research Centre, Florence, June 2000, p. 24.

2 United Nations Economic and Social Council, Committee on Economic, Social and Cultural Rights, Poverty and the International Covenant on Economic, Social and Cultural Rights, 10/05/2001, E/C.12/2001/10, 10 May 2001, para 8.

3 World Bank, *World Development Indicators 2003*, World Bank, Washington, D.C., 2003, p. 5. Currently the one or two dollar a day per person poverty thresholds are measured at 1990 prices and adjusted to take account of variations in the prices of goods and services among countries.

4 United Nations, Millennium Development Goal 1: Eradicate extreme poverty and hunger. Target 1 of MDG 1 aims to reduce by half the proportion of people living on less than one dollar a day between 1990 and 2015; Target 2 aims to halve the proportion of the world's population that suffers from hunger over the same period.

5 United Nations Development Programme, *Human Development Report 1997*, Oxford University Press for UNDP, New York, 1997, p. 17. The Human Development Index (HDI), introduced by UNDP in 1990, is a summary measure that gives equal weight to three dimensions of human development: longevity, knowledge and living standards. UNDP has also developed two human poverty indices: Human Poverty Index 1 (HPI-1), which measures deprivations in the same three basic dimensions for developing countries; and HPI-2, which adds the dimension of social exclusion to HPI-1 for selected countries of the Organisation for Economic Co-operation and Development.

6 United Nations Development Programme, *Human Development Report 2003*, Oxford University Press for UNDP, New York, 2003, p. 68.

7 These were the Demographic and Health Surveys (DHS, except for China). The total number of children in this aggregated sample was almost 1.2 million (approximately 1 in every 1,500 children in the developing world), and the information about the children's lives was reported by their mothers or main caregivers. The numerical estimates on child poverty presented in *The State of the World's Children 2005* have been updated by adding data from several DHS and Multiple Indicator Cluster Surveys (MICS), downloadable at [www.childinfo.org], to the set of surveys used in the 2003 study.

8 Gordon, David, et al., *Child Poverty in the Developing World*, The Policy Press, Bristol, October 2003. The study estimates child deprivation using data from household surveys available from 46 countries (DHS, except for China). In addition to the seven dimensions of deprivation shown here, the study also tried to measure access to basic social services, defined as children living 20 km or more from any type of school, or 50 km or more from any medical facility with doctors. As this type of information was only available in a few countries, it was not possible to construct accurate regional estimates of this aspect of severe deprivation; but information presented here on the use of health services and education sheds light on the strikingly poor access to basic social services in many developing countries. The researchers used the prevalence of two or more severe deprivations as a proxy for absolute poverty, a concept not used in the present report.

9 Morris, Saul S., et al., International Food Policy Research Institute, 'Does Geographic Targeting of Nutrition Interventions Make Sense in Cities? Evidence from Abidjan and Accra', *Discussion Paper No. 61 Brief*, Washington, D.C., April 1999.

10 Kabeer, Naila, *Gender Mainstreaming in Poverty Eradication and the Millennium Development Goals: A handbook for policy-makers and other stakeholders,* Commonwealth Secretariat/IDRC/CIDA, London, 2003, p. 76.

[11] International Labour Office, *A Future Without Child Labour: Global report under the follow-up to the ILO Declaration on Fundamental Principles and Rights at Work,* International Labour Organization, Geneva, 2002, pp. 17-18.

[12] Ibid.

[13] Ibid.

[14] Christian Children's Fund, 'Shaping a Response to Poverty: A Conceptual Overview and Implications for Responding to Children Living in Poverty', Children and Poverty Series, Part III, CCF, Richmond, 2003, p. 7.

[15] Minujin, Alberto, and Enrique Delamonica, 'Mind the Gap! Widening Child Mortality Disparities', *Journal of Human Development,* vol. 4, no. 3, November 2003, p. 403.

[16] United Nations Children's Fund, *Report on the Situation of Children and Adolescents in Brazil,* UNICEF Brazil, 2004. The illiteracy figure refers to children aged 12-17 years only.

[17] World Bank, *World Development Report 2000/2001,* Oxford University Press for the World Bank, Oxford, 2001, p. 27.

[18] United Nations Development Programme, *Human Development Report 2003,* op. cit., p. 39.

[19] Ibid., p. 73.

[20] United Nations Children's Fund, *Progress For Children,* vol. 1, New York, August 2004, pp. 8, 12.

[21] Three of the nine countries and one Indian state considered as positive role models in Mehrotra, Santosh, and Richard Jolly, eds., *Development with a Human Face: Experiences in social achievement and economic growth,* Clarendon Press, Oxford, 1997.

[22] World Bank and International Money Fund, *Global Monitoring Report 2004,* World Bank, Washington, D.C., 2004, pp. 36-37.

[23] Noorbakhsh, Farhad, Alberto Paloni and Ali Youssef, 'Human Capital and FDI inflows to developing countries: New empirical evidence', *World Development,* vol. 29, no. 9, 2001, pp. 1593-1610.

[24] United Nations Children's Fund, 'A Decade of Transition: The MONEE Project CEE/CIS/Baltics', *Regional Monitoring Report No. 8,* UNICEF Innocenti Research Centre, Florence, 2001.

[25] Erikson, Dan, Annie Lord and Peter Wolf, *Cuba's Social Services: A review of education, health and sanitation* (commissioned as background for the World Bank's *World Development Report 2004*), January 2002, p. 5.

[26] Monroy Peralta, José Guillermo, 'A desk review on children and youth in poverty reduction strategies: A human rights point of view' (unpublished article submitted to Global Policy Section, Division of Policy and Planning, UNICEF, April 2004).

[27] United Nations Children's Fund, 'A League Table of Child Poverty in Rich Nations', op. cit., p. 8.

[28] International Programme on the Elimination of Child Labour, *Investing in Every Child: An economic study of the costs and benefits of eliminating child labour,* International Labour Office, International Labour Organization, Geneva, December 2003.

[29] International Labour Office, *A Future Without Child Labour,* op. cit., p. 101.

[30] United Nations Children's Fund, 'Brazil: The protective environment in action' (internal document). Data gathered from annual sample household surveys (Pesquisa Nacional Amostral de Domicilios) for 1995-2002 undertaken by Instituto Brasileiro de Geografia e Estatisticas – the national institute for geography and statistics in Brazil.

[31] United Nations Children's Fund, 'The Many Faces of Poverty: Research on child poverty in Serbia' (final draft), Belgrade, December 2003, p. 38.

CHAPTER 2 PANELS

Poverty deprives children of their rights

[a] Calculated from annual under-five mortality rates for 2003.

[b] United Nations, We the Children: End-decade review of the follow-up to the World Summit for Children, Report of the Secretary-General, A/S-27/3, United Nations, New York, May 4, 2001.

[c] World Health Organization, 'State of the art of new vaccines – Research and Development', Initiative for Vaccine Research, WHO, Geneva, April 2003, p. 5.

[d] United Nations Children's Fund, *Facts for Life,* UNICEF, New York, 2002, pp. iv, 53.

[e] The Micronutrient Initiative and United Nations Children's Fund, *Vitamin and Mineral Deficiency: A global progress report,* The Micronutrient Initiative, Ottawa, 2003, p. 13.

[f] United Nations Children's Fund, *The State of the World's Children 2004,* UNICEF, New York, 2003.

[g] O'Malley, Kate, 'Children and Young People Participating in PRSP Processes: Lessons from Save the Children's experience', Save the Children Fund, London, 2004.

Operational definitions of deprivation for children

Gordon, David, et al., *Child Poverty in the Developing World,* op. cit.

Oportunidades: A poverty-reduction programme that works

Information supplied by UNICEF Mexico, 2004; the National Institute of Public Health, Centre for Research and Advanced Studies in Social Anthropology, 'Resultados de la Evaluación Externa del Programa de Desarrollo Humano Oportunidades, 2003' (Results of the External Evaluation of the Human Development Programme called Oportunidades, 2003), March 2004; and the Oportunidades programme.

CHAPTER 3

[1] Although the civil war in southern Sudan began in 1955, there was a period of peace between 1972 and 1983.

[2] Stockholm Peace Research Institute, 'Appendix 3A: Patterns of major armed conflicts, 1990-2003', *SIPRI Yearbook 2004,* Oxford University Press, New York, 2004.

[3] Otunnu, Olara A., 'Special Comment' on Children and Security, *Disarmament Forum,* No. 3, United Nations Institute for Disarmament Research, Geneva, 2002, pp. 3-4.

[4] Collier, P., et al., *Breaking the Conflict Trap: Civil war and development policy,* A World Bank Policy Research Report, World Bank and Oxford University Press, Washington, D.C., 2003, pp. 23-24.

[5] United Nations, Resources mobilization and enabling environment for poverty eradication in the context of the implementation of the Programme of Action for the Least Developed Countries for the Decade 2001-2010, Report of the Secretary-General, E/2004/54, United Nations, New York, 23 April 2004, p. 14.

[6] United Nations Office for the Coordination of Humanitarian Affairs, Situation Report, 'Indonesia: OCHA daily sitrep on Aceh No. 24', 8 June 2003.

[7] Coalition to Stop the Use of Child Soldiers, *Child Soldiers Newsletter,* Issue 11, London, May 2004.

[8] United Nations, Children and armed conflict, Report of the Secretary-General, A/58/546-S/2003/1053, United Nations, New York, 10 November 2003, pp. 5, 9-10.

[9] Machel, Graça, *The Impact of War on Children,* Hurst and Company for UNICEF/UNIFEM, London, 2001, p. 1.

[10] Office of the United Nations High Commissioner for Refugees, *2003 Global Refugee Trends,* UNHCR, Geneva, 15 June 2004; and Norwegian Refugee Council, *Internal displacement: A global overview of trends and developments in 2003,* Global IDP Project, Geneva, February 2004.

[11] Machel, *The Impact of War on Children,* op. cit., p. 55; and United Nations Children's Fund, *The State of the World's Children 1996,* Oxford University Press for UNICEF, New York, 1995, p. 19.

[12] Machel, *The Impact of War on Children,* op. cit., p. 57.

[13] International Campaign to Ban Landmines, *Landmine Monitor Report 2003: Toward a mine-free world,* Human Rights Watch, New York, 2003, p. 39.

[14] Ibid.

[15] Human Rights Watch, *Off Target: The conduct of the war and civilian casualties in Iraq,* Human Rights Watch, New York, December 2003.

[16] United Nations, Protection of children affected by armed conflicts, A/RES/48/157, United Nations, New York, 20 December 1993.

[17] United Nations, Promotion and Protection of the Rights of Children: Impact of armed conflict on children, Note by the Secretary-General, A/51/306, United Nations, New York, 26 August 1996.

[18] United Nations Children's Fund, *The State of the World's Children 1996*, op. cit., pp. 40-41.

[19] Information from the United Nations Treaty Collection, Multilateral Treaties deposited with the Secretary-General, United Nations, New York.

[20] United Nations, Children and armed conflict, Report of the Secretary-General, op. cit., p. 6.

[21] Rehn, Elisabeth and Ellen Johnson Sirleaf, 'Women, War and Peace: The independent experts' assessment on the impact of armed conflict on women and women's role in peace-building', *Progress of the World's Women 2002*, vol. 1, UNIFEM, New York, 2002, p. 124.

[22] United Nations, Rome Statute of the International Criminal Court, A/CONF.183/9, United Nations, New York, 17 July 1998.

[23] Gibbons, Elizabeth D., *Sanctions in Haiti: Human rights and democracy under assault*, published with the Center for Strategic and International Studies, Praeger, Westport, January 1999, pp. 20, 22-23, 95.

[24] Peace in Sri Lanka, Media Release, 'Over half a million children receive polio vaccination on sub-national immunization day', 21 October 2003.

CHAPTER 3 PANELS

Girl soldiers: The untold story

From McKay, Susan, and Dyan Mazurana, *Where Are The Girls? – Girls in fighting forces in Northern Uganda, Sierra Leone and Mozambique: Their lives during and after war*, Rights and Democracy, Montreal, supported by the Canadian International Development Agency's Child Protection Research Fund, March 2004; Mazurana, Dyan, and Susan McKay, 'Child Soldiers: What about the girls?', *Bulletin of the Atomic Scientists*, September/October 2001, vol. 57, no. 5, pp. 30-35; and Brett, Rachel, 'Girl Soldiers: Challenging the assumptions', Quaker United Nations Office, New York, 2002.

UNICEF's core commitments to children in conflict and unstable situations

United Nations Children's Fund, *Core Commitments for Children in Emergencies*, UNICEF, New York, June 2004.

CHAPTER 4

[1] Joint United Nations Programme on HIV/AIDS, United Nations Children's Fund and the United States Agency for International Development, *Children on the Brink 2004: A joint report of new orphan estimates and a framework for action*, Population, Health and Nutrition Project for USAID, Washington, D.C., July 2004, p. 7.

[2] Ibid., p. 29.

[3] Mushati, P., et al., 'Adult mortality and erosion of household viability in AIDS-afflicted towns, estates and villages in eastern Zimbabwe', paper presented at the Scientific Meeting on the Empirical Evidence for the Demographic and Socio-Economic Impact of AIDS, 26-28 March 2003, Durban, South Africa, pp. 8-10.

[4] Ibid, p. 12.

[5] Joint United Nations Programme on HIV/AIDS, United Nations Children's Fund and the United States Agency for International Development, *Children on the Brink 2004*, op. cit., p. 10.

[6] Wakhweya, Angela, et al., 'Situation Analysis of Orphans in Uganda: Orphans and their households: Caring for their future – today', Government of Uganda and Uganda AIDS Commission, November 2002, p. 74.

[7] Steinberg, M., et al., 'Hitting Home: How households cope with the impact of the HIV/AIDS epidemic: A survey of households affected by HIV/AIDS in South Africa', Henry J. Kaiser Family Foundation, Washington, D.C., October 2002.

[8] Joint United Nations Programme on HIV/AIDS and United Nations Children's Fund, *Children Orphaned by AIDS: Front-line responses from eastern and southern Africa*, UNICEF and UNAIDS, New York, December 1999, p. 4.

[9] Joint United Nations Programme on HIV/AIDS, *2004 Report on the global AIDS epidemic*, UNAIDS, Geneva, June 2004, p. 63.

[10] Musingeh, A.C.S., et al., 'HIV/AIDS and Child Labour in Zambia: A rapid assessment', Paper No. 5, International Programme on the Elimination of Child Labour, International Labour Office, International Labour Organization, Geneva/Lusaka, 2003.

[11] Mwami, J.A., A.J. Sanga and J. Nyoni, *Tanzania – Children Labour in Mining: A rapid assessment*, International Programme on the Elimination of Child Labour, International Labour Office, International Labour Organization, Geneva, January 2002.

[12] Kifle, A., 'Ethiopia – Child Domestic Workers in Addis Ababa: A rapid assessment', International Programme on the Elimination of Child Labour, International Labour Office, International Labour Organization, Geneva, July 2002, pp. ix, 17, 19, 27.

[13] Joint United Nations Programme on HIV/AIDS, United Nations Children's Fund and the United States Agency for International Development, *Children on the Brink 2004*, op. cit., p. 18.

[14] Joint United Nations Programme on HIV/AIDS, United Nations Children's Fund and partners, 'The Framework for the protection, care and support of orphans and vulnerable children living in a world with HIV and AIDS', UNAIDS, Bangkok, July 2004.

[15] Joint United Nations Programme on HIV/AIDS, *2004 Report on the global AIDS epidemic*, op. cit., p. 13.

[16] Joint United Nations Programme on HIV/AIDS, United Nations Children's Fund and the United States Agency for International Development, *Children on the Brink 2004*, op. cit., p. 14.

[17] United Nations Children's Fund, 'Global Campaign for Orphans and Children Made Vulnerable by HIV/AIDS' (internal document), 21 April 2004, p. 3.

[18] Joint United Nations Programme on HIV/AIDS, United Nations Children's Fund and the United States Agency for International Development, *Children on the Brink 2004*, op. cit., p. 14.

[19] United Nations Children's Fund, *Africa's Orphaned Generations*, UNICEF, New York, November 2003, p. 8.

[20] United Nations, The Global Coalition on Women and AIDS, Joint United Nations Programme on HIV/AIDS, 'Facing the Future Together: Report of the Secretary-General's Task Force on Women, Girls and HIV/AIDS in Southern Africa', UNAIDS, South Africa, July 2004, p. 19.

[21] Joint United Nations Programme on HIV/AIDS, United Nations Children's Fund and the United States Agency for International Development, *Children on the Brink 2004*, op. cit., p. 5.

CHAPTER 4 PANELS

The global threat of HIV/AIDS

[a] World Health Organization, *The World Health Report 2004*, Geneva, 2004, p. 2; and Joint United Nations Programme on HIV/AIDS, *2004 Report on the global AIDS epidemic*, op. cit., p. 30.

[b] Joint United Nations Programme on HIV/AIDS, United Nations Children's Fund and the United States Agency for International Development, *Children on the Brink 2004*, op. cit., p. 10.

[c] Annual prevalence rate for 2003.

[d] Joint United Nations Programme on HIV/AIDS and World Health Organization, 'A History of the HIV/AIDS Epidemic with Emphasis on Africa', Workshop on HIV/AIDS and Adult Mortality in Developing Countries, New York, 8-13 September, 2003.

[e] All other information derived from Joint United Nations Programme on HIV/AIDS, *2004 Report on the global AIDS epidemic*, op. cit.

The 'feminization' of HIV/AIDS

From Joint United Nations Programme on HIV/AIDS, United Nations Children's Fund and the United States Agency for International Development, *Children on the Brink 2004*, op. cit.; and Joint United Nations Programme on HIV/AIDS, *2004 Report on the global AIDS epidemic*, op. cit.; *AIDS epidemic update 2003*, UNAIDS, Geneva, 2003; and 'Women and AIDS: A growing challenge', Fact sheet, UNAIDS, July 2004.

Children with HIV/AIDS

Joint United Nations Programme on HIV/AIDS, United Nations Children's Fund and the United States Agency for International Development, *Children on the Brink 2004*, op. cit.

Antiretroviral treatment: Prolonging the lives of adults and children living with HIV/AIDS

[a] World Health Organization, *The World Health Report 2004*, op. cit., p. 21.

[b] World Health Organization, '"3 by 5" – Closing the Treatment Gap: Changing history', WHO, Geneva, 2004.

[c] World Health Organization, *The World Health Report 2004*, op. cit., p. 21.

[d] Chirac, Pierre, 'Increasing the Access to Antiretroviral Drugs to Moderate the Impact of AIDS: An exploration of alternative options', in *AIDS, Public Policy and Child Well-Being*, UNICEF Innocenti Research Centre, Florence, 2002; and the Joint United Nations Programme on HIV/AIDS, *2004 Report on the Global AIDS Epidemic*, op. cit., p. 103.

[e] Remarks of the Right Reverend Nyansanko Ni-Nku at the All Africa Conference of Churches Leadership Summit on HIV/AIDS, Nairobi, 8-10 June 2004, as reported in World Health Organization, 'African heads of churches summit commit to "3 by 5"', 2004.

[f] Laurent, Christian, et al., 'Effectiveness and safety of a generic fixed-dose combination of nevirapine, stavudine, and lamivudine in HIV-1-infected adults in Cameroon: Open-label multicentre trial', *The Lancet*, vol. 364, 3 July 2004, pp. 29-34.

[g] Marins, J.R.P., et al., 'Dramatic improvement in survival among Brazilian AIDS patients', *AIDS*, 2003, vol. 17, no. 11, pp. 1675-1682.

[h] World Bank, 'Provision of ARV Therapy in Resource-Limited Settings: The challenges of drug resistance and adherence', Meeting summary, Global HIV/AIDS Program of the World Bank, 17-18 June 2003.

CHAPTER 5

1 United Nations Educational, Scientific and Cultural Organization, *Education for All Global Monitoring Report 2003/4*, UNESCO, Paris, 2003, p. 311.

2 World Bank and the International Monetary Fund, *Global Monitoring Report 2004: Policies and actions for achieving the Millennium Development Goals and related outcomes*, World Bank, Washington, D.C., 2004, p. iii.

CHAPTER 5 PANELS

The human rights-based approach to development: Examples from Latin America

Based on internal briefing papers supplied by Global Policy Section, Division of Policy and Planning, UNICEF, 2004; and 'The Human Rights-Based Approach: Statement of common understanding', UNICEF, *The State of the World's Children 2004*, New York, 2003, pp. 91-93.

China's 'digital divide'

[a] 'China Internet users top 87 million', *Washington Times*, 21 July 2004.

[b] '12th Statistical Survey on the Internet Development in China', China Internet Network Information Centre, July 2003, p. 7.

[c] 'Overcoming China's Digital Divide: Best Practices and Future Action', PlaNet Finance China, 2004.

[d] 'Internet cafes banned around schools, residential areas', *Xinhua*, 24 March 2004.

[e] 'China bars under-16s from cybercafes', *BBC News*, 11 October 2002.

[f] 'No losers as China grows', *China Daily*, 20 March 2004.

[g] 'Bridging the Digital Divide – a Permanent Theme in the Telecommunication Development', Policy Statement by H. E. Zhang Chunjiang, Vice Minister of the Information Industry, China, 18 March 2002.

STATISTICAL TABLES

Economic and social statistics on the countries and territories of the world, with particular reference to children's well-being.

TABLES

General note on the data

The data presented in the following statistical tables are accompanied by definitions, sources and explanations of symbols. Data from the responsible United Nations agencies have been used whenever possible. Where such internationally standardized estimates do not exist, the tables draw on other sources, particularly data received from the appropriate UNICEF field office. Where possible, only comprehensive or representative national data have been used.

Data quality is likely to be adversely affected for countries that have recently suffered from man-made or natural disasters. This is particularly so where basic country infrastructure has been fragmented or major population movements have occurred.

Several of the indicators, such as the data for life expectancy, total fertility rates and crude birth and death rates, are part of the regular work on estimates and projections undertaken by the United Nations Population Division. These and other internationally produced estimates are revised periodically, which explains why some of the data will differ from those found in earlier UNICEF publications.

Two statistical tables have been revised considerably this year. HIV/AIDS indicators on knowledge and behaviour in table 4 have undergone a thorough review for quality and comparability, with some data being dropped from the table, but considerable new data being included. The estimates of the number of people living with HIV calculated by UNAIDS have also undergone a major revision and are now presented with uncertainty ranges. Table 9 on child protection includes additional indicators related to child marriage, and data for more countries for the other indicators related to child labour, birth registration and female genital mutilation. More details on these indicators are included in the notes following each of the tables.

In addition, substantial changes have been made to tables 1, 3 and 8. In table 1, the net primary school enrolment/attendance indicator has been computed based on attendance data from household surveys dated from 1999-2003, where available, and otherwise from administrative enrolment data reported by UNESCO/UIS (UNESCO Institute for Statistics). This represents a shift away from enrolment data towards a greater emphasis on attendance data.

Health data have seen two substantial changes this year. In table 3, the data on drinking water and sanitation have been updated, with a minor change in the method for estimating sanitation coverage. In previous estimates, certain categories of latrines that were poorly defined were counted as "improved." In the recent set of updates, an adjustment factor is applied to this category of sanitation facilities based on a more detailed breakdown by type of latrine. Where this breakdown is not available, only half of the share of the population using undefined latrines (such as traditional, pit or simple pit latrines) is counted as using an improved sanitation facility. This revision in methodology has resulted in lower sanitation coverage estimates, particularly in sub-Saharan Africa, where the use of "traditional latrines" is most widespread. As more surveys are conducted, using more complete definitions and better breakdowns of facilities, sanitation estimates will become even more precise.

The indicator on oral rehydration has also been redefined in this table, and is now defined as the percentage of under-fives with diarrhoea receiving oral rehydration, including from ORS packets, recommended home-made fluids or through increased fluids, together with continued feeding. The indicator previously only considered increased fluids and continued feeding.

Table 8 includes three columns on maternal mortality. One column presents data reported by national authorities; the second presents data that include adjustments for the well-documented problems of underreporting and misclassification of maternal deaths, as well as model-based estimates for countries with no data. An additional column has been added this year with the lifetime risk of maternal death. The maternal mortality ratio is a measure of the risk of death a woman faces once she becomes pregnant. The lifetime risk indicator reflects this cumulative risk over the course of her reproductive life. A low value for this indicator indicates a high lifetime risk of maternal mortality.

In addition to these tables, there have been changes in the regional groupings used at the end of each table. The following countries have now been included in the regional averages for the industrialized countries: Cyprus, Czech Republic, Estonia, Hungary, Latvia, Lithuania, Poland and Slovakia.

Explanation of symbols

Since the aim of this statistics chapter is to provide a broad picture of the situation of children and women worldwide, detailed data qualifications and footnotes are seen as more appropriate for inclusion elsewhere. The following symbols are common across all tables; symbols specific to a particular table are included in the table footnotes:

- \- Indicates data are not available.
- x Indicates data that refer to years or periods other than those specified in the column heading, differ from the standard definition, or refer to only part of a country. Such data are not included in the regional averages or totals.
- * Data refer to the most recent year available during the period specified in the column heading.

Under-five mortality rankings

The following list ranks countries and territories in descending order of their estimated 2003 under-five mortality rate (U5MR), a critical indicator of the well-being of children. Countries and territories are listed alphabetically in the tables that follow.

	Under-5 mortality rate Value	Rank
Sierra Leone	284	**1**
Niger	262	**2**
Angola	260	**3**
Afghanistan	257	**4**
Liberia	235	**5**
Somalia	225	**6**
Mali	220	**7**
Burkina Faso	207	**8**
Congo, Democratic Republic of the	205	**9**
Guinea-Bissau	204	**10**
Rwanda	203	**11**
Chad	200	**12**
Nigeria	198	**13**
Côte d'Ivoire	192	**14**
Burundi	190	**15**
Mauritania	183	**16**
Zambia	182	**17**
Central African Republic	180	**18**
Malawi	178	**19**
Ethiopia	169	**20**
Cameroon	166	**21**
Tanzania, United Republic of	165	**22**
Guinea	160	**23**
Mozambique	158	**24**
Benin	154	**25**
Swaziland	153	**26**
Equatorial Guinea	146	**27**
Cambodia	140	**28**
Togo	140	**29**
Uganda	140	**29**
Djibouti	138	**31**
Senegal	137	**32**
Madagascar	126	**33**
Zimbabwe	126	**33**
Iraq	125	**35**
Timor-Leste	124	**36**
Gambia	123	**37**
Kenya	123	**37**
Haiti	118	**39**
Sao Tome and Principe	118	**39**
Tajikistan	118	**39**
Yemen	113	**42**
Botswana	112	**43**
Congo	108	**44**
Myanmar	107	**45**
Pakistan	103	**46**
Turkmenistan	102	**47**
Ghana	95	**48**
Papua New Guinea	93	**49**
Sudan	93	**49**
Azerbaijan	91	**51**
Gabon	91	**51**
Lao People's Democratic Republic	91	**51**
India	87	**54**
Bhutan	85	**55**
Eritrea	85	**55**
Lesotho	84	**57**
Nepal	82	**58**
Comoros	73	**59**
Kazakhstan	73	**59**
Maldives	72	**61**
Bangladesh	69	**62**
Guyana	69	**62**
Uzbekistan	69	**62**
Kyrgyzstan	68	**65**

	Under-5 mortality rate Value	Rank
Mongolia	68	**65**
Bolivia	66	**65**
Kiribati	66	**65**
South Africa	66	**65**
Namibia	65	**65**
Marshall Islands	61	**71**
Korea, Democratic People's Republic of	55	**72**
Tuvalu	51	**73**
Guatemala	47	**74**
Georgia	45	**75**
Algeria	41	**76**
Honduras	41	**76**
Indonesia	41	**76**
Belize	39	**79**
Egypt	39	**79**
Iran (Islamic Republic of)	39	**79**
Morocco	39	**79**
Suriname	39	**79**
Turkey	39	**79**
Nicaragua	38	**85**
Vanuatu	38	**85**
China	37	**87**
El Salvador	36	**88**
Philippines	36	**88**
Brazil	35	**90**
Cape Verde	35	**90**
Dominican Republic	35	**90**
Peru	34	**93**
Armenia	33	**94**
Moldova, Republic of	32	**95**
Lebanon	31	**96**
Nauru	30	**97**
Paraguay	29	**98**
Jordan	28	**99**
Mexico	28	**99**
Palau	28	**99**
Ecuador	27	**102**
Saint Vincent and the Grenadines	27	**102**
Saudi Arabia	26	**104**
Thailand	26	**104**
Occupied Palestinian Territory	24	**106**
Panama	24	**106**
Samoa	24	**106**
Tunisia	24	**106**
Grenada	23	**110**
Micronesia (Federated States of)	23	**110**
Viet Nam	23	**110**
Saint Kitts and Nevis	22	**113**
Solomon Islands	22	**113**
Albania	21	**115**
Colombia	21	**115**
Cook Islands	21	**115**
Russian Federation	21	**115**
Venezuela	21	**115**
Argentina	20	**120**
Fiji	20	**120**
Jamaica	20	**120**
Romania	20	**120**
Trinidad and Tobago	20	**120**
Ukraine	20	**120**
Tonga	19	**126**
Mauritius	18	**127**
Saint Lucia	18	**127**
Syrian Arab Republic	18	**127**
Belarus	17	**130**

	Under-5 mortality rate Value	Rank
Bosnia and Herzegovina	17	**130**
Libyan Arab Jamahiriya	16	**132**
Bahrain	15	**133**
Bulgaria	15	**133**
Qatar	15	**133**
Seychelles	15	**133**
Sri Lanka	15	**133**
Bahamas	14	**138**
Dominica	14	**138**
Serbia and Montenegro	14	**138**
Uruguay	14	**138**
Barbados	13	**142**
Antigua and Barbuda	12	**143**
Latvia	12	**143**
Oman	12	**143**
Liechtenstein	11	**146**
Lithuania	11	**146**
The former Yugoslav Republic of Macedonia	11	**146**
Costa Rica	10	**149**
Chile	9	**150**
Estonia	9	**150**
Kuwait	9	**150**
Cuba	8	**153**
Hungary	8	**153**
Slovakia	8	**153**
United Arab Emirates	8	**153**
United States	8	**157**
Andorra	7	**158**
Croatia	7	**158**
Malaysia	7	**158**
Poland	7	**158**
Australia	6	**162**
Brunei Darussalam	6	**162**
Canada	6	**162**
Ireland	6	**162**
Israel	6	**162**
Malta	6	**162**
New Zealand	6	**162**
United Kingdom	6	**162**
Austria	5	**170**
Belgium	5	**170**
Cyprus	5	**170**
Finland	5	**170**
France	5	**170**
Germany	5	**170**
Greece	5	**170**
Korea, Republic of	5	**170**
Luxembourg	5	**170**
Netherlands	5	**170**
Portugal	5	**170**
San Marino	5	**170**
Switzerland	5	**170**
Czech Republic	4	**183**
Denmark	4	**183**
Iceland	4	**183**
Italy	4	**183**
Japan	4	**183**
Monaco	4	**183**
Norway	4	**183**
Slovenia	4	**183**
Spain	4	**183**
Singapore	3	**192**
Sweden	3	**192**
Holy See	no data	-
Niue	no data	-

TABLE 1. BASIC INDICATORS

Countries and territories	Under-5 mortality rank	Under-5 mortality rate 1960	Under-5 mortality rate 2003	Infant mortality rate (under 1) 1960	Infant mortality rate (under 1) 2003	Total population (thousands) 2003	Annual no. of births (thousands) 2003	Annual no. of under-5 deaths (thousands) 2003	GNI per capita (US$) 2003	Life expectancy at birth (years) 2003	Total adult literacy rate 2000	Net primary school enrolment/ attendance (%) 1996-2003*	% share of household income 1992-2002* lowest 40%	% share of household income 1992-2002* highest 20%
Afghanistan	**4**	360	257	245	165	23897	1136	292	250x	43	36	54s	-	-
Albania	**115**	151	21	105	18	3166	57	1	1740	74	85	97	23	37
Algeria	**76**	280	41	164	35	31800	724	30	1890	70	67	91s	19	43
Andorra	**158**	-	7	-	6	71	1	0	d	-	-	-	-	-
Angola	**3**	345	260	208	154	13625	713	185	740	40	-	58s	-	-
Antigua and Barbuda	**143**	-	12	-	11	73	1	0	9160	-	82x	98	-	-
Argentina	**120**	72	20	60	17	38428	727	15	3650	74	97	93s	10	56
Armenia	**94**	-	33	-	30	3061	29	1	950	72	98	97s	18	45
Australia	**162**	24	6	20	6	19731	241	1	21650	79	-	96	18	41
Austria	**170**	43	5	37	4	8116	68	0	26720	79	-	91	21	39
Azerbaijan	**51**	-	91	-	75	8370	148	13	810	72	97x	88s	19	45
Bahamas	**138**	68	14	51	11	314	6	0	14920x	67	95	86	-	-
Bahrain	**133**	160	15	110	12	724	14	0	10840x	74	88	84s	-	-
Bangladesh	**62**	248	69	149	46	146736	4183	289	400	62	40	83s	22	41
Barbados	**142**	90	13	74	11	270	3	0	9270	77	100	100	-	-
Belarus	**130**	47	17	37	13	9895	88	1	1590	70	100	94	21	39
Belgium	**170**	35	5	31	4	10318	111	1	25820	79	-	100	22	37
Belize	**79**	104	39	74	33	256	6	0	c	71	93	96	-	-
Benin	**25**	296	154	176	91	6736	278	43	440	51	37	54s	-	-
Bhutan	**55**	300	85	175	70	2257	77	7	660	63	47	53	-	-
Bolivia	**65**	255	66	152	53	8808	255	17	890	64	85	92s	13	49
Bosnia and Herzegovina	**130**	160	17	105	14	4161	39	1	1540	74	93x	86s	24	36
Botswana	**43**	173	112	118	82	1785	54	6	3430	39	77	84s	7	70
Brazil	**90**	177	35	115	33	178470	3502	123	2710	68	87	97	8	64
Brunei Darussalam	**162**	87	6	63	5	358	8	0	24100x	76	92	91x	-	-
Bulgaria	**133**	70	15	49	14	7897	62	1	2130	71	98	93	20	39
Burkina Faso	**8**	315	207	181	107	13002	621	129	300	46	24	27s	12	61
Burundi	**15**	250	190	148	114	6825	304	58	100	41	48	47s	15	48
Cambodia	**28**	-	140	-	97	14144	475	67	310	57	68	65s	18	48
Cameroon	**21**	255	166	151	95	16018	563	93	640	46	71	74s	15	51
Canada	**162**	33	6	28	5	31510	319	2	23930	79	-	100	20	40
Cape Verde	**90**	-	35	-	26	463	12	0	1490	70	74	99	-	-
Central African Republic	**18**	327	180	187	115	3865	144	26	260	40	47	43s	7	65
Chad	**12**	-	200	-	117	8598	416	83	250	45	43	39s	-	-
Chile	**150**	155	9	118	8	15805	284	3	4390	76	96	89	10	62
China	**87**	225	37	150	30	1304196	18706	692	1100	71	85	93	14	50
Colombia	**115**	125	21	79	18	44222	973	20	1810	72	92	90s	9	62
Comoros	**59**	265	73	200	54	768	28	2	450	61	56	30s	-	-
Congo	**44**	220	108	143	81	3724	164	18	640	48	81	96x	-	-
Congo, Democratic Republic of the	**9**	302	205	174	129	52771	2658	545	100	42	61	51s	-	-
Cook Islands	**115**	-	21	-	18	18	0	0	-	-	-	85	-	-
Costa Rica	**149**	123	10	87	8	4173	78	1	4280	78	96	91	13	52
Côte d'Ivoire	**14**	290	192	195	117	16631	587	113	660	41	49	57s	15	51
Croatia	**158**	98	7	70	6	4428	49	0	5350	74	98	88	21	40
Cuba	**153**	54	8	39	6	11300	129	1	1170x	77	97	96	-	-
Cyprus	**170**	36	5	30	4	802	10	0	12320x	78	97	95	-	-
Czech Republic	**183**	25	4	22	4	10236	90	0	6740	76	-	88	25	36
Denmark	**183**	25	4	22	3	5364	62	0	33750	77	-	99	23	36
Djibouti	**31**	289	138	186	97	703	27	4	910	46	65	34	-	-
Dominica	**138**	-	14	-	12	79	2	0	3360	-	-	91	-	-
Dominican Republic	**90**	149	35	102	29	8745	203	7	2070	67	84	83s	14	53
Ecuador	**102**	178	27	107	24	13003	295	8	1790	71	92	90s	11	58
Egypt	**79**	278	39	186	33	71931	1911	75	1390	69	55	85s	21	44
El Salvador	**88**	191	36	130	32	6515	161	6	2200	71	79	89	10	57
Equatorial Guinea	**27**	316	146	188	97	494	21	3	930x	49	83	61s	-	-
Eritrea	**55**	-	85	-	45	4141	163	14	190	53	56	61s	-	-
Estonia	**150**	52	9	40	8	1323	11	0	4960	72	100	98	18	44
Ethiopia	**20**	269	169	180	112	70678	2992	506	90	46	39	30s	22	39
Fiji	**120**	97	20	71	16	839	19	0	2360	70	93	100	-	-

	Under-5 mortality rank	Under-5 mortality rate		Infant mortality rate (under 1)		Total population (thousands) 2003	Annual no. of births (thousands) 2003	Annual no. of under-5 deaths (thousands) 2003	GNI per capita (US$) 2003	Life expectancy at birth (years) 2003	Total adult literacy rate 2000	Net primary school enrolment/ attendance (%) 1996-2003*	% share of household income 1992-2002*	
		1960	2003	1960	2003								lowest 40%	highest 20%
Finland	**170**	28	5	22	4	5207	55	0	27020	78	-	100	24	37
France	**170**	34	5	29	4	60144	772	4	24770	79	-	100	20	40
Gabon	**51**	-	91	-	60	1329	41	4	3580	57	71	93s	-	-
Gambia	**37**	364	123	207	90	1426	50	6	310	54	37	52s	12	55
Georgia	**75**	-	45	-	41	5126	52	2	830	74	100x	99s	18	44
Germany	**170**	40	5	34	4	82476	711	4	25250	78	-	83	22	37
Ghana	**48**	215	95	127	59	20922	663	63	320	58	72	74s	16	47
Greece	**170**	64	5	53	4	10976	99	0	13720	78	97	95	19	44
Grenada	**110**	-	23	-	18	80	2	0	3790	-	-	84	-	-
Guatemala	**74**	202	47	136	35	12347	419	20	1910	66	69	78s	9	64
Guinea	**23**	380	160	215	104	8480	362	58	430	49	41	54s	17	47
Guinea-Bissau	**10**	-	204	-	126	1493	74	15	140	45	38	41s	14	53
Guyana	**62**	126	69	100	52	765	16	1	900	63	99	88s	14	50
Haiti	**39**	253	118	169	76	8326	251	30	380	50	50	54s	-	-
Holy See	**-**	-	-	-	-	1	-	-	-	-	-	-	-	-
Honduras	**76**	204	41	137	32	6941	205	8	970	69	75	87	9	59
Hungary	**153**	57	8	51	7	9877	86	1	6330	72	99	91	21	38
Iceland	**183**	22	4	17	3	290	4	0	30810	80	-	100	-	-
India	**54**	242	87	146	63	1065462	25052	2180	530	64	57	77s	21	42
Indonesia	**76**	216	41	128	31	219883	4515	185	810	67	87	87s	20	43
Iran (Islamic Republic of)	**79**	281	39	164	33	68920	1424	56	2000	70	76	93s	15	50
Iraq	**35**	171	125	117	102	25175	879	110	2170x	61	39	76s	-	-
Ireland	**162**	36	6	31	6	3956	57	0	26960	77	-	94	19	43
Israel	**162**	39	6	32	5	6433	126	1	16020x	79	95	100	18	44
Italy	**183**	50	4	44	4	57423	503	2	21560	79	98	100	19	42
Jamaica	**120**	74	20	56	17	2651	54	1	2760	76	87	79s	17	46
Japan	**183**	40	4	31	3	127654	1160	5	34510	82	-	100	25	36
Jordan	**99**	139	28	97	23	5473	151	4	1850	71	90	89s	19	44
Kazakhstan	**59**	-	73	-	63	15433	250	18	1780	67	99	96s	21	40
Kenya	**37**	205	123	122	79	31987	1032	127	390	44	82	72s	15	51
Kiribati	**65**	-	66	-	49	88	2	0	880	-	-	71	-	-
Korea, Democratic People's Republic of	**72**	120	55	85	42	22664	364	20	a	63	98	-	-	-
Korea, Republic of	**170**	127	5	90	5	47700	562	3	12030	76	98	100	22	38
Kuwait	**150**	128	9	89	8	2521	50	0	16340x	77	82	85	-	-
Kyrgyzstan	**65**	-	68	-	59	5138	112	8	330	69	-	90	22	38
Lao People's Democratic Republic	**51**	235	91	155	82	5657	200	18	320	55	65	62s	19	45
Latvia	**143**	44	12	35	10	2307	18	0	4070	71	100	91	21	40
Lebanon	**96**	85	31	65	27	3653	69	2	4040	74	86	97s	-	-
Lesotho	**57**	203	84	136	63	1802	55	5	590	35	83	65s	6	67
Liberia	**5**	288	235	190	157	3367	167	39	130	41	54	70	-	-
Libyan Arab Jamahiriya	**132**	270	16	159	13	5551	128	2	5540x	73	80	96x	-	-
Liechtenstein	**146**	-	11	-	10	34	0	0	d	-	-	-	-	-
Lithuania	**146**	70	11	52	8	3444	29	0	4490	73	100	97	21	40
Luxembourg	**170**	41	5	33	5	453	5	0	43940	78	-	96	21	39
Madagascar	**33**	186	126	112	78	17404	719	91	290	54	67	62s	13	54
Malawi	**19**	361	178	205	112	12105	534	95	170	38	60	79s	13	56
Malaysia	**158**	105	7	73	7	24425	545	4	3780	73	87	95	13	54
Maldives	**61**	300	72	180	55	318	11	1	2300	68	97	96	-	-
Mali	**7**	500	220	285	122	13007	650	143	290	49	26	39s	13	56
Malta	**162**	42	6	37	5	394	4	0	9260x	78	92	98	-	-
Marshall Islands	**71**	-	61	-	53	53	1	0	2710	-	-	96	-	-
Mauritania	**16**	310	183	180	120	2893	120	22	430	53	40	44s	17	46
Mauritius	**127**	92	18	67	16	1221	19	0	4090	72	85	93	-	-
Mexico	**99**	134	28	94	23	103457	2294	64	6230	74	91	99	10	59
Micronesia (Federated States of)	**110**	-	23	-	19	109	3	0	2090	69	67	-	-	-
Moldova, Republic of	**95**	88	32	64	26	4267	49	2	590	69	99	86s	19	44
Monaco	**183**	-	4	-	4	34	0	0	d	-	-	-	-	-

	Under-5 mortality rank	Under-5 mortality rate		Infant mortality rate (under 1)		Total population (thousands) 2003	Annual no. of births (thousands) 2003	Annual no. of under-5 deaths (thousands) 2003	GNI per capita (US$) 2003	Life expectancy at birth (years) 2003	Total adult literacy rate 2000	Net primary school enrolment/ attendance (%) 1996-2003*	% share of household income 1992-2002*	
		1960	2003	1960	2003								lowest 40%	highest 20%
Mongolia	**65**	-	68	-	56	2594	58	4	480	64	98	77s	16	51
Morocco	**79**	211	39	132	36	30566	707	28	1320	69	49	88	17	47
Mozambique	**24**	313	158	180	109	18863	774	122	210	38	44	60	17	47
Myanmar	**45**	252	107	169	76	49485	1172	125	220x	57	85	84s	-	-
Namibia	**65**	168	65	102	48	1987	65	4	1870	44	82	78s	4	79
Nauru	**97**	-	30	-	25	13	0	0	-	-	-	81	-	-
Nepal	**58**	315	82	212	61	25164	822	67	240	60	42	73s	19	45
Netherlands	**170**	22	5	18	5	16149	194	1	26310	78	-	99	20	40
New Zealand	**162**	26	6	22	5	3875	53	0	15870	78	-	98	18	44
Nicaragua	**85**	193	38	130	30	5466	170	6	730	70	64	77s	11	60
Niger	**2**	354	262	211	154	11972	662	173	200	46	16	30s	10	53
Nigeria	**13**	290	198	165	98	124009	4820	954	320	51	64	60s	13	56
Niue	**-**	-	-	-	-	2	0	-	-	-	81	97	-	-
Norway	**183**	23	4	19	3	4533	53	0	43350	79	-	100	24	37
Occupied Palestinian Territory	**106**	-	24	-	22	3557	137	3	1110	73	-	92s	-	-
Oman	**143**	280	12	164	10	2851	91	1	7830x	73	72	75	-	-
Pakistan	**46**	227	103	139	81	153578	5506	567	470	61	43	56s	21	42
Palau	**99**	-	28	-	23	20	0	0	7500	-	-	97	-	-
Panama	**106**	88	24	58	18	3120	70	2	4250	75	92	99	9	60
Papua New Guinea	**49**	214	93	143	69	5711	177	16	510	58	64	77	12	57
Paraguay	**98**	90	29	66	25	5878	173	5	1100	71	93	92	9	60
Peru	**93**	234	34	142	26	27167	624	21	2150	70	90	93s	11	53
Philippines	**88**	110	36	80	27	79999	2001	72	1080	70	95	81s	14	52
Poland	**158**	70	7	62	6	38587	365	3	5270	74	100	98	19	43
Portugal	**170**	112	5	81	4	10062	110	1	12130	76	92	100	17	46
Qatar	**133**	140	15	94	11	610	10	0	12000x	72	94	94	-	-
Romania	**120**	82	20	69	18	22334	233	5	2310	71	98	93	21	38
Russian Federation	**115**	64	21	48	16	143246	1226	26	2610	67	100	93x	14	51
Rwanda	**11**	206	203	122	118	8387	368	75	220	39	67	75s	23x	39x
Saint Kitts and Nevis	**113**	-	22	-	19	42	1	0	6880	-	-	96	-	-
Saint Lucia	**127**	-	18	-	16	149	3	0	4050	73	-	99	15	48
Saint Vincent and the Grenadines	**102**	-	27	-	23	120	2	0	3300	74	-	92	-	-
Samoa	**106**	210	24	134	19	178	5	0	1600	70	99	95	-	-
San Marino	**170**	-	5	-	4	28	0	0	d	-	-	-	-	-
Sao Tome and Principe	**39**	-	118	-	75	161	5	1	320	70	-	68s	-	-
Saudi Arabia	**104**	250	26	170	22	24217	762	20	8530x	72	76	59	-	-
Senegal	**32**	300	137	173	78	10095	374	51	550	53	37	47s	17	48
Serbia and Montenegro	**138**	120	14	87	12	10527	123	2	1910	73	98x	97s,y	-	-
Seychelles	**133**	-	15	-	11	81	3	0	7480	-	-	100	-	-
Sierra Leone	**1**	390	284	220	166	4971	245	70	150	34	36	41s	3x	63x
Singapore	**192**	40	3	31	3	4253	41	0	21230	78	92	93x	14	49
Slovakia	**153**	40	8	33	7	5402	55	0	4920	74	100	87	24	35
Slovenia	**183**	45	4	37	4	1984	16	0	11830	76	100	93	23	36
Solomon Islands	**113**	185	22	120	19	477	15	0	600	69	-	-	-	-
Somalia	**6**	-	225	-	133	9890	516	116	130x	48	-	11s	-	-
South Africa	**65**	-	66	-	53	45026	1006	66	2780	47	85	90	6	67
Spain	**183**	57	4	46	4	41060	379	2	16990	79	98	100	20x	40x
Sri Lanka	**133**	133	15	83	13	19065	312	5	930	73	92	100	20	43
Sudan	**49**	208	93	123	63	33610	1100	102	460	56	58	53s	-	-
Suriname	**79**	-	39	-	30	436	9	0	1940x	71	94	89s	-	-
Swaziland	**26**	225	153	150	105	1077	36	6	1350	34	80	71s	9	64
Sweden	**192**	20	3	16	3	8876	92	0	28840	80	-	100	23	37
Switzerland	**170**	27	5	22	4	7169	61	0	39880	79	-	99	20	40
Syrian Arab Republic	**127**	200	18	134	16	17800	491	9	1160	72	74	98	-	-
Tajikistan	**39**	-	118	-	92	6245	150	18	190	69	99	80s	21	40
Tanzania, United Republic of	**22**	241	165	142	104	36977	1438	237	290	43	75	49s	18	46
Thailand	**104**	148	26	103	23	62833	1085	28	2190	69	96	86	16	50

	Under-5 mortality rank	Under-5 mortality rate 1960	Under-5 mortality rate 2003	Infant mortality rate (under 1) 1960	Infant mortality rate (under 1) 2003	Total population (thousands) 2003	Annual no. of births (thousands) 2003	Annual no. of under-5 deaths (thousands) 2003	GNI per capita (US$) 2003	Life expectancy at birth (years) 2003	Total adult literacy rate 2000	Net primary school enrolment/ attendance (%) 1996-2003*	% share of household income 1992-2002* lowest 40%	% share of household income 1992-2002* highest 20%
The former Yugoslav Republic of Macedonia	**146**	177	11	120	10	2056	29	0	1980	74	96	93	22	37
Timor-Leste	**36**	-	124	-	87	778	18	2	430	50	-	64s	-	-
Togo	**29**	267	140	158	78	4909	187	26	310	50	57	63s	-	-
Tonga	**126**	-	19	-	15	104	2	0	1490	69	-	100	-	-
Trinidad and Tobago	**120**	73	20	61	17	1303	17	0	7260	71	98	95s	16	46
Tunisia	**106**	254	24	170	19	9832	165	4	2240	73	71	94s,y	16	47
Turkey	**79**	219	39	163	33	71325	1479	58	2790	71	85	88	17	47
Turkmenistan	**47**	-	102	-	79	4867	107	11	1120	67	-	85s	16	48
Tuvalu	**73**	-	51	-	37	11	0	0	-	-	-	98	-	-
Uganda	**29**	224	140	133	81	25827	1317	184	240	47	67	87s	16	50
Ukraine	**120**	53	20	41	15	48523	409	8	970	70	100	82	22	38
United Arab Emirates	**153**	223	8	149	7	2995	49	0	18060x	75	76	81	-	-
United Kingdom	**162**	27	6	23	5	59251	646	4	28350	78	-	100	18	44
United States	**157**	30	8	26	7	294043	4262	34	37610	77	-	93	16	46
Uruguay	**138**	56	14	48	12	3415	57	1	3820	75	98	90	14	50
Uzbekistan	**62**	-	69	-	57	26093	559	39	420	70	99	78s	23	36
Vanuatu	**85**	225	38	141	31	212	6	0	1180	69	-	93	-	-
Venezuela	**115**	75	21	56	18	25699	581	12	3490	74	93	94s	11	53
Viet Nam	**110**	112	23	70	19	81377	1639	38	480	69	93	87s	19	45
Yemen	**42**	340	113	225	82	20010	901	102	520	60	46	60	20	41
Zambia	**17**	213	182	126	102	10812	453	82	380	33	78	67s	11	57
Zimbabwe	**33**	159	126	97	78	12891	409	52	480x	33	89	85s	13	56

SUMMARY INDICATORS

	Under-5 mortality rate 1960	Under-5 mortality rate 2003	Infant mortality rate 1960	Infant mortality rate 2003	Total population (thousands) 2003	Annual no. of births (thousands) 2003	Annual no. of under-5 deaths (thousands) 2003	GNI per capita (US$) 2003	Life expectancy at birth (years) 2003	Total adult literacy rate 2000	Net primary school enrolment/ attendance (%) 1996-2003*	lowest 40%	highest 20%
Sub-Saharan Africa	278	175	165	104	665496	26882	4704	496	46	61	58	11	59
Middle East and North Africa	249	56	157	45	362498	9790	548	1465	67	63	79	17	46
South Asia	244	92	148	67	1436478	37099	3413	511	63	54	75	21	42
East Asia and Pacific	208	40	137	31	1928182	31621	1265	1426	69	87	90	16	47
Latin America and Caribbean	153	32	102	27	537825	11572	370	3311	70	89	93	10	60
CEE/CIS	112	41	83	34	406157	5250	215	2036	70	97	87	17	47
Industrialized countries	39	6	32	5	949593	10829	65	28337	78	-	96	19	42
Developing countries	224	87	142	60	5083370	119986	10439	1255	62	74	78	15	50
Least developed countries	278	155	171	98	718858	27821	4312	304	49	52	59	18	46
World	198	80	127	54	6286228	133043	10643	5488	63	80	80	18	43

Countries in each category are listed on page 140.

DEFINITIONS OF THE INDICATORS

Under-five mortality rate – Probability of dying between birth and exactly five years of age expressed per 1,000 live births.

Infant mortality rate – Probability of dying between birth and exactly one year of age expressed per 1,000 live births.

GNI per capita – Gross national income (GNI) is the sum of value added by all resident producers plus any product taxes (less subsidies) not included in the valuation of output plus net receipts of primary income (compensation of employees and property income) from abroad. GNI per capita is gross national income divided by mid-year population. GNI per capita in US dollars is converted using the World Bank Atlas method.

Life expectancy at birth – The number of years newborn children would live if subject to the mortality risks prevailing for the cross-section of population at the time of their birth.

Adult literacy rate – Percentage of persons aged 15 and over who can read and write.

Net primary school enrolment/attendance – Derived from net primary school enrolment rates as reported by UNESCO/UIS (UNESCO Institute of Statistics) and from national household survey reports of attendance at primary school.

Income share – Percentage of income received by the 20 per cent of households with the highest income and by the 40 per cent of households with the lowest income.

MAIN DATA SOURCES

Under-five and infant mortality rates – UNICEF, United Nations Population Division and United Nations Statistics Division.

Total population – United Nations Population Division.

Births – United Nations Population Division.

Under-five deaths – UNICEF.

GNI per capita – World Bank.

Life expectancy – United Nations Population Division.

Adult literacy – United Nations Educational, Scientific and Cultural Organization (UNESCO) and UNESCO Institute of Statistics (UIS), including the Education for All 2000 Assessment.

School enrolment/attendance – UIS and UNESCO, including the Education for All 2000 Assessment, Multiple Indicator Cluster Surveys (MICS) and Demographic and Health Surveys (DHS).

Household income – World Bank.

NOTES

a: Range $765 or less.
b: Range $766 to $3035.
c: Range $3036 to $9385.
d: Range $9386 or more.

- \- Data not available.
- s National household survey.
- x Indicates data that refer to years or periods other than those specified in the column heading, differ from the standard definition, or refer to only part of a country.
- y Indicates data that differ from the standard definition or refer to only part of a country, but are included in the calculation of regional and global averages.
- * Data refer to the most recent year available during the period specified in the column heading.

TABLE 2. NUTRITION

Countries and territories	% of infants with low birthweight 1998-2003*	% of children (1995-2003*) who are: exclusively breastfed (<6 months)	breastfed with complementary food (6-9 months)	still breastfeeding (20-23 months)	% of under-fives (1995-2003*) suffering from: underweight moderate & severe	underweight severe	wasting moderate & severe	stunting moderate & severe	Vitamin A supplementation coverage rate (6-59 months) 2002	% of households consuming iodized salt 1997-2003*
Afghanistan	-	-	29	54	48	-	25	52	84t	1
Albania	3	6	24	6	14	4	11	32	-	62
Algeria	7	13	38	22	6	1	3	18	-	69
Andorra	-	-	-	-	-	-	-	-	-	-
Angola	12	11	77	37	31	8	6	45	88	35
Antigua and Barbuda	8	-	-	-	10x	4x	10x	7x	-	-
Argentina	7	-	-	-	5	1	3	12	-	90x
Armenia	7	30	51	13	3	0	2	13	-	84
Australia	7	-	-	-	-	-	-	-	-	-
Austria	7	-	-	-	-	-	-	-	-	-
Azerbaijan	11	7	39	16	7	1	2	13	-	26
Bahamas	7	-	-	-	-	-	-	-	-	-
Bahrain	8	34k	65	41	9	2	5	10	-	-
Bangladesh	30	46	78	87	48	13	10	45	84	70
Barbados	10x	-	-	-	6x	1x	5x	7x	-	-
Belarus	5	-	-	-	-	-	-	-	-	37
Belgium	8x	-	-	-	-	-	-	-	-	-
Belize	6	24k	54	23	6x	1x	-	-	-	90x
Benin	16	38	66	62	23	5	8	31	85	72
Bhutan	15	-	-	-	19	3	3	40	-	95
Bolivia	9	54	74	46	8	1	1	27	50	90
Bosnia and Herzegovina	4	6	-	-	4	1	6	10	-	77
Botswana	10	34	57	11	13	2	5	23	85	66
Brazil	10x	-	30	17	6	1	2	11	-	88
Brunei Darussalam	10	-	-	-	-	-	-	-	-	-
Bulgaria	10	-	-	-	-	-	-	-	-	-
Burkina Faso	19	6	49	87	34	12	13	37	97t	23x
Burundi	16	62	46	85	45	13	8	57	89	96
Cambodia	11	12	72	59	45	13	15	45	34	14
Cameroon	11	12	72	29	21	4	5	35	86	61
Canada	6	-	-	-	-	-	-	-	-	-
Cape Verde	13	57k	64	13	14x	2x	6x	16x	-	0x
Central African Republic	14	17	77	53	24	6	9	39	90	86
Chad	17x	10	68	51	28	9	11	29	85	58
Chile	5	63	47	-	1	-	0	2	-	100
China	6	67k	-	-	10	1	2	14	-	93
Colombia	9	26	58	25	7	1	1	14	-	92
Comoros	25	21	34	45	25	9	12	42	-	82
Congo	-	4k	94	13	14	3	4	19	86	-
Congo, Democratic Republic of the	12	24	79	52	31	9	13	38	62	72
Cook Islands	3	19k	-	-	-	-	-	-	-	-
Costa Rica	7	35x,k	47x	12x	5	0	2	6	-	97x
Côte d'Ivoire	17	10	54	42	21	5	8	25	97	31
Croatia	6	23	-	-	1	-	1	1	-	90
Cuba	6	41	42	9	4	0	2	5	-	83
Cyprus	-	-	-	-	-	-	-	-	-	-
Czech Republic	7	-	-	-	1x	0x	2x	2x	-	-
Denmark	5	-	-	-	-	-	-	-	-	-
Djibouti	-	-	-	-	18	6	13	26	91	-
Dominica	10	-	-	-	5x	0x	2x	6x	-	-
Dominican Republic	11	10	41	16	5	1	2	9	31	18
Ecuador	16	35	70	25	12	-	-	26	50	99
Egypt	12	30	72	31	9	1	4	16	-	56
El Salvador	13	16	77	40	10	-	1	19	-	91x
Equatorial Guinea	13	24	-	-	19	4	7	39	-	20x
Eritrea	21x	52	43	62	40	12	13	38	51	68
Estonia	4	-	-	-	-	-	-	-	-	-
Ethiopia	15	55	43	77	47	16	11	52	16	28
Fiji	10	47k	-	-	8x	1x	8x	3x	-	31x

	% of infants with low birthweight 1998-2003*	% of children (1995-2003*) who are: exclusively breastfed (<6 months)	breastfed with complementary food (6-9 months)	still breastfeeding (20-23 months)	% of under-fives (1995-2003*) suffering from: underweight moderate & severe	underweight severe	wasting moderate & severe	stunting moderate & severe	Vitamin A supplementation coverage rate (6-59 months) 2002	% of households consuming iodized salt 1997-2003*
Finland	4	-	-	-	-	-	-	-	-	-
France	7	-	-	-	-	-	-	-	-	-
Gabon	14	6	62	9	12	2	3	21	87	15
Gambia	17	26	37	54	17	4	9	19	91	8
Georgia	6	18k	12	12	3	0	2	12	-	68
Germany	7	-	-	-	-	-	-	-	-	-
Ghana	11	31	70	57	25	5	10	26	99t	50
Greece	8	-	-	-	-	-	-	-	-	-
Grenada	9	39k	-	-	-	-	-	-	-	-
Guatemala	13	51	67	47	23	4	2	49	33	67
Guinea	12	11	28	73	23	5	9	26	95	68
Guinea-Bissau	22	37	36	67	25	7	10	30	80	2
Guyana	12	11	42	31	14	3	11	11	-	-
Haiti	21	24	73	30	17	4	5	23	-	11
Holy See	-	-	-	-	-	-	-	-	-	-
Honduras	14	35	61	34	17	-	1	29	61	80
Hungary	9	-	-	-	2x	0x	2x	3x	-	-
Iceland	4	-	-	-	-	-	-	-	-	-
India	30	37k	44	66	47	18	16	46	27	50
Indonesia	9	40	75	59	26	6	-	-	82	73
Iran (Islamic Republic of)	7x	44	-	0	11	2	5	15	-	94
Iraq	15	12	51	27	16	2	6	22	-	40
Ireland	6	-	-	-	-	-	-	-	-	-
Israel	8	-	-	-	-	-	-	-	-	-
Italy	6	-	-	-	-	-	-	-	-	-
Jamaica	9	-	-	-	4	-	2	5	-	100
Japan	8	-	-	-	-	-	-	-	-	-
Jordan	10x	27	70	12	4	1	2	9	-	88
Kazakhstan	8	36	73	17	4	0	2	10	-	20
Kenya	11	13	84	57	20	4	6	31	91	91
Kiribati	5	80x,k	-	-	13x	-	11x	28x	-	-
Korea, Democratic People's Republic of	7	70	-	-	21	-	8	42	99t	-
Korea, Republic of	4	-	-	-	-	-	-	-	-	-
Kuwait	7	12k	26	9	10	3	11	24	-	-
Kyrgyzstan	7x	24	77	21	11	2	3	25	-	27
Lao People's Democratic Republic	14	23	10	47	40	13	15	41	58	75
Latvia	5	-	-	-	-	-	-	-	-	-
Lebanon	6	27k	35	11	3	0	3	12	-	87
Lesotho	14	15	51	58	18	4	5	46	-	69
Liberia	-	35	70	45	26	8	6	39	40	-
Libyan Arab Jamahiriya	7x	-	-	23	5	1	3	15	-	90x
Liechtenstein	-	-	-	-	-	-	-	-	-	-
Lithuania	4	-	-	-	-	-	-	-	-	-
Luxembourg	8	-	-	-	-	-	-	-	-	-
Madagascar	14	41	82	43	33	11	14	49	95	52
Malawi	16	44	93	77	22	-	5	45	86	49
Malaysia	10	29k	-	12	12	1	-	-	-	-
Maldives	22	10	85	-	30	7	13	25	51	44
Mali	23	25	32	69	33	11	11	38	68	74
Malta	6	-	-	-	-	-	-	-	-	-
Marshall Islands	12	63x,k	-	-	-	-	-	-	51	-
Mauritania	-	20	78	57	32	10	13	35	89t	2
Mauritius	13	16x,k	29x	-	15	2	14	10	-	0x
Mexico	9	38x,k	36x	21x	8	1	2	18	-	90
Micronesia (Federated States of)	18	60k	-	-	-	-	-	-	71	-
Moldova, Republic of	5	-	-	-	3	-	3	10	-	33
Monaco	-	-	-	-	-	-	-	-	-	-
Mongolia	8	51	55	57	13	3	6	25	84t	45
Morocco	11x	66k	53	21	9	2	4	24	-	41

TABLE 2. NUTRITION

	% of infants with low birthweight 1998-2003*	% of children (1995-2003*) who are: exclusively breastfed (<6 months)	breastfed with complementary food (6-9 months)	still breastfeeding (20-23 months)	% of under-fives (1995-2003*) suffering from: underweight moderate & severe	underweight severe	wasting moderate & severe	stunting moderate & severe	Vitamin A supplementation coverage rate (6-59 months) 2002	% of households consuming iodized salt 1997-2003*
Mozambique	14x	30	80	65	24	6	4	41	71	62x
Myanmar	15	11	67	67	35	8	9	34	92t	48
Namibia	14	19	57	37	24	5	9	24	96	63
Nauru	-	-	-	-	-	-	-	-	-	-
Nepal	21	68	66	92	48	13	10	51	83	63
Netherlands	-	-	-	-	-	-	-	-	-	-
New Zealand	6	-	-	-	-	-	-	-	-	83
Nicaragua	12	31	68	39	10	2	2	20	-	97
Niger	17	1	56	61	40	14	14	40	77t	15
Nigeria	14	17	64	34	29	9	9	38	79	97
Niue	0	-	-	-	-	-	-	-	-	-
Norway	5	-	-	-	-	-	-	-	-	-
Occupied Palestinian Territory	9	29k	78	11	4	1	3	9	-	37
Oman	8	-	92	73	24	4	13	23	97t	61
Pakistan	19x	16k	31	56	38	12	13	37	95t	17
Palau	9	59k	-	-	-	-	-	-	-	-
Panama	10x	25x	38x	21x	7	-	1	14	-	95
Papua New Guinea	11x	59	74	66	35x	-	-	-	-	-
Paraguay	9x	7k	59	15	5	-	-	-	-	83
Peru	11x	71	76	49	7	1	1	25	6	93
Philippines	20	34	58	32	31	-	6	31	86t	24
Poland	6	-	-	-	-	-	-	-	-	-
Portugal	8	-	-	-	-	-	-	-	-	-
Qatar	10	12k	48	21	6	-	2	8	-	-
Romania	9	-	-	-	6x	1x	3x	8x	-	53
Russian Federation	6	-	-	-	3	1	4	13	-	35
Rwanda	9	84	79	71	27	7	6	41	36	90
Saint Kitts and Nevis	9	56k	-	-	-	-	-	-	-	100
Saint Lucia	8	-	-	-	14x	-	6x	11x	-	-
Saint Vincent and the Grenadines	10	-	-	-	-	-	-	-	-	-
Samoa	4x	-	-	-	-	-	-	-	-	-
San Marino	-	-	-	-	-	-	-	-	-	-
Sao Tome and Principe	-	56	53	42	13	2	4	29	-	41
Saudi Arabia	11x	31k	60	30	14	3	11	20	-	-
Senegal	18	24k	64	49	23	6	8	25	83	16
Serbia and Montenegro	4	11k	33	11	2	0	4	5	-	73
Seychelles	-	-	-	-	6x	0x	2x	5x	-	-
Sierra Leone	-	4	51	53	27	9	10	34	87t	23
Singapore	8	-	-	-	14x	-	4x	11x	-	-
Slovakia	7	-	-	-	-	-	-	-	-	-
Slovenia	6	-	-	-	-	-	-	-	-	-
Solomon Islands	13x	65k	-	-	21x	4x	7x	27x	-	-
Somalia	-	9	13	8	26	7	17	23	60	-
South Africa	15	7	67	30	12	2	3	25	-	62
Spain	6x	-	-	-	-	-	-	-	-	-
Sri Lanka	22	84	-	73	29	-	14	14	-	88
Sudan	31	16	47	40	17	7	-	-	93t	1
Suriname	13	9	25	11	13	2	7	10	-	-
Swaziland	9	24	60	25	10	2	1	30	68	59
Sweden	4	-	-	-	-	-	-	-	-	-
Switzerland	6	-	-	-	-	-	-	-	-	-
Syrian Arab Republic	6	81k	50	6	7	1	4	18	-	40
Tajikistan	15	14	35	35	-	-	5	36	-	28
Tanzania, United Republic of	13	32	64	48	29	7	5	44	94t	67
Thailand	9	4k	71	27	19x	-	6x	16x	-	67
The former Yugoslav Republic of Macedonia	5	37	8	10	6	1	4	7	-	80
Timor-Leste	10	44	63	10	43	13	12	47	35	72
Togo	15	18	65	65	25	7	12	22	95	67
Tonga	0	62k	-	-	-	-	-	-	-	-

	% of infants with low birthweight 1998-2003*	% of children (1995-2003*) who are: exclusively breastfed (<6 months)	breastfed with complementary food (6-9 months)	still breastfeeding (20-23 months)	% of under-fives (1995-2003*) suffering from: underweight moderate & severe	underweight severe	wasting moderate & severe	stunting moderate & severe	Vitamin A supplementation coverage rate (6-59 months) 2002	% of households consuming iodized salt 1997-2003*
Trinidad and Tobago	23	2	19	10	7x	0x	4x	5x	-	1
Tunisia	7	46	-	22	4	1	2	12	-	97
Turkey	16	7	34	21	8	1	2	16	-	64
Turkmenistan	6	13	71	27	12	2	6	22	-	75
Tuvalu	5	-	-	-	-	-	-	-	-	-
Uganda	12	63	75	50	23	5	4	39	46	95
Ukraine	5	22	-	-	3	1	6	15	-	32
United Arab Emirates	15x	34k	52	29	14	3	15	17	-	-
United Kingdom	8	-	-	-	-	-	-	-	-	-
United States	8	-	-	-	1x	0x	1x	2x	-	-
Uruguay	8	-	-	-	5	1	1	8	-	-
Uzbekistan	7	19	49	45	8	2	7	21	79	19
Vanuatu	6	50k	-	-	20x	-	-	19x	-	-
Venezuela	7	7k	50	31	4	1	3	13	-	90
Viet Nam	9	15	-	26	33	6	6	36	55	83
Yemen	32x	18	79	41	46	-	12	53	49	39
Zambia	12	40	87	58	28	7	5	47	80	77
Zimbabwe	11	33	90	35	13	2	6	27	78	93

SUMMARY INDICATORS

	% of infants with low birthweight 1998-2003*	exclusively breastfed (<6 months)	breastfed with complementary food (6-9 months)	still breastfeeding (20-23 months)	underweight moderate & severe	underweight severe	wasting moderate & severe	stunting moderate & severe	Vitamin A supplementation coverage rate (6-59 months) 2002	% of households consuming iodized salt 1997-2003*
Sub-Saharan Africa	14	28	64	51	29	8	9	38	71	67
Middle East and North Africa	15	32	59	25	14	2	6	21	-	57
South Asia	30	36	46	67	46	16	15	44	46	49
East Asia and Pacific	8	52	-	-	17	3	3	19	78e	84
Latin America and Caribbean	10	-	48	26	7	1	2	16	-	86
CEE/CIS	9	14	42	25	6	1	4	16	-	43
Industrialized countries	7	-	-	-	-	-	-	-	-	-
Developing countries	17	38	55	51	27	8	8	31	59	69
Least developed countries	18	33	63	63	36	10	10	42	70	52
World	16	37	55	51	27	8	8	31	-	67

Countries in each category are listed on page 140.

DEFINITIONS OF THE INDICATORS

Low birthweight – Infants who weigh less than 2,500 grams.

Underweight – Moderate and severe – below minus two standard deviations from median weight for age of reference population; severe – below minus three standard deviations from median weight for age of reference population.

Wasting – Moderate and severe – below minus two standard deviations from median weight for height of reference population.

Stunting – Moderate and severe – below minus two standard deviations from median height for age of reference population.

Vitamin A – Percentage of children aged 6-59 months who have received at least one high dose of vitamin A capsules in 2002.

MAIN DATA SOURCES

Low birthweight – Demographic and Health Surveys (DHS), Multiple Indicator Cluster Surveys (MICS), other national household surveys and data from routine reporting systems.

Breastfeeding – DHS, MICS and UNICEF.

Underweight, wasting and stunting – DHS, MICS, UNICEF and World Health Organization (WHO).

Vitamin A – UNICEF and WHO.

Salt iodization – MICS, DHS and UNICEF.

NOTES

- \- Data not available.
- x Indicates data that refer to years or periods other than those specified in the column heading, differ from the standard definition, or refer to only part of a country.
- k Refers to exclusive breastfeeding for less than four months.
- * Data refer to the most recent year available during the period specified in the column heading.
- t Identifies countries that have achieved a second round of vitamin A coverage greater than or equal to 70 per cent.
- e This regional figure for East Asia and Pacific does not include China.

TABLE 3. HEALTH

Countries and territories	% of population using improved drinking water sources 2002			% of population using adequate sanitation facilities 2002			% of routine EPI vaccines financed by government 2003	% immunized 2003						% under-fives with ARI	% under-fives with ARI taken to health provider	% under-fives with diarrhoea receiving oral rehydration and continued feeding	Malaria: 1999-2003		
								1-year-old children					pregnant women	1998-2003*		1994-2003*	% under-fives sleeping under a bednet	% under-fives sleeping under a treated bednet	% under-fives with fever receiving anti-malarial drugs
	total	urban	rural	total	urban	rural	total	TB	DPT3	polio3	measles	hepB3	tetanus						
Afghanistan	13	19	11	8	16	5	0	56	54	54	50	-	40	19	28	-	-	-	-
Albania	97	99	95	89	99	81	40	95	97	97	93	97	-	1	84	51	-	-	-
Algeria	87	92	80	92	99	82	100	98	87	87	84	-	-	-	-	-	-	-	-
Andorra	100	100	100	100	100	100	-	-	99	99	96	84	-	-	-	-	-	-	-
Angola	50	70	40	30	56	16	10	62	46	45	62	-	72	-	-	32	10	2	63
Antigua and Barbuda	91	95	89	95	98	94	100	-	99	99	99	99	-	-	-	-	-	-	-
Argentina	-	97	-	-	-	-	100	99	88	91	97	-	-	-	-	-	-	-	-
Armenia	92	99	80	84	96	61	65	92	94	96	94	93	-	11	25	48	-	-	-
Australia	100	100	100	100	100	100	100	-	92	92	93	95	-	-	-	-	-	-	-
Austria	100	100	100	100	100	100	-	-	84	84	79	83	-	-	-	-	-	-	-
Azerbaijan	77	95	59	55	73	36	51	99	97	98	98	98	-	3	36	40	12	1	1
Bahamas	97	98	86	100	100	100	-	-	92	93	90	88	-	-	-	-	-	-	-
Bahrain	-	100	-	-	100	-	100	-	97	97	99	98	-	-	-	-	-	-	-
Bangladesh	75	82	72	48	75	39	100	95	85	85	77	-	89	18	27	35	-	-	-
Barbados	100	100	100	99	99	100	94	-	86	90	90	91	-	-	-	-	-	-	-
Belarus	100	100	100	-	-	-	100	99	86	99	99	99	-	-	-	-	-	-	-
Belgium	-	100	-	-	-	-	-	-	90	95	75	50	-	-	-	-	-	-	-
Belize	91	100	82	47	71	25	100	99	96	95	96	96	-	-	66	-	-	-	-
Benin	68	79	60	32	58	12	0	99	88	88	83	81	56	12	29	42	32	7	60
Bhutan	62	86	60	70	65	70	0	93	95	96	88	95	-	-	-	-	-	-	-
Bolivia	85	95	68	45	58	23	40	94	81	79	64	81	-	-	49	59	-	-	-
Bosnia and Herzegovina	98	100	96	93	99	88	70	94	87	86	84	-	-	2	80	23	-	-	-
Botswana	95	100	90	41	57	25	100	99	97	97	90	78	-	39	14	7	-	-	-
Brazil	89	96	58	75	83	35	100	99	96	99	99	91	-	-	-	28	-	-	-
Brunei Darussalam	-	-	-	-	-	-	100	99	99	99	99	99	-	-	-	-	-	-	-
Bulgaria	100	100	100	100	100	100	-	98	96	96	96	96	-	-	-	-	-	-	-
Burkina Faso	51	82	44	12	45	5	100	83	84	83	76	-	50	14	22	-	-	-	-
Burundi	79	90	78	36	47	35	6	84	74	69	75	-	46	13	40	16	3	1	31
Cambodia	34	58	29	16	53	8	7	76	69	69	65	-	43	20	35	-	-	-	-
Cameroon	63	84	41	48	63	33	100	82	73	72	61	-	65	7	25	33	11	1	66
Canada	100	100	99	100	100	99	-	-	91	88	95	-	-	-	-	-	-	-	-
Cape Verde	80	86	73	42	61	19	80	78	78	79	68	54	-	-	-	-	-	-	-
Central African Republic	75	93	61	27	47	12	0	70	40	40	35	-	63	10	32	47	31	2	69
Chad	34	40	32	8	30	0	75	72	47	48	61	-	43	12	22	50	27	1	32
Chile	95	100	59	92	96	64	100	94	99	99	99	-	-	-	-	-	-	-	-
China	77	92	68	44	69	29	100	93	90	91	84	70	-	-	-	-	-	-	-
Colombia	92	99	71	86	96	54	100	96	91	91	92	93	-	13	51	44	24	1	-
Comoros	94	90	96	23	38	15	0	75	75	75	63	27	46	10	49	31	36	9	63
Congo	46	72	17	9	14	2	0	60	50	50	50	-	59	4	38	-	-	-	-
Congo, Democratic Republic of the	46	83	29	29	43	23	0	68	49	55	54	-	48	11	36	17	12	1	45
Cook Islands	95	98	88	100	100	100	100	99	96	95	99	93	-	-	-	-	-	-	-
Costa Rica	97	100	92	92	89	97	0	87	88	88	89	86	-	-	-	-	-	-	-
Côte d'Ivoire	84	98	74	40	61	23	58	66	54	54	56	48	80	-	-	34	10	1	58
Croatia	-	-	-	-	-	-	100	98	94	95	95	-	-	-	-	-	-	-	-
Cuba	91	95	78	98	99	95	99	99	71	98	99	99	-	-	-	-	-	-	-
Cyprus	100	100	100	100	100	100	25	-	98	98	86	88	-	-	-	-	-	-	-
Czech Republic	-	-	-	-	-	-	-	98	97	97	99	86	-	-	-	-	-	-	-
Denmark	100	100	100	-	-	-	-	-	96	96	96	-	-	-	-	-	-	-	-
Djibouti	80	82	67	50	55	27	85	63	68	68	66	-	-	-	-	-	-	-	-
Dominica	97	100	90	83	86	75	70	99	99	99	99	-	-	-	-	42	-	-	-
Dominican Republic	93	98	85	57	67	43	65	90	65	60	79	81	-	20	61	53	-	-	-
Ecuador	86	92	77	72	80	59	100	99	89	99	99	58	-	-	-	-	-	-	-
Egypt	98	100	97	68	84	56	100	98	98	98	98	98	71	10	70	29	-	-	-
El Salvador	82	91	68	63	78	40	100	90	88	87	99	75	-	42	-	-	-	-	-
Equatorial Guinea	44	45	42	53	60	46	0	73	33	39	51	-	53	-	-	36	15	1	49
Eritrea	57	72	54	9	34	3	0	91	83	83	84	83	55	19	44	-	12	4	4
Estonia	-	-	-	-	93	-	-	99	94	95	95	-	-	-	-	-	-	-	-
Ethiopia	22	81	11	6	19	4	18	76	56	57	52	-	24	24	16	38	-	-	3
Fiji	-	-	-	98	99	98	100	99	94	99	91	92	-	-	-	-	-	-	-

	% of population using improved drinking water sources 2002			% of population using adequate sanitation facilities 2002			% of routine EPI vaccines financed by government 2003	% immunized 2003						% under-fives with ARI	% under-fives with ARI taken to health provider	% under-fives with diarrhoea receiving oral rehydration and continued feeding 1994-2003*	Malaria: 1999-2003		
								1-year-old children					pregnant women	1998-2003*			% under-fives sleeping under a bednet	% under-fives sleeping under a treated bednet	% under-fives with fever receiving anti-malarial drugs
	total	urban	rural	total	urban	rural	total	TB	DPT3	polio3	measles	hepB3	tetanus						
Finland	100	100	100	100	100	100	-	98	98	96	97	-	-	-	-	-	-	-	-
France	-	100	-	-	-	-	-	85	97	97	86	29	-	-	-	-	-	-	-
Gabon	87	95	47	36	37	30	100	89	38	31	55	-	54	13	48	44	-	-	-
Gambia	82	95	77	53	72	46	63	99	90	90	90	90	-	8	75	38	42	15	55
Georgia	76	90	61	83	96	69	19	87	76	75	73	49	-	4	99	-	-	-	-
Germany	100	100	100	-	-	-	-	-	89	94	92	81	-	-	-	-	-	-	-
Ghana	79	93	68	58	74	46	28	92	80	80	80	80	70	10	44	24	-	-	61
Greece	-	-	-	-	-	-	-	88	88	87	88	88	-	-	-	-	-	-	-
Grenada	95	97	93	97	96	97	100	-	97	98	99	97	-	-	-	-	-	-	-
Guatemala	95	99	92	61	72	52	0	97	83	83	75	-	-	18	64	22	6	1	-
Guinea	51	78	38	13	25	6	20	78	45	43	52	-	74	16	39	29	27	-	-
Guinea-Bissau	59	79	49	34	57	23	0	84	77	75	61	-	66	10	64	23	67	7	58
Guyana	83	83	83	70	86	60	90	95	90	91	89	90	-	5	78	40	67	6	3
Haiti	71	91	59	34	52	23	30	71	43	43	53	-	52	39	63	41	-	-	12
Holy See	-	-	-	-	-	-	-	-	-	-	-	-	-	-	-	-	-	-	-
Honduras	90	99	82	68	89	52	100	91	92	92	95	92	-	-	-	-	-	-	-
Hungary	99	100	98	95	100	85	-	99	99	99	99	-	-	-	-	-	-	-	-
Iceland	100	100	100	-	-	-	-	-	97	97	93	-	-	-	-	-	-	-	-
India	86	96	82	30	58	18	100	81	70	70	67	-	78	19	64	22	-	-	-
Indonesia	78	89	69	52	71	38	90	82	70	70	72	75	51	8	57	61	-	-	1
Iran (Islamic Republic of)	93	98	83	84	86	78	100	99	99	99	99	98	-	24	93	-	-	-	-
Iraq	81	97	50	80	95	48	100	93	81	84	90	70	70	7	76	-	-	-	-
Ireland	-	100	-	-	-	-	-	90	85	86	78	-	-	-	-	-	-	-	-
Israel	100	100	100	-	100	-	100	-	97	93	95	98	-	-	-	-	-	-	-
Italy	-	100	-	-	-	-	-	-	96	97	83	97	-	-	-	-	-	-	-
Jamaica	93	98	87	80	90	68	100	88	81	80	78	19	-	3	39	21	-	-	-
Japan	100	100	100	100	100	100	100	-	97	97	99	-	-	-	-	-	-	-	-
Jordan	91	91	91	93	94	85	100	67	97	97	96	97	-	6	72	-	-	-	-
Kazakhstan	86	96	72	72	87	52	100	99	99	99	99	99	-	3	48	22	-	-	-
Kenya	62	89	46	48	56	43	36	87	73	67	72	73	66	18	46	15	14	4	-
Kiribati	64	77	53	39	59	22	-	99	99	96	88	99	-	-	-	-	-	-	-
Korea, Democratic People's Republic of	100	100	100	59	58	60	80	88	68	99	95	-	-	-	-	-	-	-	-
Korea, Republic of	92	97	71	-	-	-	100	87	97	94	96	91	-	-	-	-	-	-	-
Kuwait	-	-	-	-	-	-	100	-	99	99	97	99	-	-	-	-	-	-	-
Kyrgyzstan	76	98	66	60	75	51	40	99	98	98	99	99	-	-	-	16	-	-	-
Lao People's Democratic Republic	43	66	38	24	61	14	0	65	50	52	42	50	36	1	36	37	-	-	-
Latvia	-	-	-	-	-	-	100	99	98	98	99	98	-	-	-	-	-	-	-
Lebanon	100	100	100	98	100	87	100	-	92	92	96	88	-	4	74	-	-	-	-
Lesotho	76	88	74	37	61	32	10	83	79	78	70	-	-	7	49	29	-	-	-
Liberia	62	72	52	26	49	7	0	43	38	39	53	-	56	39	70	-	-	-	-
Libyan Arab Jamahiriya	72	72	68	97	97	96	-	99	93	93	91	91	-	-	-	-	-	-	-
Liechtenstein	-	-	-	-	-	-	-	-	-	-	-	-	-	-	-	-	-	-	-
Lithuania	-	-	-	-	-	-	100	99	94	91	98	95	-	-	-	-	-	-	-
Luxembourg	100	100	100	-	-	-	-	-	98	98	91	49	-	-	-	-	-	-	-
Madagascar	45	75	34	33	49	27	12	72	55	58	55	55	55	6	47	47	30	0	61
Malawi	67	96	62	46	66	42	0	91	84	85	77	84	70	27	27	51	8	3	27
Malaysia	95	96	94	-	-	98	100	99	96	97	92	95	-	-	-	-	-	-	-
Maldives	84	99	78	58	100	42	98	98	98	98	96	98	-	22	22	-	-	-	-
Mali	48	76	35	45	59	38	100	63	69	65	68	79	32	10	43	45	72	8	38
Malta	100	100	100	-	100	-	-	-	94	94	90	70	-	-	-	-	-	-	-
Marshall Islands	85	80	95	82	93	59	-	93	68	80	90	74	-	-	-	-	-	-	-
Mauritania	56	63	45	42	64	9	100	84	76	75	71	-	41	10	39	-	-	-	-
Mauritius	100	100	100	99	100	99	100	92	92	93	94	92	-	-	-	-	-	-	-
Mexico	91	97	72	77	90	39	100	99	91	92	96	91	-	-	-	-	-	-	-
Micronesia (Federated States of)	94	95	94	28	61	14	6	64	92	88	91	89	-	-	-	-	-	-	-
Moldova, Republic of	92	97	88	68	86	52	49	98	98	98	96	99	-	1	78	52	-	-	-
Monaco	-	100	-	-	100	-	-	-	-	-	-	-	-	-	-	-	-	-	-
Mongolia	62	87	30	59	75	37	22	98	98	98	98	98	-	2	78	66	-	-	-
Morocco	80	99	56	61	83	31	100	92	91	91	90	90	-	-	35	-	-	-	-

TABLE 3. HEALTH

	% of population using improved drinking water sources 2002			% of population using adequate sanitation facilities 2002			% of routine EPI vaccines financed by government 2003	% immunized 2003						% under-fives with ARI	% under-fives with ARI taken to health provider	% under-fives with diarrhoea receiving oral rehydration and continued feeding 1994-2003*	Malaria: 1999-2003		
								1-year-old children					pregnant women	1998-2003*			% under-fives sleeping under a bednet	% under-fives sleeping under a treated bednet	% under-fives with fever receiving anti-malarial drugs
	total	urban	rural	total	urban	rural	total	TB	DPT3	polio3	measles	hepB3	tetanus						
Mozambique	42	76	24	27	51	14	21	87	72	70	77	72	57	10	51	33	-	-	-
Myanmar	80	95	74	73	96	63	0	79	77	76	75	-	77	4	48	48	-	-	-
Namibia	80	98	72	30	66	14	100	92	82	82	70	-	85	18	53	39	7	3	-
Nauru	-	-	-	-	-	-	100	95	80	59	40	75	-	-	-	-	-	-	-
Nepal	84	93	82	27	68	20	65	91	78	76	75	15	69	23	24	43	-	-	-
Netherlands	100	100	99	100	100	100	-	-	98	98	96	-	-	-	-	-	-	-	-
New Zealand	-	100	-	-	-	-	100	-	90	82	85	90	-	-	-	-	-	-	-
Nicaragua	81	93	65	66	78	51	74	94	86	86	93	86	-	31	57	49	-	-	2
Niger	46	80	36	12	43	4	100	64	52	51	64	-	36	12	27	43	17	6	48
Nigeria	60	72	49	38	48	30	100	48	25	39	35	-	51	10	31	28	6	1	34
Niue	100	100	100	100	100	100	100	99	95	95	86	95	-	-	-	-	-	-	-
Norway	100	100	100	-	-	-	-	-	90	90	84	-	-	-	-	-	-	-	-
Occupied Palestinian Territory	94	97	86	76	78	70	-	99	98	98	99	98	-	17	65	-	-	-	-
Oman	79	81	72	89	97	61	100	98	99	99	98	99	-	-	-	-	-	-	-
Pakistan	90	95	87	54	92	35	100	82	67	69	61	-	57	-	-	33x	-	-	-
Palau	84	79	94	83	96	52	5	-	99	99	99	99	-	-	-	-	-	-	-
Panama	91	99	79	72	89	51	100	87	86	83	83	86	-	-	-	-	-	-	-
Papua New Guinea	39	88	32	45	67	41	80	60	54	41	49	53	34	13x	75x	-	-	-	-
Paraguay	83	100	62	78	94	58	100	70	77	77	91	77	-	-	-	-	-	-	-
Peru	81	87	66	62	72	33	100	94	89	89	95	60	-	20	58	46	-	-	-
Philippines	85	90	77	73	81	61	3	91	79	80	80	40	70	-	46	37	-	-	-
Poland	-	100	-	-	-	-	-	94	99	98	97	97	-	-	-	-	-	-	-
Portugal	-	-	-	-	-	-	-	81	99	96	96	94	-	-	-	-	-	-	-
Qatar	100	100	100	100	100	100	100	99	92	93	93	98	-	-	-	-	-	-	-
Romania	57	91	16	51	86	10	100	99	97	97	97	98	-	-	-	-	-	-	-
Russian Federation	96	99	88	87	93	70	100	97	98	97	96	94	-	-	-	-	-	-	-
Rwanda	73	92	69	41	56	38	50	88	96	96	90	96	76	12	20	16	6	5	13
Saint Kitts and Nevis	99	99	99	96	96	96	97	99	99	99	98	99	-	-	-	-	-	-	-
Saint Lucia	98	98	98	89	89	89	100	95	90	91	90	14	-	-	-	-	-	-	-
Saint Vincent and the Grenadines	-	-	93	-	-	96	100	87	99	99	94	31	-	-	-	-	-	-	-
Samoa	88	91	88	100	100	100	100	73	94	95	99	97	-	-	-	-	-	-	-
San Marino	-	-	-	-	-	-	-	-	96	96	91	96	-	-	-	-	-	-	-
Sao Tome and Principe	79	89	73	24	32	20	-	99	94	94	87	43	-	5	47	44	43	23	61
Saudi Arabia	-	97	-	-	100	-	100	94	95	95	96	95	-	-	-	-	-	-	-
Senegal	72	90	54	52	70	34	100	77	73	73	60	-	75	7	27	33	15	2	36
Serbia and Montenegro	93	99	86	87	97	77	-	94	89	89	87	-	-	3	97	-	-	-	-
Seychelles	87	100	75	-	-	100	100	99	99	99	99	99	-	-	-	-	-	-	-
Sierra Leone	57	75	46	39	53	30	20	87	70	60	73	-	62	9	50	39	15	2	61
Singapore	-	100	-	-	100	-	100	97	92	92	88	92	-	-	-	-	-	-	-
Slovakia	100	100	100	100	100	100	100	98	99	98	99	99	-	-	-	-	-	-	-
Slovenia	-	-	-	-	-	-	100	98	92	93	94	-	-	-	-	-	-	-	-
Solomon Islands	70	94	65	31	98	18	-	76	71	68	78	78	-	-	-	-	-	-	-
Somalia	29	32	27	25	47	14	0	65	40	40	40	-	-	-	-	-	16	0	19
South Africa	87	98	73	67	86	44	100	97	94	94	83	94	52	19	75	37	-	-	-
Spain	-	-	-	-	-	-	-	-	98	98	97	83	-	-	-	-	-	-	-
Sri Lanka	78	99	72	91	98	89	100	99	99	98	99	-	-	-	-	-	-	-	-
Sudan	69	78	64	34	50	24	0	53	50	50	57	-	35	5	57	38	23	0	50
Suriname	92	98	73	93	99	76	100	-	74	74	71	-	-	4	58	43	77	3	-
Swaziland	52	87	42	52	78	44	100	97	95	95	94	95	-	10	60	24	0	0	26
Sweden	100	100	100	100	100	100	-	16	98	99	94	-	-	-	-	-	-	-	-
Switzerland	100	100	100	100	100	100	-	-	95	95	82	-	-	-	-	-	-	-	-
Syrian Arab Republic	79	94	64	77	97	56	100	99	99	99	98	98	-	18	66	-	-	-	-
Tajikistan	58	93	47	53	71	47	0	99	82	84	89	57	-	1	51	29	6	2	69
Tanzania, United Republic of	73	92	62	46	54	41	30	91	95	97	97	95	83	14	68	38	21	2	53
Thailand	85	95	80	99	97	100	100	99	96	97	94	95	-	-	-	-	-	-	-
The former Yugoslav Republic of Macedonia	-	-	-	-	-	-	90	95	96	96	96	-	-	-	-	-	-	-	-
Timor-Leste	52	73	51	33	65	30	0	80	70	70	60	-	-	14	57	-	48	8	47
Togo	51	80	36	34	71	15	0	84	64	63	58	-	47	9	30	25	15	2	60
Tonga	100	100	100	97	98	96	100	99	98	98	99	93	-	-	-	-	-	-	-

	% of population using improved drinking water sources 2002			% of population using adequate sanitation facilities 2002			% of routine EPI vaccines financed by government 2003	% immunized 2003						% under-fives with ARI 1998-2003*	% under-fives with ARI taken to health provider 1998-2003*	% under-fives with diarrhoea receiving oral rehydration and continued feeding 1994-2003*	Malaria: 1999-2003		
								1-year-old children					pregnant women						
	total	urban	rural	total	urban	rural	total	TB	DPT3	polio3	measles	hepB3	tetanus				% under-fives sleeping under a bednet	% under-fives sleeping under a treated bednet	% under-fives with fever receiving anti-malarial drugs
Trinidad and Tobago	91	92	88	100	100	100	100	-	91	91	88	76	-	3	74	31	-	-	-
Tunisia	82	94	60	80	90	62	100	93	95	95	90	92	-	9	43	-	-	-	-
Turkey	93	96	87	83	94	62	100	89	68	69	75	68	37	12x	37x	19	-	-	-
Turkmenistan	71	93	54	62	77	50	82	99	98	99	97	97	-	1	51	-	-	-	-
Tuvalu	93	94	92	88	92	83	100	99	93	93	95	95	-	-	-	-	-	-	-
Uganda	56	87	52	41	53	39	7	96	81	82	82	63	48	23	65	29	7	0	-
Ukraine	98	100	94	99	100	97	96	98	97	99	99	77	-	-	-	-	-	-	-
United Arab Emirates	-	-	-	100	100	100	100	98	94	94	94	92	-	-	-	-	-	-	-
United Kingdom	-	100	-	-	-	-	-	-	91	91	80	-	-	-	-	-	-	-	-
United States	100	100	100	100	100	100	56	-	96	91	93	92	-	-	-	-	-	-	-
Uruguay	98	98	93	94	95	85	100	99	91	91	95	91	-	-	-	-	-	-	-
Uzbekistan	89	97	84	57	73	48	77	98	98	99	99	99	-	0	57	33	-	-	-
Vanuatu	60	85	52	50	78	42	100	63	49	53	48	56	-	-	-	-	-	-	-
Venezuela	83	85	70	68	71	48	100	91	68	86	82	75	-	9	72	51	-	-	-
Viet Nam	73	93	67	41	84	26	55	98	99	96	93	78	79	20	71	24	96	16	7
Yemen	69	74	68	30	76	14	100	67	66	66	66	42	31	23x	32x	23x	-	-	-
Zambia	55	90	36	45	68	32	5	94	80	80	84	-	60	15	69	24	16	7	52
Zimbabwe	83	100	74	57	69	51	0	92	80	80	80	80	60	16	50	80	3	-	-
SUMMARY INDICATORS																			
Sub-Saharan Africa	57	82	44	36	55	26	45	74	60	63	62	30	53	14	39	32	14	2	38
Middle East and North Africa	87	95	77	72	88	52	89	88	87	87	88	71	-	12	69	-	-	-	-
South Asia	84	94	80	35	64	23	96	82	71	72	67	1	75	19	57	26	-	-	-
East Asia and Pacific	78	92	68	50	72	35	84	91	86	87	82	66	-	-	-	-	-	-	-
Latin America and Caribbean	89	95	69	75	84	44	92	96	89	91	93	73	-	-	-	36	-	-	-
CEE/CIS	91	98	79	81	92	62	89	95	88	89	90	81	-	-	-	25	-	-	-
Industrialized countries	100	100	100	100	100	100	69	-	95	93	92	62	-	-	-	-	-	-	-
Developing countries	79	92	70	49	73	31	80	85	76	77	75	40	64	16	52	31	-	-	-
Least developed countries	58	80	50	35	58	27	37	79	68	68	67	20	56	16	37	35	19	2	36
World	83	95	72	58	81	37	80	85	78	79	77	42	64	16	53	31	-	-	-

Countries in each category are listed on page 140.

DEFINITIONS OF THE INDICATORS

Government funding of vaccines – Percentage of vaccines routinely administered in a country to protect children that are financed by the national government (including loans).

EPI – Expanded Programme on Immunization: The immunizations in this programme include those against TB, DPT, polio and measles, as well as protecting babies against neonatal tetanus by vaccination of pregnant women. Other vaccines (e.g. against hepatitis B or yellow fever) may be included in the programme in some countries.

DPT3 – Percentage of infants that received three doses of diphtheria, pertussis (whooping cough) and tetanus vaccine.

HepB3 – Percentage of infants that received three doses of hepatitis B vaccine.

% under-fives with ARI – Percentage of children (0-4 years) with an acute respiratory infection (ARI) in the last two weeks.

% under-fives with ARI taken to health provider – Percentage of children (0-4 years) with ARI in the last two weeks taken to an appropriate health provider.

% under-fives with diarrhoea receiving oral rehydration and continued feeding – Percentage of children (0-4 years) with diarrhoea (in the two weeks preceeding the survey) who received either oral rehydration therapy (Oral Rehydration Solution or recommended home-made fluids) or increased fluids, with continued feeding.

Malaria

% under-fives sleeping under a mosquito net – Percentage of children (0-4 years) who slept under a mosquito net.

% under-fives sleeping under a treated mosquito net – Percentage of children (0-4 years) who slept under an insecticide-impregnated mosquito net.

% under-fives with fever receiving anti-malarial drugs – Percentage of children (0-4 years) who were ill with fever in the last two weeks and received any appropriate (locally defined) antimalarial drugs.

MAIN DATA SOURCES

Use of improved drinking water sources and adequate sanitation facilities – UNICEF, World Health Organization (WHO), Multiple Indicator Cluster Surveys (MICS) and Demographic and Health Surveys (DHS).

Government funding of vaccines – UNICEF and WHO.

Immunization – UNICEF and WHO.

Acute respiratory infection – DHS, MICS and other national household surveys.

Oral rehydration – DHS and MICS.

Malaria – MICS and DHS.

NOTES

- \- Data not available.
- x Indicates data that refer to years or periods other than those specified in the column heading, differ from the standard definition or refer to only part of a country.
- * Data refer to the most recent year available during the period specified in the column heading.

TABLE 4. HIV/AIDS

Countries and territories	HIV Prevalence: Adult prevalence rate (15-49 years), end-2003 estimate	Estimated number of people living with HIV, 2003 (in thousands): adults and children (0-49 years)	low estimate	high estimate	children (0-14 years)	women (15-49 years)	HIV prevalence rate in young (15-24 years) pregnant women in capital city: year	median	Knowledge and behaviour (1998-2003)* (15-24 years): % who know condom can prevent HIV: male	female	% who know healthy-looking person can have HIV: male	female	% who have comprehensive knowledge of HIV: male	female	% who used condom at last high-risk sex: male	female	Orphans: Children (0-17 years) orphaned by AIDS, 2003 estimate (in thousands)	orphaned due to all causes, 2003 estimate (in thousands)	Orphan school attendance ratio (1998-2003*)
Afghanistan	-	-	-		-	-	-	-	-	-	-	-	-	-	-	-	-	1600	-
Albania	-	-	-		-	-	-	-	-	42	-	40	-	0	-	-	-	-	-
Algeria	0.1	9.1	3.0	18	-	1.4	-	-	-	-	-	-	-	-	-	-	-	-	-
Andorra	-	-	-		-	-	-	-	-	-	-	-	-	-	-	-	-	-	-
Angola	3.9	240	97	600	23	130	-	-	-	-	-	-	-	-	-	-	110	1000	90
Antigua and Barbuda	-	-	-		-	-	-	-	-	-	-	-	-	-	-	-	-	-	-
Argentina	0.7	130	61	210	-	24	-	-	-	-	-	-	-	-	-	-	-	750	-
Armenia	0.1	2.6	1.2	4.3	-	0.9	-	-	56	41	48	53	8	7	44	0	-	-	-
Australia	0.1	14	6.8	22	-	1.0	-	-	-	-	-	-	-	-	-	-	-	-	-
Austria	0.3	10	5.0	16	-	2.2	-	-	-	-	-	-	-	-	-	-	-	-	-
Azerbaijan	<0.1	1.4	0.5	2.8	-	-	-	-	-	11	-	35	-	2	-	-	-	-	-
Bahamas	3.0	5.6	3.2	8.7	<0.2	2.5	-	-	-	-	-	-	-	-	-	-	-	7.6	-
Bahrain	0.2	<0.6	0.2	1.1	-	<0.5	-	-	-	-	-	-	-	-	-	-	-	-	-
Bangladesh	-	-	2.5	15	-	-	-	-	-	-	-	-	-	-	-	-	-	5300	-
Barbados	1.5	2.5	0.7	9.2	<0.2	0.8	-	-	-	-	-	-	-	-	-	-	-	3.7	-
Belarus	-	-	12	42	-	-	-	-	-	-	-	-	-	-	-	-	-	-	-
Belgium	0.2	10	5.3	17	-	3.5	-	-	-	-	-	-	-	-	-	-	-	-	-
Belize	2.4	3.6	1.2	10	<0.2	1.3	-	-	-	-	-	-	-	-	-	-	-	5.6	-
Benin	1.9	68	38	120	5.7	35	2002	2.3	53	45	69	56	14	8	34	19	34	340	-
Bhutan	-	-	-		-	-	-	-	-	-	-	-	-	-	-	-	-	90	-
Bolivia	0.1	4.9	1.6	11	-	1.3	-	-	-	56	74	64	-	22m	-	-	-	340	82
Bosnia and Herzegovina	<0.1	0.9	0.3	1.8	-	-	-	-	-	53	-	74	-	-	-	-	-	-	-
Botswana	37.3	350	330	380	25	190	2003	32.9	89	93	76	81	33	40	88	75	120	160	99
Brazil	0.7	660	320	1100	-	240	-	-	-	-	-	-	-	-	-	-	-	4300	-
Brunei Darussalam	<0.1	<0.2	< 0.4		-	<0.2	-	-	-	-	-	-	-	-	-	-	-	4.2	-
Bulgaria	<0.1	<0.5	< 1.0		-	-	-	-	-	-	-	-	-	-	-	-	-	-	-
Burkina Faso	4.2	300	190	470	31	150	2002	2.3	-	-	64	42	-	-	55	41	260	830	-
Burundi	6.0	250	170	370	27	130	2002	13.6	-	47	-	66	-	24	-	-	200	660	70
Cambodia	2.6	170	100	290	7.3	51	-	-	-	64	-	62	-	37	-	-	-	670	71
Cameroon	6.9	560	390	810	43	290	2002	7.0	-	46	63	57	-	16m	31	16	240	930	94p
Canada	0.3	56	26	86	-	13	-	-	-	-	-	-	-	-	-	-	-	-	-
Cape Verde	-	-	-		-	-	-	-	-	-	60	53	-	-	-	-	-	-	-
Central African Republic	13.5	260	160	410	21	130	2002	14.0	-	20	-	46	-	5	-	-	110	290	91
Chad	4.8	200	130	300	18	100	2003	4.8	-	21	-	28	-	5	-	-	96	500	96
Chile	0.3	26	13	44	-	8.7	-	-	-	0	-	-	-	-	-	-	-	230	-
China	0.1	840	430	1500	-	190	-	-	-	-	-	-	-	-	-	-	-	20600	-
Colombia	0.7	190	90	310	-	62	-	-	-	-	-	82	-	-	-	29	-	910	76
Comoros	-	-	-		-	-	-	-	-	41	-	55	-	10	-	-	-	-	59
Congo	4.9	90	39	200	10	45	-	-	-	-	-	-	-	-	-	-	97	260	-
Congo, Democratic Republic of the	4.2	1100	450	2600	110	570	-	-	-	45	-	-	-	-	-	-	770	4200	72
Cook Islands	-	-	-		-	-	-	-	-	-	-	-	-	-	-	-	-	-	-
Costa Rica	0.6	12	6.0	21	-	4.0	-	-	-	-	-	-	-	-	-	-	-	50	-
Côte d'Ivoire	7.0	570	390	820	40	300	2002	5.2	-	53	67	64	-	16m	56	25	310	940	83
Croatia	<0.1	<0.2	< 0.4		-	-	-	-	-	-	-	-	-	-	-	-	-	-	-
Cuba	0.1	3.3	1.1	6.6	-	1.1	-	-	-	89	-	91	-	52	-	-	-	130	-
Cyprus	-	-	-		-	-	-	-	-	-	-	-	-	-	-	-	-	-	-
Czech Republic	0.1	2.5	0.8	4.9	-	0.8	-	-	-	-	-	-	-	-	-	-	-	-	-
Denmark	0.2	5.0	2.5	8.2	-	0.9	-	-	-	-	-	-	-	-	-	-	-	-	-
Djibouti	2.9	9.1	2.3	24	0.7	4.7	-	-	-	-	-	-	-	-	-	-	5	33	-
Dominica	-	-	-		-	-	-	-	-	-	-	-	-	-	-	-	-	-	-
Dominican Republic	1.7	88	48	160	2.2	23	-	-	88	84	89	92	-	-	-	-	-	260	96
Ecuador	0.3	21	10	38	-	6.8	-	-	-	-	-	58	-	-	-	-	-	290	-
Egypt	<0.1	12	5.0	31	-	1.6	-	-	-	-	-	-	-	-	-	-	-	-	-
El Salvador	0.7	29	14	50	-	9.6	-	-	-	-	-	68	-	-	-	-	-	180	-
Equatorial Guinea	-	-	-		-	-	-	-	-	26	-	46	-	4	-	-	-	24	95
Eritrea	2.7	60	21	170	5.6	31	-	-	-	-	-	79	-	-	-	-	39	230	-
Estonia	1.1	7.8	2.6	15	-	2.6	-	-	-	-	-	-	-	-	-	-	-	-	-
Ethiopia	4.4	1500	950	2300	120	770	2003	11.7	-	-	54	39	-	-	30	17	720	4000	60
Fiji	0.1	0.6	0.2	1.3	-	<0.2	-	-	-	-	-	-	-	-	-	-	-	25	-

	HIV Prevalence								Knowledge and behaviour (1998-2003)* (15-24 years)								Orphans		
	Adult prevalence rate (15-49 years), end-2003	Estimated number of people living with HIV, 2003 (in thousands)					HIV prevalence rate in young (15-24 years) pregnant women in capital city		% who know condom can prevent HIV		% who know healthy-looking person can have HIV		% who have comprehensive knowledge of HIV		% who used condom at last high-risk sex		Children (0-17 years)		Orphan school attendance ratio
		adults and children (0-49 years)	low estimate	- high estimate	children (0-14 years)	women (15-49 years)											orphaned by AIDS, 2003	orphaned due to all causes, 2003	
	estimate						year	median	male	female	male	female	male	female	male	female	estimate (in thousands)	estimate (in thousands)	(1998-2003*)
Finland	0.1	1.5	0.5	3.0	-	<0.5	-	-	-	-	-	-	-	-	-	-	-	-	-
France	0.4	120	60	200	-	32	-	-	-	-	-	-	-	-	-	-	-	-	-
Gabon	8.1	48	24	91	2.5	26	-	-	71	64	81	72	22	24	48	33	14	57	98
Gambia	1.2	6.8	1.8	24	0.5	3.6	-	-	-	51	-	53	-	15	-	-	2	45	85
Georgia	0.1	3.0	2.0	12	-	1.0	-	-	-	-	-	-	-	-	-	-	-	-	-
Germany	0.1	43	21	71	-	10	-	-	-	-	-	-	-	-	-	-	-	-	-
Ghana	3.1	350	210	560	24	180	2003	3.9	-	-	77	71	-	-	-	-	170	1000	93p
Greece	0.2	9.1	4.5	15	-	1.8	-	-	-	-	-	-	-	-	-	-	-	-	-
Grenada	-	-	-		-	-	-	-	-	-	-	-	-	-	-	-	-	-	-
Guatemala	1.1	78	38	130	-	31	-	-	-	-	75	69	-	-	-	-	-	510	98
Guinea	3.2	140	51	360	9.2	72	-	-	-	-	56	60	-	-	32	17	35	420	113
Guinea-Bissau	-	-	-		-	-	-	-	-	32	-	31	-	8	-	-	-	81	103
Guyana	2.5	11	3.5	35	0.6	6.1	-	-	-	69	-	84	-	36	-	-	-	33	-
Haiti	5.6	280	120	600	19	150	-	-	72	46	78	68	24	14	30	19	-	610	87
Holy See	-	-	-		-	-	-	-	-	-	-	-	-	-	-	-	-	-	-
Honduras	1.8	63	35	110	3.9	33	-	-	-	-	90	81	-	-	-	-	-	180	-
Hungary	0.1	2.8	0.9	5.5	-	-	-	-	-	-	-	-	-	-	-	-	-	-	-
Iceland	0.2	<0.5		< 1.0	-	<0.2	-	-	-	-	-	-	-	-	-	-	-	-	-
India	-	-	2200	7600	-	-	-	-	-	-	-	-	17	21	59	51	-	35000	-
Indonesia	0.1	110	53	180	-	15	-	-	-	23	-	32	-	7	-	-	-	6100	82
Iran (Islamic Republic of)	0.1	31	10	61	-	3.8	-	-	-	-	-	-	-	-	-	-	-	2100	-
Iraq	<0.1	<0.5		< 1.0	-	-	-	-	-	-	-	-	-	-	-	-	-	-	-
Ireland	0.1	2.8	1.1	5.3	-	0.8	-	-	-	-	-	-	-	-	-	-	-	-	-
Israel	0.1	3.0	1.5	4.9	-	-	-	-	-	-	-	-	-	-	-	-	-	-	-
Italy	0.5	140	67	220	-	45	-	-	-	-	-	-	-	-	-	-	-	-	-
Jamaica	1.2	22	11	41	<0.5	10	-	-	-	-	-	-	-	-	-	-	-	45	-
Japan	<0.1	12	5.7	19	-	2.9	-	-	-	-	-	-	-	-	-	-	-	-	-
Jordan	<0.1	0.6	0.0	< 1.0	-	-	-	-	-	-	-	-	-	-	-	-	-	-	-
Kazakhstan	0.2	17	5.8	35	-	5.5	-	-	-	-	73	63	-	-	65	32	-	-	-
Kenya	6.7	1200	820	1700	100	720	-	-	68	59	86	83	47	34	47	25	650	1700	96
Kiribati	-	-	-		-	-	-	-	-	-	-	-	-	-	-	-	-	-	-
Korea, Democratic People's Republic of	-	-	-		-	-	-	-	-	-	-	-	-	-	-	-	-	710	-
Korea, Republic of	<0.1	8.3	2.7	16	-	0.9	-	-	-	-	-	-	-	-	-	-	-	630	-
Kuwait	-	-	-		-	-	-	-	-	-	-	-	-	-	-	-	-	-	-
Kyrgyzstan	0.1	3.9	1.5	8.0	-	<0.8	-	-	-	-	-	-	-	-	-	-	-	-	-
Lao People's Democratic Republic	0.1	1.7	0.6	3.6	-	<0.5	-	-	-	-	-	-	-	-	-	-	-	290	-
Latvia	0.6	7.6	3.7	12	-	2.5	-	-	-	-	-	-	-	-	-	-	-	-	-
Lebanon	0.1	2.8	0.7	4.1	-	<0.5	-	-	-	-	-	-	-	-	-	-	-	-	-
Lesotho	28.9	320	290	360	22	170	2003	27.8	-	58	-	46	-	18	-	-	100	180	87
Liberia	5.9	100	47	220	8.0	54	-	-	-	-	-	-	-	-	-	-	36	230	-
Libyan Arab Jamahiriya	0.3	10	3.3	20	-	-	-	-	-	-	-	-	-	-	-	-	-	-	-
Liechtenstein	-	-	-		-	-	-	-	-	-	-	-	-	-	-	-	-	-	-
Lithuania	0.1	1.3	0.4	2.6	-	<0.5	-	-	-	-	-	-	-	-	-	-	-	-	-
Luxembourg	0.2	<0.5		< 1.0	-	-	-	-	-	-	-	-	-	-	-	-	-	-	-
Madagascar	1.7	140	68	250	8.6	76	-	-	-	33	-	27	-	-	-	-	30	1000	65p
Malawi	14.2	900	700	1100	83	460	2003	18.0	76	66	89	84	41	34	38	32	500	1000	93
Malaysia	0.4	52	25	86	-	8.5	-	-	-	-	-	-	-	-	-	-	-	480	-
Maldives	-	-	-		-	-	-	-	-	-	-	-	-	-	-	-	-	-	-
Mali	1.9	140	44	420	13	71	2003	2.2	56	42	59	46	15	9	30	14	75	730	72
Malta	0.2	<0.5		< 1.0	-	-	-	-	-	-	-	-	-	-	-	-	-	-	-
Marshall Islands	-	-	-		-	-	-	-	-	-	-	-	-	-	-	-	-	-	-
Mauritania	0.6	9.5	4.5	17	-	5.1	-	-	-	-	39	30	-	-	-	-	2	140	-
Mauritius	-	-	-		-	-	-	-	-	-	-	-	-	-	-	-	-	-	-
Mexico	0.3	160	78	260	-	53	-	-	-	-	-	-	-	-	-	-	-	1900	-
Micronesia (Federated States of)	-	-	-		-	-	-	-	-	-	-	-	-	-	-	-	-	-	-
Moldova, Republic of	0.2	5.5	2.7	9.0	-	-	-	-	-	56	-	79	-	19	-	-	-	-	-
Monaco	-	-	-		-	-	-	-	-	-	-	-	-	-	-	-	-	-	-

	HIV Prevalence								Knowledge and behaviour (1998-2003)* (15-24 years)								Orphans		
	Adult prevalence rate (15-49 years), end-2003	Estimated number of people living with HIV, 2003 (in thousands)					HIV prevalence rate in young (15-24 years) pregnant women in capital city		% who know condom can prevent HIV		% who know healthy-looking person can have HIV		% who have comprehensive knowledge of HIV		% who used condom at last high-risk sex		Children (0-17 years)		Orphan school attendance ratio
		adults and children (0-49 years)	low estimate	high estimate	children (0-14 years)	women (15-49 years)											orphaned by AIDS, 2003	orphaned due to all causes, 2003	
	estimate						year	median	male	female	male	female	male	female	male	female	estimate (in thousands)	estimate (in thousands)	(1998-2003*)
Mongolia	<0.1	<0.5	< 1.0		-	<0.2	-	-	-	77	-	57	-	32	-	-	-	78	-
Morocco	0.1	15	5.0	30	-	-	-	-	-	-	-	-	-	-	-	-	-	-	-
Mozambique	12.2	1300	980	1700	99	670	2002	14.7	74	56	82	65	33	20	33	29	470	1500	80
Myanmar	1.2	330	170	620	7.6	97	-	-	-	-	-	-	-	-	-	-	-	1900	-
Namibia	21.3	210	180	250	15	110	-	-	86	73	87	82	41	31	69	48	57	120	92
Nauru	-	-	-		-	-	-	-	-	-	-	-	-	-	-	-	-	-	-
Nepal	0.5	61	29	110	-	16	-	-	-	-	-	-	-	-	-	-	-	1000	-
Netherlands	0.2	19	9.5	31	-	3.8	-	-	-	-	-	-	-	-	-	-	-	-	-
New Zealand	0.1	1.4	0.5	2.8	-	<0.2	-	-	-	-	-	-	-	-	-	-	-	-	-
Nicaragua	0.2	6.4	3.1	12	-	2.1	-	-	-	-	-	73	-	-	-	17	-	150	-
Niger	1.2	70	36	130	5.9	36	-	-	-	30	41	37	-	5m	30	7	24	680	-
Nigeria	5.4	3600	2400	5400	290	1900	2003	4.2	63	43	65	52	23	21	46	24	1800	7000	64p
Niue	-	-	-		-	-	-	-	-	-	-	-	-	-	-	-	-	-	-
Norway	0.1	2.1	0.7	4.0	-	<0.5	-	-	-	-	-	-	-	-	-	-	-	-	-
Occupied Palestinian Territory	-	-	-		-	-	-	-	-	38	-	49	-	-	-	-	-	-	-
Oman	0.1	1.3	0.5	3.0	-	<0.5	-	-	-	-	-	-	-	-	-	-	-	-	-
Pakistan	0.1	74	24	150	-	8.9	-	-	-	-	-	-	-	-	-	-	-	4800	-
Palau	-	-	-		-	-	-	-	-	-	-	-	-	-	-	-	-	-	-
Panama	0.9	16	7.7	26	-	6.2	-	-	-	-	-	-	-	-	-	-	-	48	-
Papua New Guinea	0.6	16	7.8	28	-	4.8	-	-	-	-	-	-	-	-	-	-	-	220	-
Paraguay	0.5	15	7.3	25	-	3.9	-	-	-	-	-	-	-	-	-	-	-	150	-
Peru	0.5	82	40	140	-	27	-	-	-	-	-	72	-	-	-	19	-	720	85p
Philippines	<0.1	9.0	3.0	18	-	2.0	-	-	-	50	-	67	-	-	-	-	-	2100	-
Poland	0.1	14	6.9	23	-	-	-	-	-	-	-	-	-	-	-	-	-	-	-
Portugal	0.4	22	11	36	-	4.3	-	-	-	-	-	-	-	-	-	-	-	-	-
Qatar	-	-	-		-	-	-	-	-	-	-	-	-	-	-	-	-	-	-
Romania	<0.1	6.5	4.8	8.9	-	-	-	-	-	-	77	70	-	-	-	-	-	-	-
Russian Federation	1.1	860	420	1400	-	290	-	-	-	-	-	-	-	-	-	-	-	-	-
Rwanda	5.1	250	170	380	22	130	2002	11.6	76	63	69	64	20	23	55	23	160	810	80
Saint Kitts and Nevis	-	-	-		-	-	-	-	-	-	-	-	-	-	-	-	-	-	-
Saint Lucia	-	-	-		-	-	-	-	-	-	-	-	-	-	-	-	-	-	-
Saint Vincent and the Grenadines	-	-	-		-	-	-	-	-	-	-	-	-	-	-	-	-	-	-
Samoa	-	-	-		-	-	-	-	-	-	-	-	-	-	-	-	-	-	-
San Marino	-	-	-		-	-	-	-	-	-	-	-	-	-	-	-	-	-	-
Sao Tome and Principe	-	-	-		-	-	-	-	-	32	-	65	-	11	-	-	-	-	-
Saudi Arabia	-	-	-		-	-	-	-	-	-	-	-	-	-	-	-	-	-	-
Senegal	0.8	44	22	89	3.1	23	2002	1.1	-	49	-	46	-	-	-	-	17	460	74p
Serbia and Montenegro	0.2	10	3.4	20	-	2.0	-	-	-	-	-	-	-	-	-	-	-	-	-
Seychelles	-	-	-		-	-	-	-	-	-	-	-	-	-	-	-	-	-	-
Sierra Leone	-	-	-		-	-	-	-	-	30	-	35	-	16	-	-	-	350	71
Singapore	0.2	4.1	1.3	8.0	-	1.0	-	-	-	-	-	-	-	-	-	-	-	-	-
Slovakia	<0.1	<0.2	< 0.4		-	-	-	-	-	-	-	-	-	-	-	-	-	-	-
Slovenia	<0.1	<0.5	< 1.0		-	-	-	-	-	-	-	-	-	-	-	-	-	-	-
Solomon Islands	-	-	-		-	-	-	-	-	-	-	-	-	-	-	-	-	-	-
Somalia	-	-	-		-	-	-	-	-	2	-	13	-	0	-	-	-	770	65
South Africa	21.5	5300	4500	6200	230	2900	2002	24.0	-	83	-	54	-	20	-	20	1100	2200	95
Spain	0.7	140	67	220	-	27	-	-	-	-	-	-	-	-	-	-	-	-	-
Sri Lanka	<0.1	3.5	1.2	6.9	-	0.6	-	-	-	-	-	-	-	-	-	-	-	340	-
Sudan	2.3	400	120	1300	21	220	-	-	-	-	-	-	-	-	-	-	-	1300	96
Suriname	1.7	5.2	1.4	18	<0.2	1.7	-	-	-	58	-	70	-	27	-	-	-	13	89
Swaziland	38.8	220	210	230	16	110	2002	39.0	-	63	-	81	-	27	-	-	65	100	91
Sweden	0.1	3.6	1.2	6.9	-	0.9	-	-	-	-	-	-	-	-	-	-	-	-	-
Switzerland	0.4	13	6.5	21	-	3.9	-	-	-	-	-	-	-	-	-	-	-	-	-
Syrian Arab Republic	<0.1	<0.5	0.3	2.1	-	<0.2	-	-	-	-	-	-	-	-	-	-	-	-	-
Tajikistan	<0.1	<0.2	< 0.4		-	-	-	-	-	5	-	8	-	-	-	-	-	-	-
Tanzania, United Republic of	8.8	1600	1200	2300	140	840	2002	7.0	72	62	68	65	29	26	31	21	980	2500	74p
The former Yugoslav Republic of Macedonia	<0.1	<0.2	< 0.4		-	-	-	-	-	-	-	-	-	-	-	-	-	-	-
Thailand	1.5	570	310	1000	12	200	-	-	-	-	-	-	-	-	-	-	-	1400	-
Timor-Leste	-	-	-		-	-	-	-	-	6	-	8	-	-	-	-	-	-	-

	HIV Prevalence								Knowledge and behaviour (1998-2003)* (15-24 years)								Orphans		
	Adult prevalence rate (15-49 years), end-2003	Estimated number of people living with HIV, 2003 (in thousands)					HIV prevalence rate in young (15-24 years) pregnant women in capital city		% who know condom can prevent HIV		% who know healthy-looking person can have HIV		% who have comprehensive knowledge of HIV		% who used condom at last high-risk sex		Children (0-17 years)		Orphan school attendance ratio
		adults and children (0-49 years)	low estimate	high estimate	children (0-14 years)	women (15-49 years)											orphaned by AIDS, 2003	orphaned due to all causes, 2003	
	estimate						year	median	male	female	male	female	male	female	male	female	estimate (in thousands)	estimate (in thousands)	(1998-2003*)
Togo	4.1	110	67	170	9.3	54	2003	9.1	-	63	73	66	-	20m	41	22	54	240	96
Tonga	-	-	-		-	-	-	-	-	-	-	-	-	-	-	-	-	-	-
Trinidad and Tobago	3.2	29	11	74	0.7	14	-	-	-	54	-	95	-	33	-	-	-	28	-
Tunisia	<0.1	1.0	0.4	2.4	-	<0.5	-	-	-	-	-	-	-	-	-	-	-	-	-
Turkey	-	-	-		-	-	-	-	-	-	-	-	-	-	-	-	-	-	-
Turkmenistan	<0.1	<0.2	< 0.4		-	-	-	-	-	19	-	42	-	3	-	-	-	-	-
Tuvalu	-	-	-		-	-	-	-	-	-	-	-	-	-	-	-	-	-	-
Uganda	4.1	530	350	880	84	270	2001	10.0	81	68	83	76	40	28	62	44	940	2000	95
Ukraine	1.4	360	180	590	-	120	-	-	-	57	-	78	-	-	-	-	-	-	-
United Arab Emirates	-	-	-		-	-	-	-	-	-	-	-	-	-	-	-	-	-	-
United Kingdom	0.1	32	16	52	-	7.0	-	-	-	-	-	-	-	-	-	-	-	-	-
United States	0.6	950	470	1600	-	240	-	-	-	-	-	-	-	-	-	-	-	-	-
Uruguay	0.3	6.0	2.8	9.7	-	1.9	-	-	-	-	-	-	-	-	-	-	-	62	-
Uzbekistan	0.1	11	4.9	30	-	3.7	-	-	50	28	58	55	7	8	50	-	-	-	-
Vanuatu	-	-	-		-	-	-	-	-	-	-	-	-	-	-	-	-	-	-
Venezuela	0.7	110	47	170	-	32	-	-	-	28	-	78	-	-	-	-	-	460	-
Viet Nam	0.4	220	110	360	-	65	-	-	-	60	-	63	-	25	-	-	-	2100	-
Yemen	0.1	12	4.0	24	-	-	-	-	-	-	-	-	-	-	-	-	-	-	-
Zambia	16.5	920	730	1100	85	470	2002	22.1	68	67	73	74	33	31	42	33	630	1100	91
Zimbabwe	24.6	1800	1500	2000	120	930	-	-	81	73	83	74	-	-	69	42	980	1300	85
SUMMARY INDICATORS																			
Sub-Saharan Africa	7.5	25000	23000	27900	1900	13100		9.5	-	52	68	56	-	22	42	25	-	-	81
Middle East and North Africa	0.3	510	230	1400	22	230		-	-	-	-	-	-	-	-	-	-	-	-
South Asia	0.7	5000	2400	7700	130	1500		-	-	-	-	-	17	21	59	51	-	-	-
East Asia and Pacific	0.2	2400	1800	3200	39	640		-	-	-	-	-	-	-	-	-	-	-	-
Latin America and Caribbean	0.7	2000	1600	2600	48	760		-	-	-	-	-	-	-	-	-	-	-	-
CEE/CIS	0.6	1300	840	1900	8.1	440		-	-	-	-	-	-	-	-	-	-	-	-
Industrialized countries	0.4	1600	1100	2300	17	410		-	-	-	-	-	-	-	-	-	-	-	-
Developing countries	1.2	34900	31600	39600	2100	16300		-	-	-	-	-	-	-	-	-	-	-	-
Least developed countries	3.2	12000	10800	14300	1000	6100		-	-	-	-	-	-	-	-	-	-	-	-
World	1.1	37800	34600	42300	2100	17000		-	-	-	-	-	-	-	-	-	-	-	-

Countries in each category are listed on page 140.

DEFINITIONS OF THE INDICATORS

Adult prevalence rate – Percentage of adults (15-49 years) living with HIV/AIDS as of end-2003.

Estimated number of people living with HIV/AIDS – Estimated number of adults and children living with HIV/AIDS as of end-2003.

HIV prevalence among pregnant women – Percentage of blood samples taken from pregnant women (15-24 years) that test positive for HIV during 'unlinked anonymous' sentinel surveillance at selected antenatal clinics.

Know condom can prevent HIV – Percentage of young women and men (15-24 years) who report through prompted questions that condom use can prevent HIV transmission.

Know healthy-looking person can have HIV – Percentage of young men and women (15-24 years) who know that a healthy-looking person can have the AIDS virus.

Comprehensive knowledge of HIV – Percentage of young women (15-24 years) who correctly identify the two major ways of preventing the sexual transmission of HIV (using condoms and limiting sex to one faithful, uninfected partner), who reject the two most common local misconceptions about HIV transmission, and who know that a healthy-looking person can have the AIDS virus.

Condom use at last high-risk sex – Percentage of young men and women (15-24 years) who say they used a condom the last time they had sex with a non-marital, non-cohabiting partner, of those who have had sex with such a partner in the last 12 months.

Children orphaned by AIDS – Estimated number of children (0-17 years) as of end-2003, who have lost one or both parents to AIDS.

Orphan school attendance ratio – Percentage of children (10-14 years) who lost both biological parents and who are currently attending school as a percentage of non-orphaned children of the same age who live with at least one parent and who are attending school.

MAIN DATA SOURCES

Adult prevalence rate – Joint United Nations Programme on HIV/AIDS (UNAIDS), *Report on the Global HIV/AIDS Epidemic*, 2004.

Estimated number of people living with HIV/AIDS – UNAIDS, *Report on the Global HIV/AIDS Epidemic*, 2004.

HIV prevalence among pregnant women – *Report on the Global HIV/AIDS Epidemic*, 2004.

Know condom can prevent HIV – Demographic and Health Surveys (DHS), Multiple Indicator Cluster Surveys (MICS), behavioural surveillance surveys (BSS) and Reproductive Health Surveys (RHS) (1998-2003) and www.measuredhs.com/hiv.data.

Know healthy-looking person can have HIV – DHS, BSS, RHS and MICS (1998-2003) and www.measuredhs.com/hiv.data.

Comprehensive knowledge of HIV – DHS, BSS, RHS and MICS (1998-2003) and www.measuredhs.com/hiv.data.

Condom use at last high-risk sex – DHS, MICS, BSS and RHS (1998-2003) and www.measuredhs.com/hiv.data.

Children orphaned by AIDS – UNAIDS, UNICEF and USAID, *Children on the Brink 2004*.

Orphan school attendance ratio – MICS and DHS (1998-2003) and www.measuredhs.com/hiv.data.

NOTES

- \- Data not available.
- m Data for the three knowledge indicators come from different sources.
- p Proportion of orphans (10-14 years) attending school is based on 25-49 cases.
- * Data refer to the most recent year available during the period specified in the column heading.

Countries and territories	Adult literacy rate 1990 male	Adult literacy rate 1990 female	Adult literacy rate 2000 male	Adult literacy rate 2000 female	Number per 100 population 2002 phones	Number per 100 population 2002 Internet users	Primary school enrolment ratio 1998-2002* (gross) male	Primary school enrolment ratio 1998-2002* (gross) female	Primary school enrolment ratio 1998-2002* (net) male	Primary school enrolment ratio 1998-2002* (net) female	Net primary school attendance (%) (1996-2003*) male	Net primary school attendance (%) (1996-2003*) female	% of primary school entrants reaching grade 5 Admin. data 1998-2001*	% of primary school entrants reaching grade 5 Survey data 1997-2003	Secondary school enrolment ratio 1998-2002* (gross) male	Secondary school enrolment ratio 1998-2002* (gross) female
Afghanistan	40	12	51	21	0	-	44	-	42x	15x	67	40	49	-	24	-
Albania	87	67	92	77	35	0	107	107	97	97	-	-	90y	-	77	80
Algeria	64	41	76	57	7	2	112	104	96	94	92	90	96	95	69	74
Andorra	-	-	-	-	80x	9x	-	-	-	-	-	-	-	-	-	-
Angola	-	-	-	-	2	0	80	69	32	28	57	58	4	76	21	17
Antigua and Barbuda	90	87	80x	83x	98	13	-	-	-	-	-	-	-	-	-	-
Argentina	96	96	97	97	40	11	120	119	100	100	93	93	93	78	97	103
Armenia	99	96	99	98	16	2	97	95	85	84	97	97	-	100	84	89
Australia	-	-	-	-	118	48	102	102	96	96	-	-	99x	-	155	153
Austria	-	-	-	-	128	41	104	103	90	91	-	-	94y	-	100	97
Azerbaijan	99	96	99x	96x	22	4	93	92	81	79	88	88	97y	99	81	79
Bahamas	94	95	95	96	80	19	92	93	85	88	-	-	78x	-	90	93
Bahrain	87	75	91	83	84	25	98	98	91	91	85	84	99	99	91	99
Bangladesh	44	24	49	30	1	0	97	98	86	88	81	84	65	86	45	49
Barbados	99	99	100	100	86	11	108	108	100	100	-	-	95	-	103	103
Belarus	100	99	100	100	35	8	111	109	95	93	-	-	72y	-	82	86
Belgium	-	-	-	-	128	33	106	105	100	100	-	-	-	-	146	163
Belize	90	88	93	93	30	11	119	116	96	96	-	-	81	-	68	74
Benin	38	16	52	24	4	1	122	86	84	58	61	47	84	92	35	16
Bhutan	51	23	61	34	3	1	82	62	58	47	-	-	91	-	7x	2x
Bolivia	87	70	92	79	17	3	114	113	94	94	93	91	78	96	86	83
Bosnia and Herzegovina	92	85	98x	89x	43	3	100	100	100	100	87	85	-	99	-	-
Botswana	66	70	75	80	33	3x	103	103	79	83	82	85	89	96	70	75
Brazil	83	81	87	87	42	8	153	144	96	97	95y	95y	80y	84x	102	113
Brunei Darussalam	91	79	95	88	66x	10x	107	106	90x	91x	-	-	93	-	85	91
Bulgaria	98	96	99	98	70	8	103	100	94	92	-	-	95y	-	94	91
Burkina Faso	25	8	34	14	1	0	51	36	41	29	32	22	64	81	12	8
Burundi	48	27	56	40	1	0	80	62	59	48	49	44	64	80	12	9
Cambodia	78	49	80	57	3	0	130	116	89	83	66	65	70	93	27	16
Cameroon	69	48	79	64	5	0	115	99	81x	71x	76	71	81	93	36	29
Canada	-	-	-	-	101	51	99	100	100	100	-	-	99x	-	107	106
Cape Verde	76	54	85	66	26	4	125	120	100	99	97	96	93	-	64	67
Central African Republic	47	21	60	35	1	0	79	53	64	45	47	39	24x	71	15x	6x
Chad	37	19	52	34	1	0	90	57	70	47	46	33	45	96	17	5
Chile	94	94	96	96	66	24	104	101	89	88	-	-	100	-	85	86
China	87	69	92	78	33	5	114	114	92	93	-	-	99	-	69	64
Colombia	89	88	92	92	29	5	110	109	87	86	90	90	61	87	62	69
Comoros	61	46	63	49	1	0	98	81	59	50	31	30	77	24	30	25
Congo	77	58	88	74	7	0	88	83	99x	93x	-	-	55x	-	37	27
Congo, Democratic Republic of the	61	34	73	50	1	0	52	47	35	34	55	48	64x	54	24	13
Cook Islands	-	-	-	-	43	20	98	93	86	83	-	-	51	-	58	63
Costa Rica	94	94	96	96	36	19	108	108	90	91	-	-	94	-	66	68
Côte d'Ivoire	51	26	60	37	8	1	92	68	72	53	62	52	69	94	30	16
Croatia	99	95	99	97	95	18	96	95	89	88	-	-	100y	-	88	89
Cuba	95	95	97	97	5x	1x	102	98	96	95	-	-	95	99	90	89
Cyprus	98	91	99	95	127	29	97	97	95	95	-	-	99	-	93	94
Czech Republic	-	-	-	-	121	26	104	103	88	88	-	-	97	-	95	97
Denmark	-	-	-	-	152	51	102	102	99	99	-	-	100	-	125	131
Djibouti	67	40	76	54	4	1	46	35	38	30	73y	62y	86	-	24	15
Dominica	-	-	-	-	42	16	102	97	93	90	-	-	85	-	89	102
Dominican Republic	80	79	84	84	32	4	125	127	99	95	81	84	66	93	60	75
Ecuador	90	85	93	90	23	4	117	117	99	100	90	90	78	-	59	59
Egypt	60	34	67	44	18	3	100	94	92	88	87	83	99	99	91	85
El Salvador	76	69	82	76	24	5	114	109	89	89	-	-	67	-	56	56
Equatorial Guinea	86	61	93	74	8	0	132	120	91	78	60	61	33	75	38	22
Eritrea	59	35	67	45	1	0	67	54	46	39	63	59	69y	74	33	22
Estonia	100	100	100	100	100	33	105	101	98	97	-	-	99	-	109	111
Ethiopia	37	20	47	31	1	0	75	53	52	41	33	28	61	65	23	15
Fiji	92	86	95	91	23	6	109	109	100	100	-	-	88	-	78	83

	Adult literacy rate				Number per 100 population 2002		Primary school enrolment ratio				Net primary school attendance (%) (1996-2003*)		% of primary school entrants reaching grade 5		Secondary school enrolment ratio 1998-2002* (gross)	
	1990		2000				1998-2002* (gross)		1998-2002* (net)				Admin. data	Survey data		
	male	female	male	female	phones	Internet users	male	female	male	female	male	female	1998-2001*	1997-2003	male	female
Finland	-	-	-	-	139	51	102	101	100	100	-	-	100	-	120	133
France	-	-	-	-	122	31	106	104	100	100	-	-	98	-	107	108
Gabon	68	45	80	62	24	2	135	134	79	78	94	93	59x	91	49	42
Gambia	32	20	44	30	10	2	82	75	76	70	54	49	70	98	40	28
Georgia	100	98	100x	99x	23	1	92	92	91	91	99	100	94y	-	76	82
Germany	-	-	-	-	138	41	101	100	82	84	-	-	100y	-	100	99
Ghana	70	47	80	63	3	1	85	78	61	59	74	74	66	93	41	34
Greece	98	92	99	96	134	15	97	96	94	95	-	-	100x	-	95	97
Grenada	-	-	-	-	39	14	97	92	89	80	-	-	-	-	-	-
Guatemala	69	53	76	61	20	3	107	99	87	83	79	75	56	72	41	38
Guinea	45	18	55	27	2	0	88	66	69	54	57	51	84	97	20	7
Guinea-Bissau	42	13	54	24	1	0	84	56	53	38	44	38	38	85	23	13
Guyana	98	96	99	98	19	14	122	118	100	97	88	88	95	97	86	89
Haiti	43	37	52	48	3	1	153	155	78	83	52	57	41x	88	21x	20x
Holy See	-	-	-	-	-	-	-	-	-	-	-	-	-	-	-	-
Honduras	69	67	75	75	10	3	105	107	87	88	-	-	58x	-	29x	37x
Hungary	99	99	100	99	104	16	102	100	91	90	-	-	98y	-	103	104
Iceland	-	-	-	-	156	65	101	101	100	100	-	-	99	-	104	111
India	62	36	68	45	5	2	107	90	91	76	80	73	59	92	56	40
Indonesia	87	73	92	82	9	4	112	110	93	92	88	87	89	97	58	58
Iran (Islamic Republic of)	72	54	83	69	22	5	94	90	80	78	94	91	94	-	79	75
Iraq	51	20	55	23	3	0	109	89	98	83	83	70	66	88	47	29
Ireland	-	-	-	-	127	27	104	104	94	95	-	-	98	-	100	109
Israel	95	88	97	93	141	30	114	113	100	100	-	-	99	-	95	94
Italy	98	97	99	98	142	35	101	100	100	100	-	-	96	-	97	95
Jamaica	78	86	83	91	70	23	101	100	95	95	77	80	90	92	82	85
Japan	-	-	-	-	119	45	101	101	100	100	-	-	100x	-	102	103
Jordan	90	72	95	84	36	6	98	99	91	92	89	90	98	-	85	87
Kazakhstan	100	98	100	99	19	2	100	99	90	89	96	96	95y	99	90	88
Kenya	81	61	89	76	5	1	97	95	69	71	71	73	71	88	34	30
Kiribati	-	-	-	-	6	2	130	132	-	-	-	-	95x	-	-	-
Korea, Democratic People's Republic of	98	93	99	96	2	0x	108x	101x	-	-	-	-	100	-	-	-
Korea, Republic of	98	93	99	96	117	55	102	102	100	100	-	-	100	-	91	91
Kuwait	79	73	84	80	72	11	95	94	85	84	-	-	99y	-	83	88
Kyrgyzstan	-	-	-	-	9	3	102	99	92	88	95y	94y	91y	100	86	87
Lao People's Democratic Republic	70	43	76	53	2	0	123	106	86	79	64	59	62	93	47	34
Latvia	100	100	100	100	69	13	99	98	91	90	-	-	98y	-	92	93
Lebanon	88	73	92	80	43	12	105	101	90	89	97	96	94	95	74	81
Lesotho	65	90	73	94	6	1	123	125	81	88	62	68	67	89	30	38
Liberia	55	23	70	37	0x	0x	122	89	79	61	59x,y	53x,y	33	-	40	28
Libyan Arab Jamahiriya	83	51	91	68	13x	2	114	114	97x	96x	-	-	89x	-	102	108
Liechtenstein	-	-	-	-	92	58	-	-	-	-	-	-	-	-	-	-
Lithuania	100	99	100	100	75	14	105	104	98	97	-	-	99y	-	99	98
Luxembourg	-	-	-	-	186	37	101	100	96	96	-	-	99	-	93	99
Madagascar	66	50	74	60	1	0	106	102	68	69	60	63	34	40	15	14
Malawi	69	36	75	47	2	0	149	143	81	81	79	80	54	79	39	29
Malaysia	87	74	91	83	57	32	95	95	95	95	-	-	97y	-	66	73
Maldives	95	95	97	97	25	5	125	124	96	96	-	-	98	-	64	68
Mali	28	10	36	16	1	0	65	49	44	32	44	33	84	94	18	9
Malta	88	89	91	93	122	30	106	106	98	98	-	-	99	-	91	89
Marshall Islands	-	-	-	-	9	2	103	98	100	91	-	-	-	-	-	-
Mauritania	46	24	51	30	10	0	88	85	68	65	46	42	55	83	25	19
Mauritius	85	75	88	81	56	10	106	106	93	93	-	-	99	-	81	78
Mexico	91	84	93	89	40	10	111	110	99	100	97	97	90	-	73	78
Micronesia (Federated States of)	63	63	66	67	9x	5	136	149	-	-	-	-	-	-	-	-
Moldova, Republic of	99	96	100	98	24	3	86	85	79	78	86	87	90y	99	71	73
Monaco	-	-	-	-	150	49	-	-	-	-	-	-	98x	-	-	-
Mongolia	99	97	99	98	14	2	97	100	85	88	76	77	89y	95	69	83
Morocco	53	25	62	36	25	2	113	101	92	85	67x,y	50x,y	84	82x	45	36

TABLE 5. EDUCATION

	Adult literacy rate				Number per 100 population 2002		Primary school enrolment ratio				Net primary school attendance (%) (1996-2003*)		% of primary school entrants reaching grade 5		Secondary school enrolment ratio 1998-2002* (gross)	
	1990		2000				1998-2002* (gross)		1998-2002* (net)				Admin. data	Survey data		
	male	female	male	female	phones	Internet users	male	female	male	female	male	female	1998-2001*	1997-2003	male	female
Mozambique	49	18	60	29	2	0	110	87	63	56	68	64	52	55	16	10
Myanmar	87	74	89	81	1	0	90	90	82	82	83	85	60	78	41	38
Namibia	77	72	83	81	14	3	106	106	76	81	77	78	94	95	57	65
Nauru	-	-	-	-	29x	3x	80	82	80	82	-	-	-	-	52	56
Nepal	47	14	59	24	2	0	130	113	75	66	79	66	78	92	50	37
Netherlands	-	-	-	-	136	51	109	107	100	99	-	-	100	-	126	122
New Zealand	-	-	-	-	107	48	99	99	99	98	-	-	97x	-	109	118
Nicaragua	61	61	64	64	7	2	104	105	82	82	75	80	54	87	52	61
Niger	18	5	24	9	0	0	47	32	41	28	36	25	71	89	8	5
Nigeria	59	38	72	56	2	0	107	86	38x	33x	64	57	80x	95	33x	28x
Niue	77	76	80	83	81x	53	121	114	100	94	-	-	76	-	95	93
Norway	-	-	-	-	158	50	101	102	100	100	-	-	100x	-	113	116
Occupied Palestinian Territory	-	-	-	-	18	3	104	105	95	95	91	92	98y	99	82	88
Oman	67	38	80	62	28	7	84	82	74	75	-	-	96	-	79	78
Pakistan	49	20	57	28	3	1	84	62	76	57	62	51	50x	91	29	19
Palau	-	-	-	-	-	-	120	112	100	93	-	-	84	-	89	89
Panama	90	88	93	91	31	4x	112	108	99	99	-	-	89	-	67	72
Papua New Guinea	64	48	71	57	1	1	77	78	82	73	32y	31y	60	-	25	20
Paraguay	92	88	94	92	34	2	114	110	91	92	87x	87x	77	90x	63	64
Peru	92	79	95	85	15	9	120	120	100	100	93	93	86	97	92	86
Philippines	92	91	95	95	23	4	113	111	92	94	80	83	79	89	78	86
Poland	100	100	100	100	55x	23	100	99	98	98	-	-	99	-	105	101
Portugal	91	84	95	90	125	19	122	120	100	100	-	-	97x	-	111	117
Qatar	92	92	94	94	72	11	108	104	95	94	-	-	88	-	88	93
Romania	99	96	99	97	43	10	100	98	93	92	-	-	94y	-	82	83
Russian Federation	100	99	100	99	36	4	114	113	93x	93x	-	-	-	-	92	92
Rwanda	63	44	74	60	2	0	118	116	83	85	75	75	40	78	15	14
Saint Kitts and Nevis	-	-	-	-	61	21	112	123	91	100	-	-	-	-	107	153
Saint Lucia	-	-	-	-	41	8x	111	112	100	98	-	-	97	-	75	97
Saint Vincent and the Grenadines	-	-	-	-	32	6	103	99	92	92	-	-	85	-	62	74
Samoa	99	97	99	98	8	2	104	101	96	94	-	-	94	-	71	79
San Marino	-	-	-	-	138	53	-	-	-	-	-	-	100x	-	-	-
Sao Tome and Principe	-	-	-	-	5	7	130	122	100	94	67	69	61	71	42	36
Saudi Arabia	76	50	83	67	38	6	68	66	61	57	-	-	94	-	73	65
Senegal	38	19	47	28	8	1	79	72	61	54	51	44	68	93	22	15
Serbia and Montenegro	97x	88x	99x	97x	49	6	99	99	75	75	98y	96y	100x	94	88	89
Seychelles	-	-	-	-	82	15	116	115	100	99	-	-	91	-	107	113
Sierra Leone	40	14	51	23	2	0	93	65	68	63	43	39	-	94	31	22
Singapore	94	83	96	88	126	50	95x	93x	93x	92x	-	-	100x	-	70x	77x
Slovakia	100	100	100	100	81	16	102	101	86	88	-	-	98y	-	89	90
Slovenia	100	100	100	100	134	38	101	100	94	93	-	-	100y	-	105	107
Solomon Islands	-	-	-	-	2	1	104x	90x	-	-	-	-	81x	-	21x	14x
Somalia	-	-	-	-	1	1	18x	9x	13x	7x	12	10	-	79	10x	6x
South Africa	82	80	86	85	41	7	107	103	89	90	86	84	65	99	83	90
Spain	98	95	99	97	133	16	108	106	100	99	-	-	98x	-	112	119
Sri Lanka	93	85	94	89	10	1	111	110	100	100	-	-	97x	-	72	77
Sudan	60	32	69	46	3	0	63	54	50	42	54	51	84	73	34	30
Suriname	94	89	96	93	39	4	127	125	97	98	88	91	99x	84	62	86
Swaziland	74	70	81	79	10	2	103	98	76	77	71	71	74	94	45	45
Sweden	-	-	-	-	162	57	109	112	100	100	-	-	97x	-	132	160
Switzerland	-	-	-	-	153	35	108	107	99	99	-	-	99	-	103	96
Syrian Arab Republic	82	48	88	60	15	1	115	108	100	95	-	-	92	-	47	42
Tajikistan	99	97	100	99	4	0	109	104	100	95	79	81	97y	94	90	74
Tanzania, United Republic of	76	51	84	67	3	0	70	69	54	54	47	51	78	96	6	5
Thailand	95	90	97	94	37	8	100	96	87	85	-	-	94	-	85	81
The former Yugoslav Republic of Macedonia	96	91	97	94	45	5	99	99	93	93	-	-	97y	-	86	83
Timor-Leste	-	-	-	-	-	-	-	-	-	-	65	63	-	-	-	-
Togo	61	29	72	43	5	4	136	112	100	84	67	59	84	88	51	22
Tonga	-	-	-	-	15	3	114	111	100	100	-	-	83	-	94	106

	Adult literacy rate				Number per 100 population 2002		Primary school enrolment ratio				Net primary school attendance (%) (1996-2003*)		% of primary school entrants reaching grade 5		Secondary school enrolment ratio 1998-2002* (gross)	
	1990		2000		phones	Internet users	1998-2002* (gross)		1998-2002* (net)				Admin. data	Survey data		
	male	female	male	female			male	female	male	female	male	female	1998-2001*	1997-2003	male	female
Trinidad and Tobago	98	96	99	98	53	11	106	104	94	94	94	95	98	100	80	85
Tunisia	72	47	81	61	18	5	114	109	97	97	95y	93y	95	-	78	81
Turkey	89	66	93	77	63	7	98	91	91	85	73	69	99x	98	86	66
Turkmenistan	-	-	-	-	8	0x	-	-	-	-	86	84	-	-	-	-
Tuvalu	-	-	-	-	7x	13	106	101	100	96	-	-	96x	-	83	73
Uganda	69	44	78	57	2	0	139	134	100	100	87	87	45	89	19	15
Ukraine	100	99	100	100	30	2	91	90	82	81	-	-	98x	-	97	97
United Arab Emirates	71	71	75	79	94	31	94	90	82	80	-	-	97	-	77	82
United Kingdom	-	-	-	-	143	42	101	101	100	100	-	-	-	-	146	170
United States	-	-	-	-	113	55	98	99	92	93	-	-	99x	-	94	92
Uruguay	96	97	97	98	47	12x	109	107	89	90	-	-	89	-	95	108
Uzbekistan	100	98	100	99	7	1	103	102	87	89	78	78	-	89	100	97
Vanuatu	-	-	-	-	6	3	112	111	92	94	-	-	95	-	28	29
Venezuela	90	88	93	92	37	5	107	105	92	93	93	94	96	96	64	74
Viet Nam	94	87	95	91	7	2	107	100	98	92	87	86	89	94	72	67
Yemen	55	13	68	25	5	1	97	64	71	47	67	40	86	88	65	27
Zambia	79	59	85	72	2	0	81	76	66	66	67	67	77	88	27	21
Zimbabwe	87	75	93	85	6	4	100	98	82	83	84	86	73	94	45	40

SUMMARY INDICATORS

Sub-Saharan Africa	60	40	69	53	5	1	92	80	64	59	60	56	63	83	29	23
Middle East and North Africa	66	39	74	52	18	3	96	87	82	76	82	76	91	91	69	63
South Asia	59	34	66	42	4	2	102	88	88	75	78	71	60	91	51	39
East Asia and Pacific	88	72	93	81	30	6	111	110	92	92	-	-	94	-	68	64
Latin America and Caribbean	87	83	90	88	36	8	122	119	95	95	92	92	82	-	83	89
CEE/CIS	98	94	98	95	38	5	101	98	89	86	79	77	-	96	90	85
Industrialized countries	-	-	-	-	123	43	101	101	95	96	-	-	-	-	105	106
Developing countries	76	58	81	66	20	4	105	96	86	80	76	72	78	89	60	54
Least developed countries	54	32	62	42	2	0	88	80	67	61	61	56	64	79	30	25
World	82	69	85	74	36	10	104	97	87	82	76	72	79	89	66	61

Countries in each category are listed on page 140.

DEFINITIONS OF THE INDICATORS

Adult literacy rate – Percentage of persons aged 15 and over who can read and write.

Gross primary school enrolment ratio – The number of children enrolled in a primary level, regardless of age, divided by the population of the age group that officially corresponds to the same level.

Gross secondary school enrolment ratio – The number of children enrolled in a secondary level, regardless of age, divided by the population of the age group that officially corresponds to the same level.

Net primary school enrolment ratio – The number of children enrolled in primary school who belong to the age group that officially corresponds to primary schooling, divided by the total population of the same age group.

Net primary school attendance – Percentage of children in the age group that officially corresponds to primary schooling who attend primary school. These data come from national household surveys.

Primary school entrants reaching grade five – Percentage of the children entering the first grade of primary school who eventually reach grade five.

MAIN DATA SOURCES

Adult literacy – UNESCO Institute for Statistics, including the Education for All 2000 Assessment.

Phone and Internet use – International Telecommunications Union, Yearbook of Statistics 2002.

Primary and secondary school enrolment – UNESCO Institute for Statistics, including the Education for All 2000 Assessment.

Net primary school attendance – Demographic and Health Surveys (DHS) and Multiple Indicator Cluster Surveys (MICS).

Reaching grade five – Administrative data: UNESCO Institute for Statistics, including the Education for All 2000 Assessment. Survey data: DHS and MICS.

NOTES

- \- Data not available.
- x Indicates data that refer to years or periods other than those specified in the column heading, differ from the standard definition or refer to only part of a country.
- y Indicates data that differ from the standard definition or refer to only part of a country, but are included in the calculation of regional and global averages.
- * Data refer to the most recent year available during the period specified in the column heading.

TABLE 6. DEMOGRAPHIC INDICATORS

Countries and territories	Population (thousands) 2003		Population annual growth rate (%)		Crude death rate		Crude birth rate		Life expectancy		Total fertility rate 2003	% of population urbanized 2003	Average annual growth rate of urban population (%)	
	under 18	under 5	1970-90	1990-2003	1970	2003	1970	2003	1970	2003			1970-90	1990-2003
Afghanistan	11910	4183	0.4	4.2	26	22	51	48	38	43	6.8	23	2.9	6.1
Albania	1062	276	2.2	-0.3	8	5	33	18	67	74	2.3	44	2.8	1.2
Algeria	12606	3349	3.0	1.8	16	5	49	23	53	70	2.8	59	4.3	2.9
Andorra	13	3	5.1	2.3	-	-	-	-	-	-	-	92	5.0	2.1
Angola	7386	2706	2.6	2.9	27	24	49	52	37	40	7.2	36	5.4	5.3
Antigua and Barbuda	25	7	-0.2	1.1	-	-	-	-	-	-	-	38	0.0	1.6
Argentina	12384	3540	1.5	1.3	9	8	23	19	66	74	2.4	90	2.0	1.6
Armenia	807	146	1.7	-1.1	5	8	23	10	72	72	1.1	64	2.3	-1.4
Australia	4740	1237	1.5	1.2	9	7	20	12	71	79	1.7	92	1.5	1.8
Austria	1581	372	0.2	0.4	13	10	15	8	70	79	1.3	66	0.2	0.4
Azerbaijan	2991	690	1.6	1.2	7	6	29	18	68	72	2.1	50	2.0	0.6
Bahamas	108	30	2.0	1.6	7	8	30	19	66	67	2.3	89	2.8	2.1
Bahrain	244	71	4.0	3.0	9	3	40	20	62	74	2.6	90	4.2	3.2
Bangladesh	65342	19408	2.5	2.3	21	8	46	29	44	62	3.4	24	7.3	3.8
Barbados	65	16	0.4	0.4	9	8	22	12	69	77	1.5	52	0.8	1.5
Belarus	2120	426	0.6	-0.3	8	13	16	9	71	70	1.2	71	2.7	0.3
Belgium	2127	559	0.2	0.3	12	10	14	11	71	79	1.7	97	0.3	0.3
Belize	113	33	2.1	2.5	8	5	40	27	66	71	3.1	48	1.8	2.5
Benin	3533	1168	2.7	2.9	25	14	53	41	42	51	5.6	45	6.3	4.8
Bhutan	1088	345	2.4	2.2	22	9	42	35	42	63	5.0	9	5.2	5.6
Bolivia	3967	1194	2.3	2.1	20	8	46	29	46	64	3.8	63	4.0	3.2
Bosnia and Herzegovina	902	203	0.9	-0.3	7	8	23	10	66	74	1.3	44	2.8	0.7
Botswana	838	248	3.3	2.1	13	23	49	30	55	39	3.7	52	11.5	3.6
Brazil	60357	16663	2.2	1.4	11	7	35	20	59	68	2.2	83	3.6	2.2
Brunei Darussalam	127	39	3.4	2.6	7	3	36	23	67	76	2.5	76	3.7	3.7
Bulgaria	1449	305	0.1	-0.8	9	15	16	8	71	71	1.1	70	1.4	-0.4
Burkina Faso	7264	2560	2.5	2.9	25	17	53	48	40	46	6.7	18	6.8	5.0
Burundi	3675	1199	2.3	1.5	20	21	44	45	44	41	6.8	10	7.2	5.0
Cambodia	6976	2107	1.7	2.9	19	10	42	34	43	57	4.7	19	2.1	5.9
Cameroon	7868	2443	2.8	2.4	21	17	46	35	44	46	4.6	51	6.2	4.3
Canada	6942	1663	1.2	1.0	7	8	16	10	73	79	1.5	80	1.3	1.4
Cape Verde	217	61	1.3	2.2	12	5	40	28	56	70	3.3	56	5.4	4.0
Central African Republic	1928	619	2.3	2.1	22	22	42	38	42	40	4.9	43	3.4	3.1
Chad	4587	1646	2.3	3.0	27	20	48	49	38	45	6.6	25	5.2	4.3
Chile	5163	1419	1.6	1.4	10	6	29	18	62	76	2.3	87	2.1	1.8
China	369191	92555	1.6	0.9	8	7	33	14	61	71	1.8	39	3.9	3.6
Colombia	16599	4737	2.2	1.8	9	5	38	22	61	72	2.6	76	3.2	2.6
Comoros	377	124	3.3	2.9	18	8	50	37	48	61	4.8	35	5.1	4.7
Congo	2001	694	3.2	3.1	14	15	44	44	54	48	6.3	53	5.1	3.9
Congo, Democratic Republic of the	28334	10220	3.0	2.7	20	21	48	50	45	42	6.7	32	2.6	3.6
Cook Islands	8	2	-0.6	0.0	-	-	-	-	-	-	-	70	-0.2	1.5
Costa Rica	1501	393	2.6	2.3	7	4	33	19	67	78	2.3	61	4.2	3.3
Côte d'Ivoire	8114	2492	4.1	2.2	20	20	51	35	44	41	4.7	45	6.0	3.1
Croatia	909	241	0.7	-0.7	10	12	15	11	69	74	1.7	59	2.2	0.0
Cuba	2747	671	1.1	0.5	7	7	30	12	69	77	1.6	76	2.1	0.7
Cyprus	213	52	0.5	1.3	10	8	19	13	71	78	1.9	69	2.8	1.7
Czech Republic	1951	441	0.2	-0.1	13	11	16	9	70	76	1.2	74	2.1	-0.1
Denmark	1169	323	0.2	0.3	10	11	16	12	73	77	1.8	85	0.5	0.4
Djibouti	347	116	6.1	2.2	24	18	50	39	40	46	5.6	84	7.5	3.0
Dominica	27	7	0.1	0.7	-	-	-	-	-	-	-	72	1.9	1.1
Dominican Republic	3358	954	2.3	1.6	11	7	42	23	58	67	2.7	59	3.9	2.2
Ecuador	5061	1422	2.7	1.8	12	6	42	23	58	71	2.7	62	4.4	2.7
Egypt	29856	8702	2.3	2.0	17	6	40	27	51	69	3.3	42	2.4	1.7
El Salvador	2655	789	1.8	1.9	12	6	44	25	57	71	2.9	60	2.9	3.3
Equatorial Guinea	248	87	0.9	2.6	23	17	39	43	40	49	5.9	48	2.2	5.1
Eritrea	2163	717	2.6	2.2	21	12	47	40	43	53	5.4	20	4.1	4.0
Estonia	276	57	0.7	-1.4	11	14	15	9	70	72	1.2	69	1.2	-1.6
Ethiopia	36987	12453	2.6	2.8	23	18	49	42	41	46	6.1	16	4.6	4.4
Fiji	321	95	1.6	1.1	8	6	34	23	60	70	2.9	52	2.5	2.8

	Population (thousands) 2003		Population annual growth rate (%)		Crude death rate		Crude birth rate		Life expectancy		Total fertility rate 2003	% of population urbanized 2003	Average annual growth rate of urban population (%)	
	under 18	under 5	1970-90	1990-2003	1970	2003	1970	2003	1970	2003			1970-90	1990-2003
Finland	1111	284	0.4	0.3	10	10	14	11	70	78	1.7	61	1.4	0.3
France	13493	3797	0.6	0.4	11	9	17	13	72	79	1.9	76	0.8	0.7
Gabon	630	191	2.9	2.6	21	12	35	31	47	57	3.9	84	6.9	4.2
Gambia	669	221	3.5	3.2	28	13	50	36	36	54	4.7	26	6.0	3.6
Georgia	1202	270	0.7	-0.5	9	10	19	10	68	74	1.4	52	1.5	-0.9
Germany	15226	3750	0.1	0.3	12	11	14	9	71	78	1.4	88	0.4	0.5
Ghana	9780	2978	2.9	2.4	17	10	48	32	49	58	4.1	45	4.0	4.1
Greece	1966	508	0.7	0.6	8	11	17	9	72	78	1.3	61	1.3	0.8
Grenada	27	7	-0.4	-0.5	-	-	-	-	-	-	-	41	-0.4	1.3
Guatemala	6116	1935	2.6	2.6	15	7	45	34	52	66	4.4	46	3.3	3.6
Guinea	4283	1471	2.3	2.5	28	16	51	43	37	49	5.8	35	5.3	5.0
Guinea-Bissau	800	292	2.8	3.0	29	20	49	50	36	45	7.1	34	5.0	5.7
Guyana	271	79	0.2	0.4	11	9	38	22	60	63	2.3	38	0.8	1.3
Haiti	3853	1127	2.1	1.4	19	15	39	30	47	50	3.9	37	4.1	3.3
Holy See	-	-	-	-	-	-	-	-	-	-	-	100	-	-
Honduras	3263	980	3.2	2.7	15	6	49	30	52	69	3.7	46	4.8	3.7
Hungary	1955	452	0.0	-0.4	11	14	15	9	69	72	1.2	65	1.2	0.0
Iceland	78	21	1.1	1.0	7	7	21	14	74	80	1.9	93	1.4	1.2
India	414965	118568	2.1	1.8	17	8	40	24	49	64	3.0	28	3.4	2.6
Indonesia	77966	21636	2.1	1.4	17	7	41	21	48	67	2.3	46	5.0	4.5
Iran (Islamic Republic of)	27281	6205	3.4	1.5	14	5	43	21	54	70	2.3	67	4.9	2.8
Iraq	12039	3834	3.1	2.9	16	9	49	35	55	61	4.7	67	4.2	2.6
Ireland	1004	276	0.9	0.9	11	8	22	15	71	77	1.9	60	1.3	1.3
Israel	2110	630	2.2	2.7	7	6	27	20	71	79	2.7	92	2.6	2.8
Italy	9779	2573	0.3	0.1	10	11	17	9	72	79	1.2	67	0.4	0.2
Jamaica	967	263	1.2	0.9	8	6	35	20	68	76	2.3	52	2.3	1.0
Japan	22153	5947	0.8	0.3	7	8	19	9	72	82	1.3	65	1.7	0.5
Jordan	2412	734	3.5	4.0	16	4	50	28	54	71	3.5	79	4.7	4.7
Kazakhstan	4849	1142	1.2	-0.7	9	9	26	16	64	67	1.9	56	1.9	-0.8
Kenya	15809	4644	3.6	2.3	17	17	52	32	50	44	3.9	39	8.0	5.9
Kiribati	37	11	1.9	1.5	-	-	-	-	-	-	-	47	3.4	4.0
Korea, Democratic People's Republic of	6968	1822	1.6	1.0	9	11	34	16	61	63	2.0	61	2.0	1.3
Korea, Republic of	11565	2932	1.5	0.8	9	6	31	12	60	76	1.4	80	4.5	1.5
Kuwait	759	245	5.3	1.3	6	2	47	20	66	77	2.6	96	6.3	1.4
Kyrgyzstan	1981	529	2.0	1.2	11	7	31	22	62	69	2.6	34	2.0	0.4
Lao People's Democratic Republic	2740	867	2.1	2.4	23	12	45	35	40	55	4.7	21	4.5	4.7
Latvia	476	90	0.7	-1.2	11	14	14	8	70	71	1.1	66	1.3	-1.7
Lebanon	1279	337	0.5	2.3	11	5	35	19	64	74	2.2	87	2.2	2.7
Lesotho	857	244	2.1	1.1	17	27	42	31	49	35	3.8	18	5.6	1.4
Liberia	1802	643	2.2	3.5	22	22	50	50	42	41	6.8	47	4.6	4.3
Libyan Arab Jamahiriya	2097	600	3.9	2.0	16	4	50	23	52	73	3.0	86	6.7	2.5
Liechtenstein	7	2	1.6	1.2	-	-	-	-	-	-	-	22	1.7	1.5
Lithuania	807	174	0.9	-0.6	9	12	17	9	71	73	1.3	67	2.4	-0.7
Luxembourg	101	29	0.5	1.4	12	8	13	13	70	78	1.7	92	1.7	1.9
Madagascar	8873	3054	2.7	2.9	21	13	46	41	44	54	5.6	27	5.3	3.8
Malawi	6386	2250	3.7	1.9	24	24	56	44	40	38	6.1	16	7.0	4.5
Malaysia	9427	2714	2.5	2.4	10	5	37	22	61	73	2.9	64	4.5	4.3
Maldives	158	51	2.9	3.0	17	6	40	36	50	68	5.3	29	6.1	3.8
Mali	7322	2581	2.4	2.8	26	16	52	50	38	49	7.0	32	4.9	5.1
Malta	92	23	0.9	0.7	9	8	17	12	70	78	1.8	92	1.5	1.0
Marshall Islands	22	6	3.7	1.4	-	-	-	-	-	-	-	66	3.8	1.5
Mauritania	1430	499	2.4	2.7	21	14	46	42	42	53	5.8	62	8.2	5.3
Mauritius	364	98	1.2	1.1	7	7	28	16	62	72	1.9	43	1.0	1.6
Mexico	39800	11145	2.5	1.7	10	5	45	22	61	74	2.5	75	3.5	2.0
Micronesia (Federated States of)	50	14	2.3	1.0	9	6	40	28	62	69	3.8	29	2.7	1.8
Moldova, Republic of	1116	239	1.0	-0.2	10	11	18	12	65	69	1.4	46	2.9	-0.3
Monaco	7	2	1.2	1.1	-	-	-	-	-	-	-	100	1.2	1.1
Mongolia	1024	265	2.8	1.2	14	7	42	22	53	64	2.4	57	4.0	1.2
Morocco	11515	3287	2.4	1.7	17	6	47	23	52	69	2.7	57	4.0	3.0

TABLE 6. DEMOGRAPHIC INDICATORS

	Population (thousands) 2003		Population annual growth rate (%)		Crude death rate		Crude birth rate		Life expectancy		Total fertility rate 2003	% of population urbanized 2003	Average annual growth rate of urban population (%)	
	under 18	under 5	1970-90	1990-2003	1970	2003	1970	2003	1970	2003			1970-90	1990-2003
Mozambique	9563	3138	1.8	2.6	24	24	48	41	40	38	5.6	36	8.3	6.6
Myanmar	18759	5325	2.1	1.5	18	11	41	24	48	57	2.8	29	2.5	2.9
Namibia	989	305	2.8	2.6	18	19	45	33	48	44	4.5	32	4.6	4.2
Nauru	5	2	1.9	2.5	-	-	-	-	-	-	-	100	1.9	2.5
Nepal	11710	3688	2.2	2.3	22	10	42	33	42	60	4.2	15	6.3	6.3
Netherlands	3545	979	0.7	0.6	8	9	17	12	74	78	1.7	66	1.0	1.3
New Zealand	1042	272	0.9	1.1	9	8	22	14	71	78	2.0	86	1.1	1.2
Nicaragua	2644	814	2.9	2.7	14	5	48	31	54	70	3.7	57	3.5	3.3
Niger	6784	2549	3.1	3.4	28	19	56	55	37	46	8.0	22	6.3	5.9
Nigeria	63563	20872	2.9	2.8	22	14	48	39	43	51	5.4	47	5.6	5.0
Niue	1	0	-	-	-	-	-	-	-	-	-	-	-	-
Norway	1057	281	0.4	0.5	10	10	17	12	74	79	1.8	79	0.9	1.2
Occupied Palestinian Territory	1871	641	3.4	3.9	20	4	52	39	54	73	5.5	71	4.4	4.4
Oman	1233	409	4.5	3.3	17	3	50	32	50	73	4.9	78	13.0	5.1
Pakistan	73711	23528	2.9	2.5	18	10	43	36	48	61	5.0	34	3.9	3.3
Palau	9	2	1.5	2.3	-	-	-	-	-	-	-	69	2.3	2.2
Panama	1143	339	2.4	2.0	8	5	38	23	65	75	2.7	57	3.0	2.5
Papua New Guinea	2704	833	2.4	2.5	19	9	42	31	43	58	4.0	13	3.9	2.5
Paraguay	2653	803	2.9	2.6	9	5	37	30	65	71	3.8	57	4.3	3.8
Peru	10681	3030	2.5	1.7	14	6	42	23	53	70	2.8	74	3.4	2.2
Philippines	34124	9758	2.6	2.1	11	5	40	25	57	70	3.1	61	4.5	3.8
Poland	8537	1869	0.8	0.1	8	10	17	10	70	74	1.3	62	1.5	0.2
Portugal	2013	560	0.7	0.1	11	11	21	11	67	76	1.4	55	3.6	1.3
Qatar	189	56	7.2	2.0	13	4	35	17	60	72	3.2	92	7.5	2.3
Romania	4723	1138	0.7	-0.3	9	13	21	11	68	71	1.3	55	2.1	-0.1
Russian Federation	29723	6119	0.6	-0.3	9	15	15	9	70	67	1.1	73	1.4	-0.3
Rwanda	4377	1509	2.9	1.6	20	22	52	44	44	39	5.7	18	5.5	11.0
Saint Kitts and Nevis	14	4	-0.7	0.2	-	-	-	-	-	-	-	32	-0.7	-0.4
Saint Lucia	54	14	1.4	1.0	8	6	41	21	64	73	2.3	30	2.2	2.0
Saint Vincent and the Grenadines	45	12	1.0	0.7	11	6	41	20	61	74	2.2	58	3.0	3.4
Samoa	84	25	0.6	0.8	10	6	39	29	55	70	4.1	22	0.9	1.1
San Marino	5	1	0.9	1.4	-	-	-	-	-	-	-	89	2.9	1.2
Sao Tome and Principe	76	25	2.3	2.5	13	6	46	33	55	70	3.9	38	4.4	2.8
Saudi Arabia	10868	3542	5.3	2.9	19	4	48	32	52	72	4.5	88	7.7	3.8
Senegal	5058	1631	2.8	2.4	25	12	49	37	41	53	4.9	50	3.7	4.1
Serbia and Montenegro	2468	617	0.8	0.3	9	11	19	12	68	73	1.6	52	2.1	0.4
Seychelles	42	14	1.5	1.0	-	-	-	-	-	-	-	50	4.8	1.1
Sierra Leone	2518	903	2.1	1.6	30	29	49	49	34	34	6.5	39	4.8	3.6
Singapore	1048	242	1.9	2.6	5	5	23	10	69	78	1.3	100	1.9	2.6
Slovakia	1217	274	0.7	0.2	10	10	19	10	70	74	1.3	57	2.3	0.3
Slovenia	365	85	0.7	0.3	10	10	17	8	70	76	1.1	51	2.3	0.3
Solomon Islands	235	75	3.4	3.1	10	5	46	33	54	69	4.4	16	5.6	4.5
Somalia	5401	2020	3.4	2.5	24	18	50	52	40	48	7.2	35	4.7	3.8
South Africa	17770	4778	2.4	1.5	14	18	38	22	53	47	2.6	57	2.5	2.7
Spain	7136	1915	0.8	0.3	9	9	20	9	72	79	1.2	76	1.4	0.5
Sri Lanka	5734	1513	1.6	1.0	8	7	29	16	64	73	2.0	21	1.4	0.9
Sudan	15401	4900	2.7	2.3	22	12	48	33	43	56	4.3	39	5.1	5.2
Suriname	162	47	0.4	0.6	8	6	37	21	63	71	2.4	76	2.1	1.8
Swaziland	551	165	3.2	1.9	20	26	50	34	46	34	4.5	24	7.5	2.1
Sweden	1898	445	0.3	0.3	10	11	14	10	74	80	1.6	83	0.4	0.3
Switzerland	1390	333	0.5	0.4	9	10	16	9	73	79	1.4	68	1.6	0.3
Syrian Arab Republic	8012	2322	3.4	2.6	13	4	47	28	55	72	3.3	50	4.0	2.8
Tajikistan	2737	723	2.9	1.3	10	6	40	24	63	69	3.0	25	2.2	-0.6
Tanzania, United Republic of	19303	6189	3.2	2.7	20	18	50	39	45	43	5.1	35	9.1	6.5
Thailand	19183	5288	2.0	1.1	9	7	37	17	60	69	1.9	32	3.7	1.7
The former Yugoslav Republic of Macedonia	543	144	1.0	0.6	8	8	24	15	66	74	1.9	59	2.0	0.8
Timor-Leste	354	79	1.0	0.4	22	13	47	23	39	50	3.8	8	0.1	0.2
Togo	2479	811	2.7	2.7	20	15	47	38	44	50	5.3	35	6.6	4.3
Tonga	45	13	0.3	0.3	8	7	36	26	62	69	3.7	33	2.0	0.9

	Population (thousands) 2003		Population annual growth rate (%)		Crude death rate		Crude birth rate		Life expectancy		Total fertility rate 2003	% of population urbanized 2003	Average annual growth rate of urban population (%)	
	under 18	under 5	1970-90	1990-2003	1970	2003	1970	2003	1970	2003			1970-90	1990-2003
Trinidad and Tobago	374	86	1.1	0.5	7	7	27	14	66	71	1.6	75	1.6	1.2
Tunisia	3357	807	2.4	1.4	14	6	39	17	54	73	2.0	64	3.7	2.1
Turkey	25817	7096	2.3	1.6	13	6	39	21	56	71	2.4	66	4.5	2.5
Turkmenistan	1981	497	2.6	2.2	11	6	37	22	60	67	2.7	45	2.3	2.2
Tuvalu	4	1	2.1	1.4	-	-	-	-	-	-	-	55	5.4	3.7
Uganda	14724	5358	3.1	3.1	19	16	51	51	46	47	7.1	12	4.7	3.8
Ukraine	9983	2034	0.5	-0.5	9	14	15	8	71	70	1.2	67	1.5	-0.5
United Arab Emirates	905	246	11.0	3.0	12	2	39	16	61	75	2.8	85	11.2	3.2
United Kingdom	13275	3352	0.2	0.3	12	10	16	11	72	78	1.6	89	0.9	0.4
United States	75893	20794	1.0	1.1	9	8	17	15	71	77	2.1	80	1.1	1.6
Uruguay	993	283	0.5	0.7	10	9	21	17	69	75	2.3	93	0.9	1.0
Uzbekistan	10600	2691	2.7	1.8	10	6	37	21	63	70	2.4	37	3.1	1.2
Vanuatu	101	31	2.8	2.7	14	5	44	30	53	69	4.1	23	4.5	4.3
Venezuela	9943	2834	3.0	2.1	7	5	37	23	65	74	2.7	88	3.8	2.5
Viet Nam	30594	7685	2.2	1.6	18	6	41	20	49	69	2.3	26	2.7	3.4
Yemen	11129	3809	3.2	4.0	26	9	54	45	38	60	7.0	26	5.6	5.4
Zambia	5819	1919	3.3	2.1	17	28	51	42	49	33	5.6	36	4.6	1.4
Zimbabwe	6557	1890	3.5	1.6	13	28	49	32	55	33	3.9	35	6.1	3.0
SUMMARY INDICATORS														
Sub-Saharan Africa	340099	112679	2.8	2.5	21	18	48	40	44	46	5.4	36	4.8	4.4
Middle East and North Africa	153400	44212	3.0	2.2	17	6	45	27	51	67	3.4	57	4.4	2.9
South Asia	584618	171284	2.2	1.9	18	8	41	26	48	63	3.3	28	3.7	2.8
East Asia and Pacific	593672	154424	1.8	1.1	10	7	35	16	58	69	2.0	41	3.9	3.5
Latin America and Caribbean	197133	55677	2.2	1.6	11	6	37	22	60	70	2.5	77	3.3	2.2
CEE/CIS	107963	25526	1.0	0.2	9	11	21	13	66	70	1.6	63	2.0	0.2
Industrialized countries	206750	54425	0.7	0.6	10	9	17	12	71	78	1.7	76	1.1	0.9
Developing countries	1924210	552742	2.1	1.6	14	9	39	24	53	62	2.9	42	3.8	3.0
Least developed countries	355097	116936	2.5	2.5	22	15	47	39	43	49	5.1	27	4.9	4.4
World	2183635	618227	1.8	1.4	12	9	33	21	56	63	2.7	48	2.7	2.2

Countries in each category are listed on page 140.

DEFINITIONS OF THE INDICATORS

Life expectancy at birth – The number of years newborn children would live if subject to the mortality risks prevailing for the cross-section of population at the time of their birth.

Crude death rate – Annual number of deaths per 1,000 population.

Crude birth rate – Annual number of births per 1,000 population.

Total fertility rate – Number of children that would be born per woman if she were to live to the end of her childbearing years and bear children at each age in accordance with prevailing age-specific fertility rates.

Urban population – Percentage of population living in urban areas as defined according to the national definition used in the most recent population census.

MAIN DATA SOURCES

Child population – United Nations Population Division.

Crude death and birth rates – United Nations Population Division.

Life expectancy – United Nations Population Division.

Fertility – United Nations Population Division.

Urban population – United Nations Population Division.

NOTES - Data not available.

TABLE 7. ECONOMIC INDICATORS

Countries and territories	GNI per capita (US$) 2003	GDP per capita average annual growth rate (%)		Average annual rate of inflation (%) 1990-2003	% of population below $1 a day 1992-2002*	% of central government expenditure allocated to: (1992-2002*)			ODA inflow in millions US$ 2002	ODA inflow as a % of recipient GNI 2002	Debt service as a % of exports of goods and services	
		1960-90	1990-2003			health	education	defence			1990	2002
Afghanistan	250x	0.1x	-	-	-	-	-	-	1285	-	-	-
Albania	1740	-	5.1	29x	2	4	2	4	317	7	4x	3
Algeria	1890	2.4	0.6	15	2	4	24	17	361	1	62	19x
Andorra	d	-	-	-	-	-	-	-	-	-	-	-
Angola	740	-	0.4	518	-	6x	15x	34x	421	5	7	10
Antigua and Barbuda	9160	-	1.5	2x	-	-	-	-	14	2	-	-
Argentina	3650	0.6	1.1	5	3	2	6	4	151x	0x	30	13
Armenia	950	-	2.8	120	13	-	-	-	293	12	-	6
Australia	21650	2.0	2.5	2	-	14	9	6	-	-	-	-
Austria	26720	3.3	1.8	2	-	13	10	2	-	-	-	-
Azerbaijan	810	-	1.4x	65x	4	1	3	11	349	6	-	4
Bahamas	14920x	1.2	0.2x	3x	-	16	20	3	-	-	-	-
Bahrain	10840x	-	1.5x	0x	-	7	13	14	71	1	-	-
Bangladesh	400	0.2	3.1	4	36	5x	11x	10x	913	2	17	6
Barbados	9270	3.0	1.4	3x	-	-	-	-	3	0	14	4x
Belarus	1590	-	0.8	250	2	4	4	5	-	-	-	2
Belgium	25820	3.0	1.8	2	-	14	2	3	-	-	-	-
Belize	c	3.2	2.3x	1x	-	8	20	5	22	3	6	36
Benin	440	0.4	2.2	7	-	6x	31x	17x	220	9	7	8
Bhutan	660	-	3.7	9x	-	11	17	0	73	14	5	5
Bolivia	890	-0.3	1.0	7	14	9	24	6	681	9	31	26
Bosnia and Herzegovina	1540	-	15.4x	3x	-	-	-	-	587	11	-	6
Botswana	3430	8.7	2.2	9	24	5	26	8	38	1	4	2x
Brazil	2710	3.6	1.2	118	8	6	6	3	376	0	19	61
Brunei Darussalam	24100x	-1.8x	-0.7x	1x	-	-	-	-	-	-	-	-
Bulgaria	2130	-	0.6	75	5	11	5	7	-	-	5x	12
Burkina Faso	300	1.1	1.7	5	45	7	17	14	473	16	6	13
Burundi	100	2.0	-3.6	13	58	2	15	23	172	24	41	47
Cambodia	310	-	3.4x	4x	34	-	-	-	487	13	-	0
Cameroon	640	2.5	0.2	4	17	3	12	10	632	7	18	11x
Canada	23930	2.3x	2.2	2	-	1	2	6	-	-	-	-
Cape Verde	1490	-	3.4	4	-	-	-	-	92	16	5	7
Central African Republic	260	-0.6	-0.4	4	67	-	-	-	60	6	8	12x
Chad	250	-1.2	-0.1	7	-	8x	8x	-	233	13	2	7x
Chile	4390	1.2	4.1	7	2	13	19	8	-23	0	20	32
China	1100	5.5	8.5	5	17	0	2	12	1476	0	10	8
Colombia	1810	2.3	0.4	18	8	9	20	13	441	1	39	39
Comoros	450	-	-1.3	4	-	-	-	-	32	14	2	3x
Congo	640	2.8	-1.4	8	-	-	-	-	420	19	32	0
Congo, Democratic Republic of the	100	-1.4	-6.4	620	-	0	0	18	807	17	5	0x
Cook Islands	-	-	-	-	-	-	-	-	4	-	-	-
Costa Rica	4280	1.6	2.6	15	2	28	20	0	5	0	21	8
Côte d'Ivoire	660	1.0	-0.4	7	16	4x	21x	4x	1069	10	26	12
Croatia	5350	-	2.4	61x	2	16	8	5	166	1	-	25
Cuba	1170x	-	3.5x	1*	-	23x	10x	-	61	-	-	-
Cyprus	12320x	6.2x	3.2	3	-	6	12	4	-	-	-	-
Czech Republic	6740	-	1.5	10x	2	16	9	5	-	-	-	9
Denmark	33750	2.1	2.0	9	-	1	13	5	-	-	-	-
Djibouti	910	-	-3.3	3x	-	-	-	-	78	13	-	4x
Dominica	3360	-	1.2	3x	-	-	-	-	30	13	4	7
Dominican Republic	2070	3.0	4.0	9	2	11	16	4	157	1	7	6
Ecuador	1790	2.0	0.1	4	18	11x	18x	13x	216	1	27	26
Egypt	1390	3.5	2.5	7	3	3	15	9	1286	1	18	10
El Salvador	2200	-0.4	2.1	6	31	5	24	7	233	2	14	7
Equatorial Guinea	930x	-	20.9	14	-	-	-	-	13x	0x	3	0x
Eritrea	190	-	1.3x	10x	-	-	-	-	230	29	-	4
Estonia	4960	-	2.7	36	2	16	7	5	-	-	-	13
Ethiopia	90	-	1.9	5	26	6	16	9	1307	20	33	9
Fiji	2360	1.9	1.5	3x	-	9	18	6	34	2	12	6

	GNI per capita (US$) 2003	GDP per capita average annual growth rate (%) 1960-90	GDP per capita average annual growth rate (%) 1990-2003	Average annual rate of inflation (%) 1990-2003	% of population below $1 a day 1992-2002*	% of central government expenditure allocated to: (1992-2002*) health	education	defence	ODA inflow in millions US$ 2002	ODA inflow as a % of recipient GNI 2002	Debt service as a % of exports of goods and services 1990	2002
Finland	27020	3.4	2.5	2	-	3	10	4	-	-	-	-
France	24770	2.9	1.5	1	-	16x	7x	6x	-	-	-	-
Gabon	3580	3.1	-0.2	5	-	-	-	-	72	2	4	11
Gambia	310	1.1x	0.1	5	59	7x	12x	4x	61	14	18	3x
Georgia	830	3.9x	-2.7	225x	3	5	5	5	313	10	-	8
Germany	25250	2.2x	1.2	2	-	19	0	4	-	-	-	-
Ghana	320	-1.4	2.1	26	45	7	22	5	653	12	20	7
Greece	13720	3.5	2.4	7	-	7	11	8	-	-	-	-
Grenada	3790	-	2.3	2x	-	10	17	0	9	2	2	13
Guatemala	1910	1.4	1.1	9	16	11	17	11	249	1	11	7
Guinea	430	-	1.7	5	-	3x	11x	29x	250	8	18	12
Guinea-Bissau	140	-0.2x	-2.5	23	-	1x	3x	4x	59	32	21	40x
Guyana	900	-0.1	3.6	11x	2	-	-	-	65	10	-	9
Haiti	380	0.1	-2.8	20x	-	-	-	-	156	4	4	4x
Holy See	-	-	-	-	-	-	-	-	-	-	-	-
Honduras	970	1.2	0.2	16	24	10x	19x	7x	435	7	30	11
Hungary	6330	3.9	2.6	17x	2	6	5	3	-	-	30	34
Iceland	30810	3.6	2.1	4	-	24	10	0	-	-	-	-
India	530	1.7	4.0	7	35	2	2	15	1463	0	25	15
Indonesia	810	4.3	2.0	15	8	1	4	3	1308	1	31	20
Iran (Islamic Republic of)	2000	-3.5x	2.4	24	2	6	7	12	116	0	1	4
Iraq	2170x	-1.1	-	0x	-	-	-	-	116	-	-	-
Ireland	26960	3.1	6.6	4	-	16	14	3	-	-	-	-
Israel	16020x	3.1	1.5	8	-	13	15	20	-	-	-	-
Italy	21560	3.3	1.5	3	-	11x	8x	4x	-	-	-	-
Jamaica	2760	0.1	0.0	18	2	7	15	2	24	0	20	18
Japan	34510	4.8	1.0	0	-	2	6	4	-	-	-	-
Jordan	1850	2.5x	0.9	2	2	10	16	19	534	6	18	7
Kazakhstan	1780	-	0.4	120	2	2	3	6	188	1	-	34
Kenya	390	2.3	-0.6	12	23	7	26	6	393	4	26	12
Kiribati	880	-5.3x	2.7	3x	-	-	-	-	21	25	-	22
Korea, Democratic People's Republic of	a	-	-	-	-	-	-	-	267	-	-	-
Korea, Republic of	12030	6.3	4.6	4x	2	0	18	13	-55x	0x	10	10x
Kuwait	16340x	-6.2x	-1.7x	3x	-	7	15	17	-	-	-	-
Kyrgyzstan	330	-	-2.5	72	2	11	20	10	186	13	-	26x
Lao People's Democratic Republic	320	-	3.7	29x	26	-	-	-	278	16	8	7x
Latvia	4070	4.0x	1.1	32	2	11	6	4	-	-	-	14
Lebanon	4040	-	2.9	12	-	2	7	11	456	3	1	41
Lesotho	590	4.4	2.4	10	43	9	27	7	76	8	4	11
Liberia	130	-1.9	5.3	54x	36	5x	11x	9x	52	11	-	0
Libyan Arab Jamahiriya	5540x	1.1x	-	-	-	-	-	-	7x	-	-	-
Liechtenstein	d	-	-	-	-	-	-	-	-	-	-	-
Lithuania	4490	-	0.6	46	2	13	7	6	-	-	-	15
Luxembourg	43940	2.6	3.6	3	-	13	10	1	-	-	-	-
Madagascar	290	-1.3	-0.9	16	49	8	21	5x	373	10	32	9
Malawi	170	1.5	1.0	31	42	7x	12x	5x	377	22	23	6
Malaysia	3780	4.1	3.4	3	2	6	23	11	86	0	12	7
Maldives	2300	-	4.5x	0x	-	9	18	10	27	4	4	4
Mali	290	0.0x	2.4	7	73	2x	9x	8x	472	17	8	5
Malta	9260x	7.1	3.6x	3x	-	10	11	2	11	0	0	3x
Marshall Islands	2710	-	-2.7	5x	-	-	-	-	62	49	-	-
Mauritania	430	0.8	2.2	5	26	4x	23x	-	355	31	24	20x
Mauritius	4090	2.9x	4.0	6	-	9	15	1	24	1	6	7
Mexico	6230	2.4	1.4	16	10	5	25	3	136	0	16	23
Micronesia (Federated States of)	2090	-	-1.4	2x	-	-	-	-	112	47	-	-
Moldova, Republic of	590	-	-5.7	79	22	4	5	2	142	8	-	18
Monaco	d	-	-	-	-	-	-	-	-	-	-	-
Mongolia	480	-	0.4	41	14	6	9	9	208	20	-	6
Morocco	1320	2.3	1.0	2	2	3	18	13	636	2	18	24

TABLE 7. ECONOMIC INDICATORS

	GNI per capita (US$) 2003	GDP per capita average annual growth rate (%) 1960-90	GDP per capita average annual growth rate (%) 1990-2003	Average annual rate of inflation (%) 1990-2003	% of population below $1 a day 1992-2002*	% of central government expenditure allocated to: (1992-2002*) health	education	defence	ODA inflow in millions US$ 2002	ODA inflow as a % of recipient GNI 2002	Debt service as a % of exports of goods and services 1990	2002
Mozambique	210	-	4.6	25	38	5x	10x	35x	2058	56	21	5
Myanmar	220x	1.4	5.7x	25x	-	3	8	29	121	-	17	3x
Namibia	1870	-	0.9	10	35	10x	22x	7x	135	4	-	-
Nauru	-	-	-	4x	-	-	-	-	12	-	-	-
Nepal	240	0.8	2.1	7	38	5	18	8	365	7	12	9
Netherlands	26310	2.4	2.1	2	-	10	2	4	-	-	-	-
New Zealand	15870	1.1	2.1	2	-	17	16	4	-	-	-	-
Nicaragua	730	-1.5	1.5	28	45	13	15	6	517	14	2	11
Niger	200	-2.2	-0.7	5	64	-	-	-	298	15	12	6x
Nigeria	320	0.4	0.0	23	70	1x	3x	3x	314	1	22	8
Niue	-	-	-	-	-	-	-	-	4	-	-	-
Norway	43350	3.5	2.8	3	-	5	7	6	-	-	-	-
Occupied Palestinian Territory	1110	-	-6.0x	9x	-	-	-	-	1616	45	-	-
Oman	7830x	7.6	0.9x	2x	-	7	15	33	41	0	12	14x
Pakistan	470	2.9	1.1	9	13	1	1	18	2144	4	16	16
Palau	7500	-	-0.3x	3x	-	-	-	-	31	22	-	-
Panama	4250	1.8	2.3	3	7	18	16	4x	35	0	3	19
Papua New Guinea	510	0.9	0.2	7x	-	7	22	4	203	7	37	12x
Paraguay	1100	3.0	-0.6	11	15	7	22	11	57	1	12	10
Peru	2150	0.4	2.1	18	18	6	7	8	491	1	6	30
Philippines	1080	1.5	1.2	8	15	2	19	5	560	1	23	19
Poland	5270	-	4.7	18	2	2	5	4	-	-	4	22
Portugal	12130	4.1	2.3	5	2	9x	11x	6x	-	-	-	-
Qatar	12000x	-	-	-	-	-	-	-	-	-	-	-
Romania	2310	2.0x	0.5	78	2	15	6	5	-	-	0	18
Russian Federation	2610	3.8x	-1.5	107	6	1	3	12	-	-	-	10
Rwanda	220	1.1	0.7	11	36x	5x	26x	-	356	19	10	13
Saint Kitts and Nevis	6880	3.7x	3.2	3x	-	-	-	-	29	10	3	22
Saint Lucia	4050	-	0.2	3x	-	-	-	-	34	5	2	5
Saint Vincent and the Grenadines	3300	7.1	3.0	3x	-	12	16	0	5	1	3	7
Samoa	1600	-	3.1x	4x	-	-	-	-	38	15	5	5x
San Marino	d	-	-	-	-	-	-	-	-	-	-	-
Sao Tome and Principe	320	-	-0.2	39	-	-	-	-	26	57	28	31
Saudi Arabia	8530x	0.2x	-0.6x	2x	-	6x	14x	36x	27	0	-	-
Senegal	550	-0.6	1.4	4	26	3	14	7	449	10	14	11
Serbia and Montenegro	1910	-	3.6x	54x	-	-	-	-	1931	17	-	2
Seychelles	7480	3.1	2.2	2	-	7	7	3	8	1	8	2
Sierra Leone	150	0.6	-5.2	25	57x	10x	13x	10x	353	49	8	18x
Singapore	21230	6.8	3.5	1x	-	6	23	29	-	-	-	-
Slovakia	4920	-	2.4	9	2	17	9	4	-	-	-	20
Slovenia	11830	-	4.1x	10x	2	15	12	3	171	1	-	16x
Solomon Islands	600	2.4x	-2.8	9x	-	-	-	-	26	10	10	7x
Somalia	130x	-1.0	-	-	-	1x	2x	38x	194	-	25x	-
South Africa	2780	1.3	0.2	9	7	-	-	-	657	1	-	12
Spain	16990	3.2	2.3	4	-	15	2	4	-	-	-	-
Sri Lanka	930	2.8	3.3	9	7	6	10	18	344	2	10	9
Sudan	460	0.2	3.3	48	-	1	8	28	351	3	4	0
Suriname	1940x	-0.6x	0.5x	75x	-	-	-	-	12	1	-	-
Swaziland	1350	2.0x	0.2	12	-	8	20	8	25	2	6	2
Sweden	28840	2.2	2.0	2	-	7	7	6	-	-	-	-
Switzerland	39880	1.6	0.4	1	-	0	3	6	-	-	-	-
Syrian Arab Republic	1160	2.9	1.4	7	-	2	9	24	81	0	20	2
Tajikistan	190	-	-4.5	153	10	2	4	9	168	15	-	6
Tanzania, United Republic of	290	-	1.0	17	20	6x	8x	16x	1233	13	25	8
Thailand	2190	4.6	2.8	3	2	8	17	6	296	0	14	21
The former Yugoslav Republic of Macedonia	1980	-	-0.5	49	2	-	-	-	277	8	-	15
Timor-Leste	430	-	-	-	-	-	-	-	220	57	-	-
Togo	310	1.2	-0.7	6	-	5x	20x	11x	51	4	8	0
Tonga	1490	-	2.0	2x	-	7x	13x	-	22	15	2	6

	GNI per capita (US$) 2003	GDP per capita average annual growth rate (%) 1960-90	GDP per capita average annual growth rate (%) 1990-2003	Average annual rate of inflation (%) 1990-2003	% of population below $1 a day 1992-2002*	% of central government expenditure allocated to: (1992-2002*) health	education	defence	ODA inflow in millions US$ 2002	ODA inflow as a % of recipient GNI 2002	Debt service as a % of exports of goods and services 1990	2002
Trinidad and Tobago	7260	1.6	3.0	6	12	9	15	2	-7	0	18	5
Tunisia	2240	3.3x	3.1	4	2	6	20	5	475	2	22	13
Turkey	2790	1.9x	1.3	69	2	3	10	8	636	0	27	34
Turkmenistan	1120	-	-1.3	223	12	-	-	-	41	1	-	30x
Tuvalu	-	-	-	-	-	-	-	-	12	-	-	-
Uganda	240	-	3.8	9	82	2x	15x	26x	638	11	47	5
Ukraine	970	-	-4.7	155	3	3	7	5	-	-	-	13
United Arab Emirates	18060x	-4.8x	-2.1x	3x	-	8	18	31	-	-	-	-
United Kingdom	28350	2.1	2.4	3	-	15	4	7	-	-	-	-
United States	37610	2.2	2.0	2	-	22	2	16	-	-	-	-
Uruguay	3820	0.9	0.9	24	2	7	8	4	13	0	31	35
Uzbekistan	420	-	-0.5	163	22	-	-	-	189	2	-	23
Vanuatu	1180	-	-0.3	2x	-	-	-	-	28	13	2	1x
Venezuela	3490	-0.5	-1.5	39	15	6	21	6	57	0	22	25
Viet Nam	480	-	5.9	13x	18	4	14	-	1277	4	7x	5
Yemen	520	-	2.4	19	16	4	22	19	584	6	4	3
Zambia	380	-1.2	-0.9	42	64	13	14	4	641	19	13	21
Zimbabwe	480x	1.1	-0.8x	35	36x	8	24	7	201	0x	19	6x

SUMMARY INDICATORS

	GNI per capita (US$) 2003	GDP growth 1960-90	GDP growth 1990-2003	Inflation 1990-2003	% below $1 a day	health	education	defence	ODA inflow US$ millions 2002	ODA % of GNI 2002	Debt service 1990	Debt service 2002
Sub-Saharan Africa	496	1.1	0.4	38	43	-	-	-	17060	5	17	10
Middle East and North Africa	1465	2.2	2.0	15	3	4	14	13	6829	2	20	10
South Asia	511	1.7	3.6	7	32	2	2	15	6614	1	21	14
East Asia and Pacific	1426	5.3	6.2	6	15	1	8	11	7193	0	16	11
Latin America and Caribbean	3311	2.3	1.3	44	10	6	16	4	4533	0	20	29
CEE/CIS	2036	-	-0.5	102	6	4	5	9	-	-	-	17
Industrialized countries	28337	3.0	1.8	2	-	15	4	10	-	-	-	-
Developing countries	1255	3.0	3.7	25	22	3	10	10	44592	1	19	17
Least developed countries	304	0.0	1.8	62	39	-	-	-	17482	9	12	7
World	5488	3.0	2.1	7	21	12	5	10	48194	0	18	17

Countries in each category are listed on page 140.

DEFINITIONS OF THE INDICATORS

GNI per capita – Gross national income (GNI) is the sum of value added by all resident producers plus any product taxes (less subsidies) not included in the valuation of output plus net receipts of primary income (compensation of employees and property income) from abroad. GNI per capita is gross national income divided by mid-year population. GNI per capita in US dollars is converted using the World Bank Atlas method.

GDP per capita – Gross domestic product (GDP) is the sum of value added by all resident producers plus any product taxes (less subsidies) not included in the valuation of output. GDP per capita is gross domestic product divided by mid-year population. Growth is calculated from constant price GDP data in local currency.

% of population below $1 a day – Percentage of population living on less than $1.08 a day at 1993 international prices (equivalent to $1 a day in 1985 prices, adjusted for purchasing power parity). As a result of revisions in purchasing power parity exchange rates, poverty rates for individual countries cannot be compared with poverty rates reported in previous editions.

ODA – Net official development assistance.

Debt service – The sum of interest payments and repayments of principal on external public and publicly guaranteed long-term debts.

MAIN DATA SOURCES

GNI per capita – World Bank.

GDP per capita – World Bank.

Rate of inflation – World Bank.

% of population below $1 a day – World Bank.

Expenditure on health, education and defence – International Monetary Fund (IMF).

ODA – Organisation for Economic Co-operation and Development (OECD).

Debt service – World Bank.

NOTES

a: Range $765 or less.
b: Range $766 to $3035.
c: Range $3036 to $9385.
d: Range $9386 or more.

- Data not available.
x Indicates data that refer to years or periods other than those specified in the column heading, differ from the standard definition or refer to only part of a country.
* Data refer to the most recent year available during the period specified in the column heading.

TABLE 8. WOMEN

Countries and territories	Life expectancy: females as a % of males 2003	Adult literacy rate: females as a % of males 2000	Gross enrolment ratios: females as a % of males		Contraceptive prevalence (%) 1995-2003*	Antenatal care coverage (%) 1995-2003*	Skilled attendant at delivery (%) 1995-2003*	Maternal mortality ratio†		
			primary school 1998-2002*	secondary school 1998-2002*				1985-2003* reported	2000 adjusted	2000 Lifetime risk of maternal death. 1 in:
Afghanistan	101	41	-	-	10	37	14	1600	1900	6
Albania	108	84	100	104	75	95	94	20	55	610
Algeria	105	75	93	107	57	81	92	140	140	190
Andorra	-	-	-	-	-	-	-	-	-	-
Angola	107	-	86	81	6	66	45	-	1700	7
Antigua and Barbuda	-	104x	-	-	53	100	100	65	-	-
Argentina	110	100	99	106	74x	95x	99	46	82	410
Armenia	110	99	98	106	61	92	97	22	55	1200
Australia	107	-	100	99	76x	100x	100	-	8	5800
Austria	108	-	99	97	51	100x	100x	-	4	16000
Azerbaijan	110	97x	99	98	55	66	84	25	94	520
Bahamas	110	101	101	103	62x	-	99x	-	60	580
Bahrain	105	91	100	109	62	97	98	46	28	1200
Bangladesh	101	61	101	109	54	40	14	380	380	59
Barbados	107	100	100	100	55	89	91	0	95	590
Belarus	116	100	98	105	50	100	100	18	35	1800
Belgium	108	-	99	112	78x	-	100x	-	10	5600
Belize	104	100	97	109	56	96	83	140	140	190
Benin	109	46	70	46	19	81	66	500	850	17
Bhutan	104	56	76	29x	31	-	24	260	420	37
Bolivia	107	86	99	97	58	83	65	390	420	47
Bosnia and Herzegovina	108	91x	100	-	48	99	100	10	31	1900
Botswana	103	107	100	107	48	97	94	330	100	200
Brazil	113	100	94	111	77	86	88	75	260	140
Brunei Darussalam	106	93	99	107	-	100x	99	0	37	830
Bulgaria	111	99	97	97	42	-	-	15	32	2400
Burkina Faso	102	41	71	67	14	73	31	480	1000	12
Burundi	102	71	78	75	16	78	25	-	1000	12
Cambodia	108	71	89	59	24	38	32	440	450	36
Cameroon	105	81	86	81	26	75	60	430	730	23
Canada	107	-	101	99	75	-	98	-	6	8700
Cape Verde	109	78	96	105	53	99	89	76	150	160
Central African Republic	105	58	67	40x	28	62	44	1100	1100	15
Chad	105	65	63	29	8	42	16	830	1100	11
Chile	108	100	97	101	56x	95x	100	17	31	1100
China	106	85	100	93	87	90	97	50	56	830
Colombia	109	100	99	111	77	91	86	78	130	240
Comoros	105	78	83	83	26	74	62	520	480	33
Congo	106	84	94	73	-	-	-	-	510	26
Congo, Democratic Republic of the	105	68	90	54	31	68	61	950	990	13
Cook Islands	-	-	95	109	63	-	100	6	-	-
Costa Rica	106	100	100	103	75x	70	98	29	43	690
Côte d'Ivoire	101	62	74	53	15	88	63	600	690	25
Croatia	111	98	99	101	-	-	100	2	8	6100
Cuba	105	100	96	99	73	100	100	34	33	1600
Cyprus	106	96	100	101	-	-	100x	0	47	890
Czech Republic	109	-	99	102	72	99x	99	3	9	7700
Denmark	107	-	100	105	78x	-	100x	10	5	9800
Djibouti	104	71	76	63	-	67	61	74	730	19
Dominica	-	-	95	115	50	100	100	67	-	-
Dominican Republic	107	100	102	125	70	99	99	180	150	200
Ecuador	108	97	100	100	66	69	69	80	130	210
Egypt	106	66	94	93	60	69	69	84	84	310
El Salvador	109	93	96	100	67	76	69	170	150	180
Equatorial Guinea	105	80	91	58	-	86	65	-	880	16
Eritrea	106	67	81	67	8	70	28	1000	630	24
Estonia	115	100	96	102	70x	-	-	46	63	1100
Ethiopia	104	66	71	65	8	27	6	870	850	14
Fiji	105	96	100	106	44	-	100	38	75	360

	Life expectancy: females as a % of males 2003	Adult literacy rate: females as a % of males 2000	Gross enrolment ratios: females as a % of males		Contraceptive prevalence (%) 1995-2003*	Antenatal care coverage (%) 1995-2003*	Skilled attendant at delivery (%) 1995-2003*	Maternal mortality ratio†		
			primary school 1998-2002*	secondary school 1998-2002*				1985-2003* reported	2000 adjusted	2000 Lifetime risk of maternal death. 1 in:
Finland	109	-	99	111	77x	100x	100x	6	6	8200
France	110	-	98	101	75x	99x	99x	10	17	2700
Gabon	103	78	99	86	33	94	86	520	420	37
Gambia	105	68	91	70	18	91	55	730	540	31
Georgia	111	99x	100	108	41	95	96	67	32	1700
Germany	108	-	99	99	75x	-	100x	8	8	8000
Ghana	105	79	92	83	25	92	44	210x	540	35
Greece	107	97	99	102	-	-	-	1	9	7100
Grenada	-	-	95	-	54	98	99	1	-	-
Guatemala	109	80	93	93	40	84	41	150	240	74
Guinea	101	49	75	35	6	71	35	530	740	18
Guinea-Bissau	107	44	67	57	8	62	35	910	1100	13
Guyana	110	99	97	103	37	81	86	190	170	200
Haiti	102	92	101	95x	27	79	24	520	680	29
Holy See	-	-	-	-	-	-	-	-	-	-
Honduras	107	100	102	128x	62	83	56	110	110	190
Hungary	112	99	98	101	77x	-	-	5	16	4000
Iceland	105	-	100	107	-	-	-	-	0	-
India	102	66	84	71	47	60	43	540	540	48
Indonesia	106	89	98	100	60	92	68	310	230	150
Iran (Islamic Republic of)	104	83	96	95	74	77	90	37	76	370
Iraq	105	42	82	62	44	77	72	290	250	65
Ireland	107	-	100	109	-	-	100	6	5	8300
Israel	105	96	99	99	68x	-	99x	5	17	1800
Italy	108	99	99	98	60	-	-	7	5	13900
Jamaica	106	110	99	104	66	99	95	110	87	380
Japan	109	-	100	101	59x	-	100	8	10	6000
Jordan	104	88	101	102	56	99	100	41	41	450
Kazakhstan	118	99	99	98	66	91	99	50	210	190
Kenya	104	85	98	88	38	88	41	590	1000	19
Kiribati	-	-	102	-	21	88x	85	-	-	-
Korea, Democratic People's Republic of	109	97	94x	-	62x	-	97	110	67	590
Korea, Republic of	110	97	100	100	81	-	100	20	20	2800
Kuwait	105	95	99	106	50	95	98	5	5	6000
Kyrgyzstan	111	-	97	101	60	97	98	44	110	290
Lao People's Democratic Republic	105	70	86	72	32	27	19	530	650	25
Latvia	116	100	99	101	48	-	100	25	42	1800
Lebanon	104	87	96	109	63	87	89	100x	150	240
Lesotho	116	129	102	127	30	85	60	-	550	32
Liberia	104	53	73	70	10	85	51	580	760	16
Libyan Arab Jamahiriya	106	75	100	106	45	81	94	77	97	240
Liechtenstein	-	-	-	-	-	-	-	-	-	-
Lithuania	115	100	99	99	47	-	-	13	13	4900
Luxembourg	108	-	99	106	-	-	100x	0	28	1700
Madagascar	104	81	96	93	19	71	46	490	550	26
Malawi	101	63	96	74	31	94	61	1100	1800	7
Malaysia	107	91	100	111	55x	-	97	50	41	660
Maldives	99	100	99	106	32	81	70	140	110	140
Mali	102	44	75	50	8	57	41	580	1200	10
Malta	106	102	100	98	-	-	98x	-	0	-
Marshall Islands	-	-	95	-	37x	-	95	-	-	-
Mauritania	106	59	97	76	8	64	57	750	1000	14
Mauritius	111	92	100	96	26	-	99	21	24	1700
Mexico	109	96	99	107	70	86	86	63	83	370
Micronesia (Federated States of)	102	102	110	-	45	-	93	120	-	-
Moldova, Republic of	110	98	99	103	62	99	99	44	36	1500
Monaco	-	-	-	-	-	-	-	-	-	-
Mongolia	106	99	103	120	67	97	99	110	110	300
Morocco	106	58	89	80	63	68	40	230	220	120

TABLE 8. WOMEN

	Life expectancy: females as a % of males 2003	Adult literacy rate: females as a % of males 2000	Gross enrolment ratios: females as a % of males		Contraceptive prevalence (%) 1995-2003*	Antenatal care coverage (%) 1995-2003*	Skilled attendant at delivery (%) 1995-2003*	Maternal mortality ratio†		
			primary school 1998-2002*	secondary school 1998-2002*				1985-2003* reported	2000 adjusted	2000 Lifetime risk of maternal death. 1 in:
Mozambique	108	48	79	63	17	76	48	1100	1000	14
Myanmar	110	91	100	93	33	76	56	230	360	75
Namibia	106	98	100	114	44	91	78	270	300	54
Nauru	-	-	103	108	-	-	-	-	-	-
Nepal	99	41	87	74	39	28	11	540	740	24
Netherlands	107	-	98	97	79x	-	100	7	16	3500
New Zealand	106	-	100	108	75	95x	100	15	7	6000
Nicaragua	107	100	101	117	69	86	67	97	230	88
Niger	101	38	68	63	14	41	16	590	1600	7
Nigeria	101	78	80	85x	13	58	35	-	800	18
Niue	-	104	94	98	-	-	100	-	-	-
Norway	108	-	101	103	74x	-	100x	6	16	2900
Occupied Palestinian Territory	105	-	101	107	51	96	97	-	100	140
Oman	105	78	98	99	32	100	95	23	87	170
Pakistan	100	49	74	66	28	43	23	530	500	31
Palau	-	-	93	100	47x	-	100	0	-	-
Panama	107	98	96	107	58x	72	90	70	160	210
Papua New Guinea	103	80	101	80	26	78	53	370x	300	62
Paraguay	107	98	96	102	57	89	71	180	170	120
Peru	108	89	100	93	69	84	59	190	410	73
Philippines	106	100	98	110	49	88	60	170	200	120
Poland	112	100	99	96	49x	-	99x	4	13	4600
Portugal	110	95	98	105	66x	-	100	8	5	11100
Qatar	107	100	96	106	43	94x	98	10	140	170
Romania	111	98	98	101	64	-	98	34	49	1300
Russian Federation	120	99	99	100	-	-	99	37	67	1000
Rwanda	102	81	98	93	13	92	31	1100	1400	10
Saint Kitts and Nevis	-	-	110	143	41	100x	99	250	-	-
Saint Lucia	105	-	101	129	47	100x	100	35	-	-
Saint Vincent and Grenadines	104	-	96	119	58	99	100	93	-	-
Samoa	110	99	97	111	30	-	100	-	130	150
San Marino	-	-	-	-	-	-	-	-	-	-
Sao Tome and Principe	109	-	94	86	29	91	79	100	-	-
Saudi Arabia	104	81	97	89	32	90	91	-	23	610
Senegal	108	60	91	68	11	79	58	560	690	22
Serbia and Montenegro	107	98x	100	101	58	-	99	7	11	4500
Seychelles	-	-	99	106	-	-	-	-	-	-
Sierra Leone	107	45	70	71	4	68	42	1800	2000	6
Singapore	106	92	98x	110x	74x	-	100	6	30	1700
Slovakia	111	100	99	101	74x	-	-	16	3	19800
Slovenia	110	100	99	102	74x	98x	100x	17	17	4100
Solomon Islands	104	-	87x	67x	11	-	85	550x	130	120
Somalia	107	-	50x	60x	1x	32	34	-	1100	10
South Africa	111	99	96	108	56	94	84	150	230	120
Spain	109	98	98	106	81	-	-	6	4	17400
Sri Lanka	108	95	99	107	70	95	97	92	92	430
Sudan	105	67	86	88	7	60	86x	550	590	30
Suriname	108	97	98	139	42	91	85	150	110	340
Swaziland	106	98	95	100	28	87	70	230	370	49
Sweden	107	-	103	121	78x	-	100x	5	2	29800
Switzerland	108	-	99	93	82	-	-	5	7	7900
Syrian Arab Republic	104	68	94	89	48	71	76x	65	160	130
Tajikistan	108	99	95	82	34	71	71	45	100	250
Tanzania, United Republic of	104	80	99	83	25	49	36	530	1500	10
Thailand	112	97	96	95	79	92	99	36	44	900
The former Yugoslav Republic of Macedonia	106	97	100	97	-	100	98	11	23	2100
Timor-Leste	104	-	-	-	7	43	24	-	660	30

	Life expectancy: females as a % of males 2003	Adult literacy rate: females as a % of males 2000	Gross enrolment ratios: females as a % of males		Contraceptive prevalence (%) 1995-2003*	Antenatal care coverage (%) 1995-2003*	Skilled attendant at delivery (%) 1995-2003*	Maternal mortality ratio†		
			primary school 1998-2002*	secondary school 1998-2002*				1985-2003* reported	2000 adjusted	2000 Lifetime risk of maternal death. 1 in:
Togo	106	60	82	43	26	73	49	480	570	26
Tonga	102	-	97	113	41	-	92	-	-	-
Trinidad and Tobago	109	99	98	106	38	92	96	45	160	330
Tunisia	106	75	96	104	66	92	90	69	120	320
Turkey	108	83	93	77	64	68	81	130x	70	480
Turkmenistan	110	-	-	-	62	98	97	9	31	790
Tuvalu	-	-	95	88	-	-	99	-	-	-
Uganda	103	73	96	79	23	92	39	510	880	13
Ukraine	115	100	99	100	89	-	100	22	35	2000
United Arab Emirates	106	105	96	106	28	97	96	3	54	500
United Kingdom	107	-	100	116	82x	-	99	7	13	3800
United States	108	-	101	98	76	99x	99	8	17	2500
Uruguay	110	101	98	114	84	94	100	26	27	1300
Uzbekistan	108	99	99	97	68	97	96	34	24	1300
Vanuatu	104	-	99	104	15x	-	89	68	130	140
Venezuela	108	99	98	116	77	94	94	60	96	300
Viet Nam	107	96	93	93	79	86	85	95	130	270
Yemen	104	37	66	42	23	45	22	350	570	19
Zambia	98	85	94	78	34	93	43	730	750	19
Zimbabwe	96	91	98	89	54	93	73	700	1100	16

SUMMARY INDICATORS

Sub-Saharan Africa	104	77	87	79	22	66	41		940	16
Middle East and North Africa	105	70	91	91	52	72	72		220	100
South Asia	102	64	86	76	45	54	35		560	43
East Asia and Pacific	107	87	99	94	79	88	87		110	360
Latin America and Caribbean	110	98	98	107	72	86	82		190	160
CEE/CIS	114	97	97	94	66	80	92		64	770
Industrialized countries	108	-	100	101	74	-	99		13	4000
Developing countries	105	81	91	90	60	70	59		440	61
Least developed countries	104	68	91	83	27	56	32		890	17
World	106	87	93	92	61	70	62		400	74

Countries in each category are listed on page 140.

DEFINITIONS OF THE INDICATORS

Life expectancy at birth – The number of years newborn children would live if subject to the mortality risks prevailing for the cross-section of population at the time of their birth.

Adult literacy rate – Percentage of persons aged 15 and over who can read and write.

Gross enrolment ratios: females as a % of males – Girls' gross enrolment ratio divided by that of boys, as a percentage. The gross enrolment ratio is the number of children enrolled in a schooling level (primary or secondary), regardless of age, divided by the population of the age group that officially corresponds to that level.

Contraceptive prevalence – Percentage of women in union aged 15-49 years currently using contraception.

Antenatal care – Percentage of women aged 15-49 years attended at least once during pregnancy by skilled health personnel (doctors, nurses or midwives).

Skilled attendant at delivery – Percentage of births attended by skilled health personnel (doctors, nurses or midwives).

Maternal mortality ratio – Annual number of deaths of women from pregnancy-related causes per 100,000 live births. This 'reported' column shows country reported figures that are not adjusted for underreporting and misclassification.

Lifetime risk of maternal death – The lifetime risk of maternal death takes into account both the probability of becoming pregnant and the probability of dying as a result of that pregnancy accumulated across a woman's reproductive years.

MAIN DATA SOURCES

Life expectancy – United Nations Population Division.

Adult literacy – United Nations Educational, Scientific and Cultural Organization (UNESCO), including the Education for All 2000 Assessment.

School enrolment – UIS (UNESCO Institute of Statistics) and UNESCO, including the Education For All 2000 Assessment.

Contraceptive prevalence – Demographic and Health Surveys (DHS), Multiple Indicator Cluster Surveys (MICS), United Nations Population Division and UNICEF.

Antenatal care – DHS, MICS, World Health Organization (WHO) and UNICEF.

Skilled attendant at delivery – DHS, MICS, WHO and UNICEF.

Maternal mortality – WHO and UNICEF.

Lifetime risk – WHO and UNICEF.

† The maternal mortality data in the column headed 'reported' are those reported by national authorities. Periodically, UNICEF, WHO and UNFPA evaluate these data and make adjustments to account for the well-documented problems of underreporting and misclassification of maternal deaths and to develop estimates for countries with no data. The column with 'adjusted' estimates for the year 2000 reflects the most recent of these reviews.

NOTES

- \- Data not available.
- x Indicates data that refer to years or periods other than those specified in the column heading, differ from the standard definition or refer to only part of a country.
- * Data refer to the most recent year available during the period specified in the column heading.

TABLE 9. CHILD PROTECTION

Countries and territories	Child labour (5-14 years) 1999-2003*			Child marriage 1986-2003*			Birth registration 1999-2003*			Female genital mutilation/cutting 1998-2003* women[a] (15-49 years)			Female genital mutilation/cutting 1998-2003* daughters[b]
	total	male	female	urban	rural	total	total	urban	rural	total	urban	rural	total
Afghanistan	8	11	5	-	-	-	10	-	-	-	-	-	-
Albania	23	26	19	-	-	-	99	99	99	-	-	-	-
Angola	22	21	23	-	-	-	29	34	19	-	-	-	-
Armenia	-	-	-	12	31	19	-	-	-	-	-	-	-
Azerbaijan	8	9	7	-	-	-	97	98	96	-	-	-	-
Bahrain	5	6	3	-	-	-	-	-	-	-	-	-	-
Bangladesh	8y	10y	5y	48	70	65	7	9	7	-	-	-	-
Benin	26y	23y	29y	25	45	37	62	71	58	17	13	20	6
Bolivia	21	22	20	17	35	21	82	83	79	-	-	-	-
Bosnia and Herzegovina	11	12	10	-	-	-	98	98	99	-	-	-	-
Botswana	-	-	-	13	9	10	58	66	52	-	-	-	-
Brazil	7y	9y	4y	22	30	24	76	-	-	-	-	-	-
Burkina Faso	57y	-	-	32	70	62	-	-	-	72	82	70	40
Burundi	24	26	23	36y	17y	17y	75	71	75	-	-	-	-
Cambodia	-	-	-	19	26	25	22	30	21	-	-	-	-
Cameroon	51	52	50	30	51	43	79	94	72	-	-	-	-
Central African Republic	56	54	57	54y	59y	57y	73	88	63	36	29	41	-
Chad	57	60	55	65	74	71	25	53	18	45	43	46	-
Colombia	5	7	4	18	34	21	91	95	84	-	-	-	-
Comoros	27	27	28	23	33	30	83	87	83	-	-	-	-
Congo, Democratic Republic of the	28y	26y	29y	-	-	-	34	30	37	-	-	-	-
Costa Rica	50y	71y	29y	-	-	-	-	-	-	-	-	-	-
Côte d'Ivoire	35	34	36	24	43	33	72	88	60	45	39	48	24
Cuba	-	-	-	-	-	-	100	100	100	-	-	-	-
Dominican Republic	9	11	6	37	51	41	75	82	66	-	-	-	-
Ecuador	6y	9y	4y	21y	34y	26y	-	-	-	-	-	-	-
Egypt	6	6	5	11	26	20	-	-	-	97	95	99	50
El Salvador	-	-	-	32y	46y	38y	-	-	-	-	-	-	-
Equatorial Guinea	27	27	27	-	-	-	32	43	24	-	-	-	-
Eritrea	-	-	-	24	59	47	-	-	-	89	86	91	63
Ethiopia	43y	47y	37y	-	-	-	-	-	-	80	80	80	48
Gabon	-	-	-	30	49	34	89	90	87	-	-	-	-
Gambia	22	23	22	-	-	-	32	37	29	-	-	-	-
Georgia	-	-	-	-	-	-	95	97	92	-	-	-	-
Ghana	57y	57y	58y	25	42	36	21	-	-	5	4	7	-
Guatemala	24y	-	-	26	45	35	-	-	-	-	-	-	-
Guinea	-	-	-	-	-	-	67	88	56	99	98	99	54
Guinea-Bissau	54	54	54	-	-	-	42	32	47	-	-	-	-
Guyana	19	21	17	-	-	-	97	99	96	-	-	-	-
Haiti	-	-	-	-	-	-	70	78	66	-	-	-	-
India	14	14	15	26	54	46	35	54	29	-	-	-	-
Indonesia	4y	5y	4y	14	35	24	62	79	51	-	-	-	-
Iraq	8	11	5	-	-	-	98	98	98	-	-	-	-
Jamaica	-	-	-	-	-	-	96	95	96	-	-	-	-
Jordan	-	-	-	11	12	11	-	-	-	-	-	-	-
Kazakhstan	-	-	-	12	17	14	-	-	-	-	-	-	-
Kenya	25	26	24	21	26	25	63	82	56	38	23	42	11
Korea, Democratic People's Republic of	-	-	-	-	-	-	99	99	99	-	-	-	-
Kyrgyzstan	-	-	-	19	22	21	-	-	-	-	-	-	-
Lao People's Democratic Republic	24	23	25	-	-	-	59	71	56	-	-	-	-
Lebanon	6	8	4	-	-	11	-	-	-	-	-	-	-
Lesotho	17	19	14	-	-	-	51	41	53	-	-	-	-
Liberia	-	-	-	38y	58y	48y	-	-	-	-	-	-	-
Madagascar	30	35	26	32	44	40	75	88	72	-	-	-	-
Malawi	17	18	16	32	50	47	-	-	-	-	-	-	-
Maldives	-	-	-	-	-	-	73	-	-	-	-	-	-
Mali	30	33	28	46	74	65	48	71	41	92	90	93	73
Mauritania	10y	-	-	32	42	37	55	72	42	71	65	77	66
Mexico	16y	15y	16y	31y	21y	28y	-	-	-	-	-	-	-
Moldova, Republic of	28	29	28	-	-	-	98	98	98	-	-	-	-
Mongolia	30	30	30	-	-	-	98	98	97	-	-	-	-
Morocco	-	-	-	13y	24y	18y	-	-	-	-	-	-	-
Mozambique	-	-	-	47	60	57	-	-	-	-	-	-	-
Myanmar	-	-	-	-	-	-	39	65	31	-	-	-	-
Namibia	-	-	-	9	10	10	71	82	64	-	-	-	-
Nepal	-	-	-	38	59	56	34	37	34	-	-	-	-
Nicaragua	10y	-	-	36	55	43	-	-	-	-	-	-	-

	Child labour (5-14 years) 1999-2003*			Child marriage 1986-2003*			Birth registration 1999-2003*			Female genital mutilation/cutting 1998-2003* women[a] (15-49 years)			daughters[b]
	total	male	female	urban	rural	total	total	urban	rural	total	urban	rural	total
Niger	65	68	62	46	86	77	46	85	40	5	2	5	4
Nigeria	39y	-	-	27	52	43	68	82	56	19	28	14	10
Occupied Palestinian Territory	-	-	-	-	-	-	100	100	99	-	-	-	-
Pakistan	-	-	-	21y	37y	32y	-	-	-	-	-	-	-
Paraguay	8y	10y	6y	18y	32y	24y	-	-	-	-	-	-	-
Peru	-	-	-	12	35	19	-	-	-	-	-	-	-
Philippines	11	12	10	11	20	15	83	87	78	-	-	-	-
Romania	1y	-	-	-	-	-	-	-	-	-	-	-	-
Rwanda	31	31	30	21	19	20	65	61	66	-	-	-	-
Sao Tome and Principe	14	15	13	-	-	-	70	73	67	-	-	-	-
Senegal	33	36	30	15	53	36	62	82	51	-	-	-	-
Sierra Leone	57	57	57	-	-	-	46	66	40	-	-	-	-
Somalia	32	29	36	-	-	-	-	-	-	-	-	-	-
South Africa	-	-	-	5	12	8	-	-	-	-	-	-	-
Sri Lanka	-	-	-	10y	15y	14y	-	-	-	-	-	-	-
Sudan	13	14	12	19y	34y	27y	64	82	46	90	92	88	58
Suriname	-	-	-	-	-	-	95	94	94	-	-	-	-
Swaziland	8	8	8	-	-	-	53	72	50	-	-	-	-
Syrian Arab Republic	8y	10y	6y	-	-	-	-	-	-	-	-	-	-
Tajikistan	18	19	17	-	-	-	75	77	74	-	-	-	-
Tanzania, United Republic of	32	34	30	23	48	39	6	22	3	18	10	20	7
Thailand	-	-	-	13y	23y	21y	-	-	-	-	-	-	-
Timor-Leste	-	-	-	-	-	-	22	32	20	-	-	-	-
Togo	60	62	59	17	41	31	82	93	78	-	-	-	-
Trinidad and Tobago	2	3	2	37y	32y	34y	95	-	-	-	-	-	-
Tunisia	-	-	-	7y	14y	10y	-	-	-	-	-	-	-
Turkey	-	-	-	19	30	23	-	-	-	-	-	-	-
Turkmenistan	-	-	-	12	7	9	-	-	-	-	-	-	-
Uganda	34	34	33	34	59	54	4	11	3	-	-	-	-
Uzbekistan	15	18	12	14	16	15	100	100	100	-	-	-	-
Venezuela	7	9	5	-	-	-	92	-	-	-	-	-	-
Viet Nam	23	23	22	5	14	12	72	91	68	-	-	-	-
Yemen	-	-	-	41	52	48	-	-	-	23	26	22	20
Zambia	11	10	11	32	49	42	10	16	6	-	-	-	-
Zimbabwe	26y	-	-	21	36	29	40	54	33	-	-	-	-

DEFINITIONS OF THE INDICATORS

Child labour – Percentage of children aged 5 to 14 years of age involved in child labour activities at the moment of the survey. A child is considered to be involved in child labour activities under the following classification: (a) children 5 to 11 years of age that during the week preceding the survey did at least one hour of economic activity or at least 28 hours of domestic work, and (b) children 12 to 14 years of age that during the week preceding the survey did at least 14 hours of economic activity or at least 42 hours of economic activity and domestic work combined.

Child labour background variables – Sex of the child; urban or rural place of residence; poorest 20% or richest 20% of the population constructed from household assets (a more detailed description of the household wealth estimation procedure can be found at www.childinfo.org); mother's education, reflecting mothers with and without some level of education.

Birth registration – Percentage of children less than five years of age that were registered at the moment of the survey. The numerator of this indicator includes children whose birth certificate was seen by the interviewer or whose mother or caretaker says the birth has been registered.

Child marriage – Percentage of women 20-24 years of age that were married or in union before they were 18 years old.

Female genital mutilation/cutting – (a) Women – the percentage of women aged 15 to 49 years of age who have been mutilated/cut. (b) Daughters – the percentage of women aged 15 to 49 with at least one mutilated/cut daughter. Female genital mutilation/cutting (FGM/C) involves the cutting or alteration of the female genitalia for social reasons. Generally, there are three recognized types of FGM/C: clitoridectomy, excision and infibulation. Clitoridectomy is the removal of the prepuce with or without excision of all or part of the clitoris. Excision is the removal of the prepuce and clitoris along with all or part of the labia minora. Infibulation is the most severe form and consists of removal of all or part of the external genitalia, followed by joining together of the two sides of the labia minora using threads, thorns or other materials to narrow the vaginal opening. A more detailed analysis of this data can be found at www.measuredhs.com and www.prb.org.

MAIN DATA SOURCES

Child labour – Multiple Indicator Cluster Survey (MICS) and Demographic and Health Surveys (DHS).

Child marriage – DHS.

Birth registration – MICS and DHS.

Female genital mutilation/cutting – DHS conducted during the period 1998-2003 and MICS conducted during the period 1999-2001.

NOTES

- \- Data not available.
- y Indicates data that differ from the standard definition or refer to only part of a country but are included in the calculation of regional and global averages.
- * Data refer to the most recent year available during the period specified in the column heading.

Summary indicators

Averages given at the end of each table are calculated using data from the countries and territories as grouped below.

Sub-Saharan Africa

Angola; Benin; Botswana; Burkina Faso; Burundi; Cameroon; Cape Verde; Central African Republic; Chad; Comoros; Congo; Congo, Democratic Republic of the; Côte d'Ivoire; Equatorial Guinea; Eritrea; Ethiopia; Gabon; Gambia; Ghana; Guinea; Guinea-Bissau; Kenya; Lesotho; Liberia; Madagascar; Malawi; Mali; Mauritania; Mauritius; Mozambique; Namibia; Niger; Nigeria; Rwanda; Sao Tome and Principe; Senegal; Seychelles; Sierra Leone; Somalia; South Africa; Swaziland; Tanzania, United Republic of; Togo; Uganda; Zambia; Zimbabwe

Middle East and North Africa

Algeria; Bahrain; Djibouti; Egypt; Iran, Islamic Republic of; Iraq; Jordan; Kuwait; Lebanon; Libyan Arab Jamahiriya; Morocco; Occupied Palestinian Territory; Oman; Qatar; Saudi Arabia; Sudan; Syrian Arab Republic; Tunisia; United Arab Emirates; Yemen

South Asia

Afghanistan; Bangladesh; Bhutan; India; Maldives; Nepal; Pakistan; Sri Lanka

East Asia and Pacific

Brunei Darussalam; Cambodia; China; Cook Islands; Fiji; Indonesia; Kiribati; Korea, Democratic People's Republic of; Korea, Republic of; Lao People's Democratic Republic; Malaysia; Marshall Islands; Micronesia, Federated States of; Mongolia; Myanmar; Nauru; Niue; Palau; Papua New Guinea; Philippines; Samoa; Singapore; Solomon Islands; Thailand; Timor-Leste; Tonga; Tuvalu; Vanuatu; Viet Nam

Latin America and Caribbean

Antigua and Barbuda; Argentina; Bahamas; Barbados; Belize; Bolivia; Brazil; Chile; Colombia; Costa Rica; Cuba; Dominica; Dominican Republic; Ecuador; El Salvador; Grenada; Guatemala; Guyana; Haiti; Honduras; Jamaica; Mexico; Nicaragua; Panama; Paraguay; Peru; Saint Kitts and Nevis; Saint Lucia; Saint Vincent and the Grenadines; Suriname; Trinidad and Tobago; Uruguay; Venezuela

CEE/CIS

Albania; Armenia; Azerbaijan; Belarus; Bosnia and Herzegovina; Bulgaria; Croatia; Georgia; Kazakhstan; Kyrgyzstan; Moldova, Republic of; Romania; Russian Federation; Serbia and Montenegro; Tajikistan; the former Yugoslav Republic of Macedonia; Turkey; Turkmenistan; Ukraine; Uzbekistan

Industrialized countries

Andorra; Australia; Austria; Belgium; Canada; Cyprus; Czech Republic; Denmark; Estonia; Finland; France; Germany; Greece; Holy See; Hungary; Iceland; Ireland; Israel; Italy; Japan; Latvia; Liechtenstein; Lithuania; Luxembourg; Malta; Monaco; Netherlands; New Zealand; Norway; Poland; Portugal; San Marino; Slovakia; Slovenia; Spain; Sweden; Switzerland; United Kingdom; United States

Developing countries

Afghanistan; Algeria; Angola; Antigua and Barbuda; Argentina; Armenia; Azerbaijan; Bahamas; Bahrain; Bangladesh; Barbados; Belize; Benin; Bhutan; Bolivia; Botswana; Brazil; Brunei Darussalam; Burkina Faso; Burundi; Cambodia; Cameroon; Cape Verde; Central African Republic; Chad; Chile; China; Colombia; Comoros; Congo; Congo, Democratic Republic of the; Cook Islands; Costa Rica; Côte d'Ivoire; Cuba; Cyprus; Djibouti; Dominica; Dominican Republic; Ecuador; Egypt; El Salvador; Equatorial Guinea; Eritrea; Ethiopia; Fiji; Gabon; Gambia; Georgia; Ghana; Grenada; Guatemala; Guinea; Guinea-Bissau; Guyana; Haiti; Honduras; India; Indonesia; Iran, Islamic Republic of; Iraq; Israel; Jamaica; Jordan; Kazakhstan; Kenya; Kiribati; Korea, Democratic People's Republic of; Korea, Republic of; Kuwait; Kyrgyzstan; Lao People's Democratic Republic; Lebanon; Lesotho; Liberia; Libyan Arab Jamahiriya; Madagascar; Malawi; Malaysia; Maldives; Mali; Marshall Islands; Mauritania; Mauritius; Mexico; Micronesia, Federated States of; Mongolia; Morocco; Mozambique; Myanmar; Namibia; Nauru; Nepal; Nicaragua; Niger; Nigeria; Niue; Occupied Palestinian Territory; Oman; Pakistan; Palau; Panama; Papua New Guinea; Paraguay; Peru; Philippines; Qatar; Rwanda; Saint Kitts and Nevis; Saint Lucia; Saint Vincent/Grenadines; Samoa; Sao Tome and Principe; Saudi Arabia; Senegal; Seychelles; Sierra Leone; Singapore; Solomon Islands; Somalia; South Africa; Sri Lanka; Sudan; Suriname; Swaziland; Syrian Arab Republic; Tajikistan; Tanzania, United Republic of; Thailand; Timor-Leste; Togo; Tonga; Trinidad and Tobago; Tunisia; Turkey; Turkmenistan; Tuvalu; Uganda; United Arab Emirates; Uruguay; Uzbekistan; Vanuatu; Venezuela; Viet Nam; Yemen; Zambia; Zimbabwe

Least developed countries

Afghanistan; Angola; Bangladesh; Benin; Bhutan; Burkina Faso; Burundi; Cambodia; Cape Verde; Central African Republic; Chad; Comoros; Congo, Democratic Republic of the; Djibouti; Equatorial Guinea; Eritrea; Ethiopia; Gambia; Guinea; Guinea-Bissau; Haiti; Kiribati; Lao People's Democratic Republic; Lesotho; Liberia; Madagascar; Malawi; Maldives; Mali; Mauritania; Mozambique; Myanmar; Nepal; Niger; Rwanda; Samoa; Sao Tome and Principe; Senegal; Sierra Leone; Solomon Islands; Somalia; Sudan; Tanzania, United Republic of; Timor-Leste; Togo; Tuvalu; Uganda; Vanuatu; Yemen; Zambia

Measuring human development

An introduction to table 10

If development is to assume a more human face, then there arises a corresponding need for a means of measuring human as well as economic progress. From UNICEF's point of view, in particular, there is a need for an agreed method of measuring the level of child well-being and its rate of change.

The under-five mortality rate (U5MR) is used in table 10 (next page) as the principal indicator of such progress.

The U5MR has several advantages. First, it measures an end result of the development process rather than an 'input' such as school enrolment level, per capita calorie availability, or the number of doctors per thousand population – all of which are means to an end.

Second, the U5MR is known to be the result of a wide variety of inputs: the nutritional health and the health knowledge of mothers; the level of immunization and ORT use; the availability of maternal and child health services (including prenatal care); income and food availability in the family; the availability of clean water and safe sanitation; and the overall safety of the child's environment.

Third, the U5MR is less susceptible than, say, per capita GNI to the fallacy of the average. This is because the natural scale does not allow the children of the rich to be one thousand times as likely to survive, even if the man-made scale does permit them to have one thousand times as much income. In other words, it is much more difficult for a wealthy minority to affect a nation's U5MR, and it therefore presents a more accurate, if far from perfect, picture of the health status of the majority of children (and of society as a whole).

For these reasons, the U5MR is chosen by UNICEF as its single most important indicator of the state of a nation's children. That is why tables 1 and 10 rank the nations of the world not in ascending order of their per capita GNI but in descending order of their under-five mortality rates.

The speed of progress in reducing the U5MR can be measured by calculating its average annual reduction rate (AARR). Unlike the comparison of absolute changes, the AARR reflects the fact that the lower limits to U5MR are approached only with increasing difficulty. As lower levels of under-five mortality are reached, for example, the same absolute reduction obviously represents a greater percentage of reduction. The AARR therefore shows a higher rate of progress for, say, a 10-point reduction if that reduction happens at a lower level of under-five mortality. (A fall in U5MR of 10 points from 100 to 90 represents a reduction of 10 per cent, whereas the same 10-point fall from 20 to 10 represents a reduction of 50 per cent).

When used in conjunction with GDP growth rates, the U5MR and its reduction rate can therefore give a picture of the progress being made by any country or region, and over any period of time, towards the satisfaction of some of the most essential of human needs.

As table 10 shows, there is no fixed relationship between the annual reduction rate of the U5MR and the annual rate of growth in per capita GDP. Such comparisons help to throw the emphasis on to the policies, priorities, and other factors which determine the ratio between economic and social progress.

Finally, the table gives the total fertility rate for each country and territory and the average annual rate of reduction. It will be seen that many of the nations that have achieved significant reductions in their U5MR have also achieved significant reductions in fertility.

TABLE 10. THE RATE OF PROGRESS

Countries and territories	Under-5 mortality rank	Under-5 mortality rate 1960	Under-5 mortality rate 1990	Under-5 mortality rate 2003	Average annual rate of reduction (%) 1960-90	Average annual rate of reduction (%) 1990-2003	Reduction since 1990 (%)	GDP per capita average annual growth rate (%) 1960-90	GDP per capita average annual growth rate (%) 1990-2003	Total fertility rate 1960	Total fertility rate 1990	Total fertility rate 2003	Average annual rate of reduction (%) 1960-90	Average annual rate of reduction (%) 1990-2003
Afghanistan	**4**	360	260	257	1.1	0.1	1	0.1x	-	7.7	7.1	6.8	0.3	0.4
Albania	**115**	151	45	21	4.0	5.9	53	-	5.1	5.9	3.0	2.3	2.3	2.2
Algeria	**76**	280	69	41	4.7	4.0	41	2.4	0.6	7.3	4.7	2.8	1.5	4.3
Andorra	**158**	-	-	7	-	-	-	-	-	-	-	-	-	-
Angola	**3**	345	260	260	0.9	0.0	0	-	0.4	6.4	7.2	7.2	-0.4	0.0
Antigua and Barbuda	**143**	-	-	12	-	-	-	-	1.5	-	-	-	-	-
Argentina	**120**	72	28	20	3.1	2.6	29	0.6	1.1	3.1	2.9	2.4	0.2	1.6
Armenia	**94**	-	60	33	-	4.6	45	-	2.8	4.5	2.4	1.1	2.1	6.5
Australia	**162**	24	10	6	2.9	3.9	40	2.0	2.5	3.3	1.9	1.7	1.8	0.9
Austria	**170**	43	9	5	5.2	4.5	44	3.3	1.8	2.7	1.5	1.3	2.0	1.2
Azerbaijan	**51**	-	105	91	-	1.1	13	-	1.4x	5.5	2.8	2.1	2.3	2.4
Bahamas	**138**	68	29	14	2.8	5.6	52	1.2	0.2x	4.4	2.6	2.3	1.8	1.0
Bahrain	**133**	160	19	15	7.1	1.8	21	-	1.5x	7.1	3.8	2.6	2.1	3.2
Bangladesh	**62**	248	144	69	1.8	5.7	52	0.2	3.1	6.8	4.6	3.4	1.3	2.5
Barbados	**142**	90	16	13	5.8	1.6	19	3.0	1.4	4.5	1.7	1.5	3.2	1.0
Belarus	**130**	47	17	17	3.4	0.0	0	-	0.8	2.7	1.9	1.2	1.2	3.8
Belgium	**170**	35	9	5	4.5	4.5	44	3.0	1.8	2.6	1.6	1.7	1.6	-0.5
Belize	**79**	104	49	39	2.5	1.8	20	3.2	2.3x	6.5	4.5	3.1	1.2	3.1
Benin	**25**	296	185	154	1.6	1.4	17	0.4	2.2	6.9	6.7	5.6	0.1	1.5
Bhutan	**55**	300	166	85	2.0	5.1	49	-	3.7	5.9	5.8	5.0	0.1	1.2
Bolivia	**65**	255	120	66	2.5	4.6	45	-0.3	1.0	6.7	4.9	3.8	1.0	2.1
Bosnia and Herzegovina	**130**	160	22	17	6.6	2.0	23	-	15.4x	4.0	1.7	1.3	2.9	2.2
Botswana	**43**	173	58	112	3.6	-5.1	-93	8.7	2.2	6.7	4.8	3.7	1.1	2.2
Brazil	**90**	177	60	35	3.6	4.1	42	3.6	1.2	6.2	2.8	2.2	2.6	2.0
Brunei Darussalam	**162**	87	11	6	6.9	4.7	45	-1.8x	-0.7x	6.9	3.2	2.5	2.6	2.1
Bulgaria	**133**	70	16	15	4.9	0.5	6	-	0.6	2.2	1.7	1.1	0.9	3.6
Burkina Faso	**8**	315	210	207	1.4	0.1	1	1.1	1.7	6.7	7.3	6.7	-0.3	0.7
Burundi	**15**	250	190	190	0.9	0.0	0	2.0	-3.6	6.8	6.8	6.8	0.0	0.0
Cambodia	**28**	-	115	140	-	-1.5	-22	-	3.4x	6.3	5.6	4.7	0.4	1.5
Cameroon	**21**	255	139	166	2.0	-1.4	-19	2.5	0.2	5.8	5.9	4.6	-0.1	2.1
Canada	**162**	33	9	6	4.3	3.1	33	2.3x	2.2	3.8	1.7	1.5	2.7	1.0
Cape Verde	**90**	-	60	35	-	4.1	42	-	3.4	7.0	5.2	3.3	1.0	3.8
Central African Republic	**18**	327	180	180	2.0	0.0	0	-0.6	-0.4	5.6	5.6	4.9	0.0	1.1
Chad	**12**	-	203	200	-	0.1	1	-1.2	-0.1	6.0	6.7	6.6	-0.4	0.1
Chile	**150**	155	19	9	7.0	5.7	53	1.2	4.1	5.3	2.6	2.3	2.4	1.0
China	**87**	225	49	37	5.1	2.2	24	5.5	8.5	5.7	2.2	1.8	3.2	1.7
Colombia	**115**	125	36	21	4.1	4.1	42	2.3	0.4	6.8	3.1	2.6	2.6	1.5
Comoros	**59**	265	120	73	2.6	3.8	39	-	-1.3	6.8	6.2	4.8	0.3	2.1
Congo	**44**	220	110	108	2.3	0.1	2	2.8	-1.4	5.9	6.3	6.3	-0.2	0.0
Congo, Democratic Republic of the	**9**	302	205	205	1.3	0.0	0	-1.4	-6.4	6.2	6.7	6.7	-0.3	0.0
Cook Islands	**115**	-	32	21	-	3.2	34	-	-	-	-	-	-	-
Costa Rica	**149**	123	17	10	6.6	4.1	41	1.6	2.6	7.2	3.2	2.3	2.7	2.8
Côte d'Ivoire	**14**	290	157	192	2.0	-1.5	-22	1.0	-0.4	7.2	6.5	4.7	0.3	2.7
Croatia	**158**	98	13	7	6.7	4.8	46	-	2.4	2.3	1.7	1.7	1.0	0.0
Cuba	**153**	54	13	8	4.7	3.7	38	-	3.5x	4.2	1.7	1.6	3.0	0.5
Cyprus	**170**	36	12	5	3.7	6.7	58	6.2x	3.2	3.5	2.4	1.9	1.3	1.9
Czech Republic	**183**	25	11	4	2.7	7.8	64	-	1.5	2.3	1.8	1.2	0.8	3.4
Denmark	**183**	25	9	4	3.4	6.2	56	2.1	2.0	2.6	1.6	1.8	1.6	-1.0
Djibouti	**31**	289	175	138	1.7	1.8	21	-	-3.3	7.8	6.3	5.6	0.7	1.0
Dominica	**138**	-	23	14	-	3.8	39	-	1.2	-	-	-	-	-
Dominican Republic	**90**	149	65	35	2.8	4.8	46	3.0	4.0	7.4	3.4	2.7	2.6	1.9
Ecuador	**102**	178	57	27	3.8	5.7	53	2.0	0.1	6.7	3.8	2.7	1.9	2.8
Egypt	**79**	278	104	39	3.3	7.5	63	3.5	2.5	7.0	4.4	3.3	1.5	2.4
El Salvador	**88**	191	60	36	3.9	3.9	40	-0.4	2.1	6.8	3.7	2.9	2.0	2.0
Equatorial Guinea	**27**	316	206	146	1.4	2.6	29	-	20.9	5.5	5.9	5.9	-0.2	0.0
Eritrea	**55**	-	147	85	-	4.2	42	-	1.3x	6.9	6.2	5.4	0.4	1.2
Estonia	**150**	52	17	9	3.7	4.9	47	-	2.7	2.0	1.9	1.2	0.2	3.8
Ethiopia	**20**	269	204	169	0.9	1.4	17	-	1.9	6.9	6.9	6.1	0.0	1.0
Fiji	**120**	97	31	20	3.8	3.4	35	1.9	1.5	6.4	3.4	2.9	2.1	1.3

	Under-5 mortality rank	Under-5 mortality rate			Average annual rate of reduction (%)		Reduction since 1990 (%)	GDP per capita average annual growth rate (%)		Total fertility rate			Average annual rate of reduction (%)	
		1960	1990	2003	1960-90	1990-2003		1960-90	1990-2003	1960	1990	2003	1960-90	1990-2003
Finland	**170**	28	7	5	4.6	2.6	29	3.4	2.5	2.7	1.7	1.7	1.5	0.0
France	**170**	34	9	5	4.4	4.5	44	2.9	1.5	2.8	1.8	1.9	1.5	-0.5
Gabon	**51**	-	92	91	-	0.1	1	3.1	-0.2	4.1	5.4	3.9	-0.9	2.7
Gambia	**37**	364	154	123	2.9	1.7	20	1.1x	0.1	6.4	5.9	4.7	0.3	1.9
Georgia	**75**	-	47	45	-	0.3	4	3.9x	-2.7	2.9	2.1	1.4	1.1	3.4
Germany	**170**	40	9	5	5.0	4.5	44	2.2x	1.2	2.4	1.4	1.4	1.8	0.0
Ghana	**48**	215	125	95	1.8	2.1	24	-1.4	2.1	6.9	5.7	4.1	0.6	2.7
Greece	**170**	64	11	5	5.9	6.1	55	3.5	2.4	2.2	1.5	1.3	1.3	1.2
Grenada	**110**	-	37	23	-	3.7	38	-	2.3	-	-	-	-	-
Guatemala	**74**	202	82	47	3.0	4.3	43	1.4	1.1	6.9	5.6	4.4	0.7	2.0
Guinea	**23**	380	240	160	1.5	3.1	33	-	1.7	7.0	6.6	5.8	0.2	1.1
Guinea-Bissau	**10**	-	253	204	-	1.7	19	-0.2x	-2.5	5.8	7.1	7.1	-0.7	0.0
Guyana	**62**	126	90	69	1.1	2.0	23	-0.1	3.6	6.5	2.6	2.3	3.1	1.0
Haiti	**39**	253	150	118	1.7	1.8	21	0.1	-2.8	6.3	5.4	3.9	0.5	2.7
Holy See	**-**	-	-	-	-	-	-	-	-	-	-	-	-	-
Honduras	**76**	204	59	41	4.1	2.8	31	1.2	0.2	7.5	5.1	3.7	1.3	2.7
Hungary	**153**	57	16	8	4.2	5.3	50	3.9	2.6	2.0	1.8	1.2	0.4	3.4
Iceland	**183**	22	5	4	4.9	1.7	20	3.6	2.1	4.0	2.2	1.9	2.0	1.2
India	**54**	242	123	87	2.3	2.7	29	1.7	4.0	5.9	4.0	3.0	1.3	2.4
Indonesia	**76**	216	91	41	2.9	6.1	55	4.3	2.0	5.5	3.3	2.3	1.7	3.0
Iran (Islamic Republic of)	**79**	281	72	39	4.5	4.7	46	-3.5x	2.4	7.0	5.0	2.3	1.1	6.5
Iraq	**35**	171	50	125	4.1	-7.0	-150	-1.1	-	7.2	5.9	4.7	0.7	1.9
Ireland	**162**	36	9	6	4.6	3.1	33	3.1	6.6	3.8	2.1	1.9	2.0	0.8
Israel	**162**	39	12	6	3.9	5.3	50	3.1	1.5	3.9	3.0	2.7	0.9	0.9
Italy	**183**	50	10	4	5.4	7.0	60	3.3	1.5	2.4	1.3	1.2	2.0	0.7
Jamaica	**120**	74	20	20	4.4	0.0	0	0.1	0.0	5.4	2.8	2.3	2.2	1.6
Japan	**183**	40	6	4	6.3	3.1	33	4.8	1.0	2.0	1.6	1.3	0.7	1.7
Jordan	**99**	139	40	28	4.2	2.7	30	2.5x	0.9	7.7	5.4	3.5	1.2	3.6
Kazakhstan	**59**	-	63	73	-	-1.1	-16	-	0.4	4.5	2.7	1.9	1.7	2.9
Kenya	**37**	205	97	123	2.5	-1.8	-27	2.3	-0.6	8.0	6.1	3.9	0.9	3.7
Kiribati	**65**	-	88	66	-	2.2	25	-5.3x	2.7	-	-	-	-	-
Korea, Democratic People's Republic of	**72**	120	55	55	2.6	0.0	0	-	-	4.4	2.4	2.0	2.0	1.5
Korea, Republic of	**170**	127	9	5	8.8	4.5	44	6.3	4.6	6.0	1.6	1.4	4.4	1.1
Kuwait	**150**	128	16	9	6.9	4.4	44	-6.2x	-1.7x	7.3	3.6	2.6	2.4	2.7
Kyrgyzstan	**65**	-	80	68	-	1.3	15	-	-2.5	5.1	3.7	2.6	1.1	2.9
Lao People's Democratic Republic	**51**	235	163	91	1.2	4.5	44	-	3.7	6.2	6.1	4.7	0.1	2.2
Latvia	**143**	44	18	12	3.0	3.1	33	4.0x	1.1	1.9	1.9	1.1	0.0	4.6
Lebanon	**96**	85	37	31	2.8	1.4	16	-	2.9	6.3	3.1	2.2	2.4	2.9
Lesotho	**57**	203	120	84	1.8	2.7	30	4.4	2.4	5.8	5.0	3.8	0.5	2.3
Liberia	**5**	288	235	235	0.7	0.0	0	-1.9	5.3	6.7	6.9	6.8	-0.1	0.1
Libyan Arab Jamahiriya	**132**	270	42	16	6.2	7.4	62	1.1x	-	7.1	4.9	3.0	1.2	4.1
Liechtenstein	**146**	-	-	11	-	-	-	-	-	-	-	-	-	-
Lithuania	**146**	70	14	11	5.4	1.9	21	-	0.6	2.5	1.9	1.3	0.9	3.2
Luxembourg	**170**	41	9	5	5.1	4.5	44	2.6	3.6	2.3	1.6	1.7	1.2	-0.5
Madagascar	**33**	186	168	126	0.3	2.2	25	-1.3	-0.9	6.9	6.3	5.6	0.3	1.0
Malawi	**19**	361	241	178	1.3	2.3	26	1.5	1.0	6.9	7.0	6.1	0.0	1.1
Malaysia	**158**	105	21	7	5.4	8.5	67	4.1	3.4	6.8	3.8	2.9	1.9	2.3
Maldives	**61**	300	115	72	3.2	3.6	37	-	4.5x	7.0	6.4	5.3	0.3	1.6
Mali	**7**	500	250	220	2.3	1.0	12	0.0x	2.4	7.1	7.0	7.0	0.0	0.0
Malta	**162**	42	14	6	3.7	6.5	57	7.1	3.6x	3.4	2.0	1.8	1.8	0.9
Marshall Islands	**71**	-	92	61	-	3.2	34	-	-2.7	-	-	-	-	-
Mauritania	**16**	310	183	183	1.8	0.0	0	0.8	2.2	6.5	6.2	5.8	0.2	0.6
Mauritius	**127**	92	25	18	4.3	2.5	28	2.9x	4.0	5.8	2.2	1.9	3.2	1.2
Mexico	**99**	134	46	28	3.6	3.8	39	2.4	1.4	6.9	3.4	2.5	2.4	2.6
Micronesia (Federated States of)	**110**	-	31	23	-	2.3	26	-	-1.4	7.0	5.0	3.8	1.1	2.3
Moldova, Republic of	**95**	88	37	32	2.9	1.1	14	-	-5.7	3.3	2.4	1.4	1.1	4.5
Monaco	**183**	-	-	4	-	-	-	-	-	-	-	-	-	-

TABLE 10. THE RATE OF PROGRESS

	Under-5 mortality rank	Under-5 mortality rate			Average annual rate of reduction (%)		Reduction since 1990 (%)	GDP per capita average annual growth rate (%)		Total fertility rate			Average annual rate of reduction (%)	
		1960	1990	2003	1960-90	1990-2003		1960-90	1990-2003	1960	1990	2003	1960-90	1990-2003
Mongolia	**65**	-	104	68	-	3.3	35	-	0.4	6.0	4.1	2.4	1.3	4.5
Morocco	**79**	211	85	39	3.0	6.0	54	2.3	1.0	7.2	4.0	2.7	2.0	3.3
Mozambique	**24**	313	235	158	1.0	3.1	33	-	4.6	6.5	6.3	5.6	0.1	1.0
Myanmar	**45**	252	130	107	2.2	1.5	18	1.4	5.7x	6.0	4.0	2.8	1.4	3.0
Namibia	**65**	168	86	65	2.2	2.2	24	-	0.9	6.2	5.8	4.5	0.2	2.1
Nauru	**97**	-	-	30	-	-	-	-	-	-	-	-	-	-
Nepal	**58**	315	145	82	2.6	4.4	43	0.8	2.1	5.9	5.1	4.2	0.5	1.6
Netherlands	**170**	22	8	5	3.4	3.6	38	2.4	2.1	3.1	1.6	1.7	2.2	-0.5
New Zealand	**162**	26	11	6	2.9	4.7	45	1.1	2.1	4.0	2.1	2.0	2.1	0.4
Nicaragua	**85**	193	68	38	3.5	4.5	44	-1.5	1.5	7.3	4.9	3.7	1.3	2.3
Niger	**2**	354	320	262	0.3	1.5	18	-2.2	-0.7	7.9	8.1	8.0	-0.1	0.1
Nigeria	**13**	290	235	198	0.7	1.3	16	0.4	0.0	6.9	6.5	5.4	0.2	1.5
Niue	**-**	-	-	-	-	-	-	-	-	-	-	-	-	-
Norway	**183**	23	9	4	3.1	6.2	56	3.5	2.8	2.9	1.8	1.8	1.6	0.0
Occupied Palestinian Territory	**106**	-	40	24	-	3.9	40	-	-6.0x	7.7	6.4	5.5	0.6	1.3
Oman	**143**	280	30	12	7.4	7.0	60	7.6	0.9x	7.2	6.7	4.9	0.2	2.6
Pakistan	**46**	227	130	103	1.9	1.8	21	2.9	1.1	6.3	6.0	5.0	0.2	1.5
Palau	**99**	-	34	28	-	1.5	18	-	-0.3x	-	-	-	-	-
Panama	**106**	88	34	24	3.2	2.7	29	1.8	2.3	5.9	3.0	2.7	2.3	0.9
Papua New Guinea	**49**	214	101	93	2.5	0.6	8	0.9	0.2	6.3	5.1	4.0	0.7	2.0
Paraguay	**98**	90	37	29	3.0	1.9	22	3.0	-0.6	6.5	4.7	3.8	1.1	1.8
Peru	**93**	234	80	34	3.6	6.6	58	0.4	2.1	6.9	3.9	2.8	1.9	2.8
Philippines	**88**	110	63	36	1.9	4.3	43	1.5	1.2	7.0	4.3	3.1	1.6	2.7
Poland	**158**	70	19	7	4.3	7.7	63	-	4.7	3.0	2.0	1.3	1.4	3.6
Portugal	**170**	112	15	5	6.7	8.5	67	4.1	2.3	3.1	1.6	1.4	2.2	1.1
Qatar	**133**	140	25	15	5.7	3.9	40	-	-	7.0	4.4	3.2	1.5	2.7
Romania	**120**	82	32	20	3.1	3.6	38	2.0x	0.5	2.3	1.9	1.3	0.6	3.2
Russian Federation	**115**	64	21	21	3.7	0.0	0	3.8x	-1.5	2.7	1.8	1.1	1.4	4.1
Rwanda	**11**	206	173	203	0.6	-1.2	-17	1.1	0.7	8.1	6.9	5.7	0.5	1.6
Saint Kitts and Nevis	**113**	-	36	22	-	3.8	39	3.7x	3.2	-	-	-	-	-
Saint Lucia	**127**	-	24	18	-	2.2	25	-	0.2	6.9	3.4	2.3	2.4	3.3
Saint Vincent and the Grenadines	**102**	-	26	27	-	-0.3	-4	7.1	3.0	7.2	3.0	2.2	2.9	2.6
Samoa	**106**	210	42	24	5.4	4.3	43	-	3.1x	7.3	4.8	4.1	1.4	1.3
San Marino	**170**	-	10	5	-	5.3	50	-	-	-	-	-	-	-
Sao Tome and Principe	**39**	-	118	118	-	0.0	0	-	-0.2	5.9	5.2	3.9	0.4	2.4
Saudi Arabia	**104**	250	44	26	5.8	4.0	41	0.2x	-0.6x	7.2	6.2	4.5	0.5	2.7
Senegal	**32**	300	148	137	2.4	0.6	7	-0.6	1.4	7.0	6.3	4.9	0.4	2.1
Serbia and Montenegro	**138**	120	26	14	5.1	4.8	46	-	3.6x	2.7	2.1	1.6	0.8	2.3
Seychelles	**133**	-	21	15	-	2.6	29	3.1	2.2	-	-	-	-	-
Sierra Leone	**1**	390	302	284	0.9	0.5	6	0.6	-5.2	6.2	6.5	6.5	-0.2	0.0
Singapore	**192**	40	8	3	5.4	7.5	63	6.8	3.5	5.5	1.7	1.3	3.9	2.2
Slovakia	**153**	40	15	8	3.3	4.8	47	-	2.4	3.1	2.0	1.3	1.5	3.6
Slovenia	**183**	45	9	4	5.4	6.2	56	-	4.1x	2.4	1.5	1.1	1.6	2.6
Solomon Islands	**113**	185	36	22	5.5	3.8	39	2.4x	-2.8	6.4	5.8	4.4	0.3	2.3
Somalia	**6**	-	225	225	-	0.0	0	-1.0	-	7.3	7.3	7.2	0.0	0.1
South Africa	**65**	-	60	66	-	-0.7	-10	1.3	0.2	6.5	3.6	2.6	2.0	2.7
Spain	**183**	57	9	4	6.2	6.2	56	3.2	2.3	2.8	1.4	1.2	2.3	1.3
Sri Lanka	**133**	133	32	15	4.7	5.8	53	2.8	3.3	5.7	2.6	2.0	2.6	2.2
Sudan	**49**	208	120	93	1.8	2.0	23	0.2	3.3	6.7	5.5	4.3	0.7	2.1
Suriname	**79**	-	48	39	-	1.6	19	-0.6x	0.5x	6.6	2.7	2.4	3.0	1.0
Swaziland	**26**	225	110	153	2.4	-2.5	-39	2.0x	0.2	6.9	6.0	4.5	0.5	2.4
Sweden	**192**	20	6	3	4.0	5.3	50	2.2	2.0	2.3	2.0	1.6	0.5	1.9
Switzerland	**170**	27	8	5	4.1	3.6	38	1.6	0.4	2.4	1.5	1.4	1.6	0.6
Syrian Arab Republic	**127**	200	44	18	5.0	6.9	59	2.9	1.4	7.5	5.4	3.3	1.1	4.1
Tajikistan	**39**	-	128	118	-	0.6	8	-	-4.5	6.3	4.9	3.0	0.8	4.1
Tanzania, United Republic of	**22**	241	163	165	1.3	-0.1	-1	-	1.0	6.8	6.3	5.1	0.3	1.8
Thailand	**104**	148	40	26	4.4	3.3	35	4.6	2.8	6.4	2.3	1.9	3.4	1.6

	Under-5 mortality rank	Under-5 mortality rate			Average annual rate of reduction (%)		Reduction since 1990 (%)	GDP per capita average annual growth rate (%)		Total fertility rate			Average annual rate of reduction (%)	
		1960	1990	2003	1960-90	1990-2003		1960-90	1990-2003	1960	1990	2003	1960-90	1990-2003
The former Yugoslav Republic of Macedonia	**146**	177	33	11	5.6	8.5	67	-	-0.5	4.2	2.0	1.9	2.5	0.4
Timor-Leste	**36**	-	160	124	-	2.0	23	-	-	6.4	5.0	3.8	0.8	2.3
Togo	**29**	267	152	140	1.9	0.6	8	1.2	-0.7	7.1	6.3	5.3	0.4	1.4
Tonga	**126**	-	27	19	-	2.7	30	-	2.0	7.3	4.7	3.7	1.5	2.0
Trinidad and Tobago	**120**	73	24	20	3.7	1.4	17	1.6	3.0	5.1	2.5	1.6	2.4	3.7
Tunisia	**106**	254	52	24	5.3	5.9	54	3.3x	3.1	7.1	3.6	2.0	2.3	4.9
Turkey	**79**	219	78	39	3.4	5.3	50	1.9x	1.3	6.4	3.4	2.4	2.1	2.9
Turkmenistan	**47**	-	97	102	-	-0.4	-5	-	-1.3	6.4	4.3	2.7	1.3	3.9
Tuvalu	**73**	-	56	51	-	0.7	9	-	-	-	-	-	-	-
Uganda	**29**	224	160	140	1.1	1.0	13	-	3.8	6.9	7.1	7.1	-0.1	0.0
Ukraine	**120**	53	22	20	2.9	0.7	9	-	-4.7	2.5	1.8	1.2	1.1	3.4
United Arab Emirates	**153**	223	14	8	9.2	4.3	43	-4.8x	-2.1x	6.9	4.2	2.8	1.7	3.4
United Kingdom	**162**	27	10	6	3.3	3.9	40	2.1	2.4	2.7	1.8	1.6	1.4	1.0
United States	**157**	30	10	8	3.7	1.7	20	2.2	2.0	3.5	2.0	2.1	1.9	-0.4
Uruguay	**138**	56	24	14	2.8	4.1	42	0.9	0.9	2.9	2.5	2.3	0.5	0.7
Uzbekistan	**62**	-	79	69	-	1.0	13	-	-0.5	6.7	4.0	2.4	1.7	4.3
Vanuatu	**85**	225	70	38	3.9	4.7	46	-	-0.3	7.2	4.9	4.1	1.3	1.5
Venezuela	**115**	75	27	21	3.4	1.9	22	-0.5	-1.5	6.6	3.5	2.7	2.1	2.2
Viet Nam	**110**	112	53	23	2.5	6.4	57	-	5.9	6.9	3.7	2.3	2.1	4.0
Yemen	**42**	340	142	113	2.9	1.8	20	-	2.4	8.3	8.1	7.0	0.1	1.2
Zambia	**17**	213	180	182	0.6	-0.1	-1	-1.2	-0.9	6.6	6.3	5.6	0.2	1.0
Zimbabwe	**33**	159	80	126	2.3	-3.5	-58	1.1	-0.8x	7.2	5.6	3.9	0.8	3.0

SUMMARY INDICATORS

	Under-5 mortality rate 1960	1990	2003	AARR 1960-90	AARR 1990-2003	Reduction since 1990 (%)	GDP 1960-90	GDP 1990-2003	TFR 1960	1990	2003	AARR 1960-90	AARR 1990-2003
Sub-Saharan Africa	278	188	175	1.3	0.6	7	1.1	0.4	6.8	6.3	5.4	0.3	1.3
Middle East and North Africa	249	81	56	3.7	2.8	31	2.2	2.0	7.1	5.0	3.4	1.2	3.2
South Asia	244	129	92	2.1	2.6	29	1.7	3.6	6.0	4.3	3.3	1.1	2.2
East Asia and Pacific	208	58	40	4.3	2.9	31	5.3	6.2	5.8	2.5	2.0	2.8	1.9
Latin America and Caribbean	153	54	32	3.5	4.0	41	2.3	1.3	6.0	3.2	2.5	2.1	2.1
CEE/CIS	112	51	41	2.6	1.7	20	-	-0.5	3.2	2.3	1.6	1.1	3.0
Industrialized countries	39	10	6	4.5	3.9	40	3.0	1.8	2.8	1.7	1.7	1.7	0.0
Developing countries	224	105	87	2.5	1.4	17	3.0	3.7	6.0	3.6	2.9	1.7	1.8
Least developed countries	278	181	155	1.4	1.2	14	0.0	1.8	6.7	5.9	5.1	0.4	1.2
World	198	95	80	2.4	1.3	16	3.0	2.1	5.0	3.2	2.7	1.5	1.4

Countries in each category are listed on page 140.

DEFINITIONS OF THE INDICATORS

Under-five mortality rate – Probability of dying between birth and exactly five years of age expressed per 1,000 live births.

Reduction since 1990 (%) – Percentage reduction in the under-five mortality rate (U5MR) from 1990 to 2003. The United Nations Millennium Declaration in 2000 established a goal of a two-thirds (67%) reduction in U5MR from 1990 to 2015. Hence this indicator provides a current assessment of progress towards this goal.

GDP per capita – Gross domestic product (GDP) is the sum of value added by all resident producers plus any product taxes (less subsidies) not included in the valuation of output. GDP per capita is gross domestic product divided by mid-year population. Growth is calculated from constant price GDP data in local currency.

Total fertility rate – The number of children that would be born per woman if she were to live to the end of her child-bearing years and bear children at each age in accordance with prevailing age-specific fertility rates.

MAIN DATA SOURCES

Under-five mortality – UNICEF, United Nations Population Division and United Nations Statistics Division.

GDP per capita – World Bank.

Fertility – United Nations Population Division.

NOTES

- \- Data not available.
- x Indicates data that refer to years or periods other than those specified in the column heading, differ from the standard definition or refer to only part of a country.

INDEX

GLOSSARY

AIDS: acquired immune deficiency syndrome

AVSI: Associazione Volontari per il Servizio Internazionale

CEE/CIS: Central and Eastern Europe, Commonwealth of Independent States

DHS: Demographic and Health Surveys

GDI: Gender-Related Development Index

GDP: gross domestic product

GEM: Gender Empowerment Measure

GNI: gross national income

HIV: human immunodeficiency virus

HDI: Human Development Index

HPI: Human Poverty Index

MDGs: Millennium Development Goals

MICS: Multiple Indicator Cluster Surveys

OECD: Organisation for Economic Co-operation and Development

PMTCT: prevention of mother-to-child transmission (of HIV)

PRSP: Poverty Reduction Strategy Paper

SARS: Severe Acute Respiratory Syndrome

SIPRI: Stockholm International Peace Research Institute

UNAIDS: Joint United Nations Programme on HIV/AIDS

UNDP: United Nations Development Programme

UNESCO: United Nations Educational, Scientific and Cultural Organization

UNICEF: United Nations Children's Fund

UNITA: National Union for the Total Independence of Angola

USAID: United States Agency for International Development

unicef

UNICEF Offices

UNICEF Headquarters
UNICEF House
3 United Nations Plaza
New York, NY 10017, USA

UNICEF Regional Office for Europe
Palais des Nations
CH-1211 Geneva 10, Switzerland

UNICEF Central and Eastern Europe, Commonwealth of Independent States and Baltic States Regional Office
Palais des Nations
CH-1211 Geneva 10, Switzerland

UNICEF Eastern and Southern Africa Regional Office
P.O. Box 44145
Nairobi 00100, Kenya

UNICEF West and Central Africa Regional Office
P.O. Box 29720 Yoff
Dakar, Senegal

UNICEF The Americas and Caribbean Regional Office
Apartado 3667
Balboa Ancón
Panama City, Panama

UNICEF East Asia and the Pacific Regional Office
P.O. Box 2-154
Bangkok 10200, Thailand

UNICEF Middle East and North Africa Regional Office
P.O. Box 1551
Amman 11821, Jordan

UNICEF South Asia Regional Office
P.O. Box 5815
Lekhnath Marg
Kathmandu, Nepal

Further information is available at our website <www.unicef.org>